SOMALIA COVER-UP

SOMALIA COVER-UP

A Commissioner's Journal

Peter Desbarats

M&S

Canadian Cataloguing in Publication Data

Desbarats, Peter, 1933-
  Somalia cover-up : a commissioner's journal

Includes index.
ISBN 0-7710-2684-6

1. Desbarats, Peter, 1933- – Diaries.   2. Commission of Inquiry into the Deployment of Canadian Forces to Somalia.   3. Canada. Dept. of National Defence.   4. Canada – Politics and government – 1993- .*
5. Somalia Affair, 1992- .*   6. Political corruption – Canada.
I. Title.

FC603.D47 1997   971.064'8   C97-931616-2   F1028.D47 1997

The publishers acknowledge the support of the Canada Council for the Arts and the Ontario Arts Council for their publishing program.

Set in Sabon by IBEX, Toronto
Printed and bound in Canada

McClelland & Stewart Inc.
The Canadian Publishers
481 University Avenue
Toronto, Ontario
M5G 2E9

1 2 3 4 5 6   02 01 00 99 98 97

For Hazel

CONTENTS

SOMALIA COVER-UP

PROLOGUE

The screams of the dying sixteen-year-old Somali could be heard clearly in the Canadian camp in the hot desert night. Many of our soldiers dropped by the bunker, which was not much more than a hole in the ground, protected by a crude roof. They saw the blood, the swollen face and lips. They knew what was going on and they did nothing to stop it.

Many more, dozens of soldiers perhaps, hearing the screams or hearing others talking about what was going on, also did nothing. The agony of Shidane Arone on that night of March 16, 1993, lasted for hours, seemed to go on forever. Before dawn he finally slipped away from his torturers, but his death will be remembered as long as there are Canadian soldiers on peace operations.

And there is no escape for us, although we as a nation haven't yet fully understood this.

The death of Shidane Arone during what was ironically called Operation Deliverance became a symbol of the lowest point in the history of the Canadian military.

1

It was December 1992 when about nine hundred members of the Canadian Airborne Regiment left a Canadian winter to fly into the heat and dust of the Horn of Africa – the northeast cusp of what used to be called the Dark Continent. Somalia was in chaos. An ancient land that had survived colonialism and the Cold War was now the victim of its own tribal warlords. Hundreds of thousands of Somalis were starving before the television cameras. Prodded by news media, the rich communities of the West underwent one of their periodic spasms of generosity.

Under the leadership of the United States, Canada and other United Nations member states rushed into Somalia to deliver these people from disaster. And when Operation Deliverance – or Operation Restore Hope, as the Americans called it – was over, about five months later they rushed out again, leaving behind as much confusion and anarchy as before. Since then, nothing much has changed in Somalia, except that starvation has taken a brief respite until the next drought or upsurge in civil war.

But a lot has changed in Canada. To begin with, there is no more Canadian Airborne Regiment. The first Canadian regiment ever to be disbanded in disgrace disappeared on March 5, 1995, nineteen months after its return from Africa. The vortex of public indignation that swallowed the Airborne has continued to consume reputations ever since. Some of our most senior military officers have been sucked into oblivion. And the honour of Canada's military continues to drain away as questions about the "Somalia affair" are answered one by one, in a process that has itself been lingering, painful, and as yet incomplete.

It wasn't only the death of Shidane Arone that killed the Airborne and led to the military's own prolonged ordeal. The immediate cause of the regiment's disbandment was the televising of 1992 hazing rituals by soldiers of its French-speaking 1er Commando. When these were broadcast in January 1995, Canadians were sickened by videos that showed new recruits eating urine-soaked bread, leading a black soldier about on a leash with the initials KKK painted on his body, and other drunken obscenities. When the soldiers threw up all over the nation's television screens, the nation in turn vomited the Airborne out of its system.

But the poison remained because what had happened in Somalia and at the base in Petawawa, Ontario, was not an aberration, as the miliary leadership tried to pretend, but a symptom of corruption within the leadership itself. The Airborne was only the most brutal manifestation of the disease. Amputating it did nothing to resolve the real problems except to allow the leadership to pretend that they had cured it. This was more dangerous than doing nothing.

Canadians, too, wanted to believe that the murder of Shidane Arone was the work of a "few bad apples." We do not consider ourselves to be a militaristic people. We are a middle power on the world scene, but there is something at which we are first-rate, or believed ourselves to be. Ever since a future Canadian prime minister, the late Lester B. Pearson, won the Nobel Peace Prize for persuading the UN to intervene in the Suez Crisis a half-century ago, we are the only country in the world to have turned peacekeeping into a national vocation. Since then, it has been a rare UN intervention that has not involved Canadian soldiers in some fashion.

So the images of Shidane Arone bleeding to death at the hands of a grinning Canadian trooper dumbfounded us. The fact that Master Cpl. Clayton Matchee was a native Canadian, as was another soldier involved in the brutality, Pte. Kyle Brown, confused us even more. The subsequent attempted suicide of Matchee, while he was in custody in Somalia, reminded us of the many, many suicides among the enormous population of native inmates in our prisons. And what were we to make of the stories about Arone repeating the word "Canada" over and over as he was beaten?

And what of the slurred profanity and racist cries of Airborne soldiers in the hazing videos? What were they trying to tell us? And the swastika tattoos on the bodies of some Canadian soldiers, the Confederate flags they displayed in defiance of their own officers? What did all this mean?

The élite Canadian Airborne Regiment was our standby UN unit, our gift to a world in turmoil. But the terrible viruses of violence and racism carried within the regiment were something its soldiers had picked up here. We had thought of our peacekeepers as our ambassadors to the world, carrying Canadian values of toleration and moderation to less fortunate nations. Now we had to cope with the incredible suggestion that they were carrying our values when they ran amok in Somalia.

We wanted to believe that it was an aberration. We wanted it all to go away, but instead it kept getting worse. The murder of Shidane Arone was compounded in horror by an emerging picture of cover-up in Somalia and at National Defence Headquarters in Ottawa. We saw a veneer of deception and hypocrisy being spread over the crime in an effort to conceal or diminish it.

Then it turned out that another Somali had been killed by Canadian soldiers less than two weeks before Arone's death, and this also had apparently been hushed up. When a courageous Canadian army doctor alleged murder in this case, he was first ignored, then vilified as some sort of lunatic. But Maj. Barry Armstrong had done his duty in pressing the case when others were avoiding theirs.

The more we learned about Operation Deliverance, the less we wanted to know. But at the same time, this Frankenstein's monster that was blundering about Somalia had an awful fascination for us. It was struggling to tell us something about ourselves.

After the Airborne regiment was disbanded, a series of courts martial punished a number of soldiers, non-commissioned officers, and one major. Everyone above that rank who might have borne some responsibility for the crime was either acquitted or never charged. The same immunity seemed to apply to the senior officers and civil servants in Ottawa who had sent this monster to Somalia, who had been responsible for its creation and training over the years, and who had certified it as operationally ready for its mission in Africa. They carried on as usual, promoting one another, preparing jobs for one another in defence industries after they retired with generous military pensions. Nothing seemed to touch or affect them, neither the anger and horror of the Canadian public nor the scorn of many of their own troops.

An in-house inquiry by the military conducted in the immediate aftermath of the Somalia mission had done little to satisfy public demand for an accounting. Consequently, Defence Minister David Collenette announced his intention in the spring of 1995 to launch a public inquiry and, in response to public opinion, gave it an unusually broad mandate to look into every aspect of the Somalia mission including: pre-deployment when the Airborne was chosen and trained; the events in Somalia and the immediate response there and in Ottawa; and post-deployment to pursue allegations of cover-up in Ottawa to the highest levels in National Defence Headquarters and, if need be, the cabinet. Nothing less than this would have satisfied Canadians at the time.

My own summons to take part in this inquiry, as I explain at the start of my journal, came entirely unexpectedly in March 1995. Up to that time, my feelings about Somalia were those of the average citizen. I had been horrified by the news reports but had paid little special attention to them. Like most Canadians, my time and energy was taken up with earning a living, family concerns, and events in my community of London, Ontario.

But, as I quickly began to appreciate, this was a unique opportunity. This would be the first major, comprehensive public inquiry into the Canadian military in our history. It would probe to the heart of the Somalia affair, answer all the unanswered questions, end the endless and damaging speculation that had sapped the morale of our troops, clean up the mess, and set the Canadian Forces on a new course, perhaps under new leadership. This was an invitation that no one could refuse, particularly not a journalist such as myself, whose whole instinct was to try to get to the bottom of the story.

And so I and my two fellow commissioners began what turned out to be a long, disappointing, and disillusioning journey.

A Hopeful Beginning
March to October 1995

It seems laughable now, but the Privy Council's initial, informal estimate of the time required for the Somalia inquiry was about nine months – a few months to organize ourselves, public hearings in the summer of 1995, and then a few months to write and submit the report by the end of the year.

One of my first discoveries was that there is no such legal entity as the inquiry. Each commissioner is appointed independently, and although one is named to be chair, all have equal powers of inquiry. So at the very beginning of the process there were just three individuals shaking hands for the first time, nothing else. No staff. No offices. No instructions apart from the terms of reference provided by the government and a few academic and legal texts on the conduct of public inquiries.

The spring day in 1995 when I met Judge Gilles Létourneau in his office in Ottawa's Supreme Court Building marked the start of the inquiry for me. The other commissioner, Judge Robert Rutherford, joined us a few weeks later.

The first task was to create an organization from scratch. The keystone in this process was the secretary of the inquiry, who acted as its executive director/general manager. Judge Létourneau recruited Stanley Cohen, a lawyer from the Justice Department who had worked with him when he chaired the Law Reform Commission. This was an inspired choice. Stan Cohen was not only a brilliant administrator, but a constant source of wise counsel during the many crises that we encountered. Stan rapidly started to hire our first lawyers, researchers, and support staff.

Office space was located in the Vanguard Building at the corner of Slater and O'Connor streets in downtown Ottawa, an undistinguished thirteen-storey structure that has been the home to innumerable royal commissions and federal inquiries over the decades. (I had worked there in 1980–81 with the Royal Commission on Newspapers and still remembered its stuffy atmosphere, winter and summer, and bleak, almost Soviet architecture and decor.) Our offices were on the eleventh floor; on the ninth, we constructed a public hearing room with basic facilities for simultaneous translation and television coverage. By June, we were a going concern, holding regular meetings of the three commissioners and staff, collecting thousands of documents from the military, deciding on procedures, assembling a library of essential legal and research documents, meeting military officials for the first of many briefings, and announcing an initial round of public hearings.

We wanted to make a fast, public start to advertise the fact that we were in business, so public policy hearings started on June 19 to discuss procedure, receive testimony on military affairs and general issues, and test our new hearing room. While these hearings were being televised, our lawyers were contacting and interviewing possible witnesses for the investigatory hearings scheduled for the beginning of October.

We also decided to visit military bases in Quebec, Ontario, and Alberta to talk to some of the Somalia veterans, to persuade soldiers of our sincerity, and to encourage them to help us.

Thousands of documents were starting to come in, far more than any of us had anticipated. Already we were noticing worrisome gaps in the documentation. Missing pages often seemed to be associated with key events.

We were about eight months into the inquiry, and well into our schedule of public hearings, when I started to keep a journal. I'm not an inveterate diarist, and at first I was somewhat surprised to find myself regularly recording impressions on my laptop during the empty Ottawa evenings and the flights to and from London. Then it became a habit, this "talking to myself" from time to time, as I appreciated the significance of what we were doing and my unique opportunity for observing.

At the end of October 1995, as I made my first entry in the journal, I had a little catching up to do. I went back to the beginning of my involvement in the inquiry, and then found myself going back even further.

Monday, October 30, 1995
London

When the call came one evening last spring, on the kitchen phone in our home in London, it was a complete surprise. I was nearing the end of my second and final term as dean of journalism at the University of Western Ontario, where I had been since 1981; Hazel and I were looking forward to a year's sabbatical before I would return to Western to teach until I reached mandatory retirement four years later. The future seemed comfortably predictable.

The woman on the other end of the line identified herself as someone from the Privy Council Office (PCO) in Ottawa and said, without any further preamble, that my name had come up to the top of a short list to serve on a federal inquiry.

I assumed it was to look at the CBC. I knew that Ottawa was putting together a small task force to undertake yet another study of our public broadcasting system. That appointment would have made some sort of sense, given my background in journalism. But the woman from the PCO obviously hadn't been considering that at all.

"Why would you think that?" she said. "It's for the Somalia inquiry."

It was my turn to be astonished. Like most Canadians, I knew that the army's mission in Somalia had turned into a fiasco. Because of its problems there, including the cold-blooded murder of a sixteen-year-old Somali, the proud Canadian Airborne Regiment had been unable to withstand another scandal after its return from Africa – the broadcasting of videotapes showing a drunken regimental initiation ceremony with undertones of racism. The regiment had been disbanded, and the federal government had promised an inquiry as soon as a number of courts martial arising from the murder had been completed.

But the invitation to serve on the Somalia inquiry puzzled me at first.

My military background consisted of marching up and down the hallway of our long Montreal upper flat at the age of nine, with my younger brother behind me, following my father, who was a lieutenant in the Royal Montreal Regiment. He was rehearsing for a regimental parade. Always a rather shy man, he was nervous about having to march down the middle of Sherbrooke Street at the head of his soldiers and, at exactly the right moment in front of the reviewing stand, order his men to smartly "Eyes Right!" Down the hallway we marched, and at the door of the dining room, answering his command, we swivelled our heads to the right while my mother applauded. A few days later, she stood with us near the reviewing stand while my father marched past and we watched everything go perfectly, thanks to our rehearsal.

I remember seeing my mother crying in the kitchen as she fried sausages for supper, after my father announced that he had transferred voluntarily from the army reserves to active service. In his early thirties, he was too old for the draft. Running the small and precarious family printing business that he had taken over from his father, he was hardly in a financial position to join up. But at that time, which must have been about 1941 or 1942, the war was going badly, and my father thought that it was his duty to go active. It was a characteristic decision. Throughout his relatively short life, until he died instantly from a heart attack in his mid-fifties, he was almost naïvely honest, not a very canny businessman but one whom everyone liked and respected. He was a virtuous man. Years later, when I encountered his former customers, they would always remember this quality.

His sense of duty took him into the active army at a time when there was every probability that he would end up overseas. My mother was bewildered, frightened, and furious. It was one of the few times, perhaps the only time, that he defied her. As his mother had been earlier in his life, his wife was the dominant partner in the relationship, but on this occasion, in the face of calls to honour and patriotism, she was powerless.

Of course I thought it was wonderful. The idea of having my father in uniform overcame any sympathy that I might have had for my mother. I could envision going to church with him on Sundays, and it turned out to be just as thrilling as I had imagined. My father was six-foot-two, slender, and always more youthful-looking than his age. He became a heroic figure in my life for those wartime years.

Over the next few summers, holidays were spent in boarding houses in rural Quebec, near wherever my father's camp was located. When we travelled there, with my younger brother and baby sister, I was the man of the family. Although I also remember having occasional nightmares about Nazi invasions of Canada, the wartime years were happy ones. There were victory gardens in every vacant lot, local fairs and carnivals to raise money for the war, and a mock anti-aircraft emplacement that we kids built in a field near the house, with a log for a cannon, to fire at the bombers that swooped low over Montreal West on their way to the airfield at Dorval and the long flights overseas.

In those years, my generation formed its notions of a proud and heroic military service. We never quite lost the worshipful admiration that we had felt for fathers, uncles, and older brothers who had fought and died for us. In later years, this feeling was transmuted slowly into pride for a military service that became known as the peacekeeper of the world. Canada always seemed to be among the first to volunteer soldiers for peacekeeping, as well as maintaining its commitment to NATO and Europe.

My generation had also lost contemporaries in the Korean War in the 1950s.

It was shortly after that when my brief inclination toward a military career was nipped in the bud. I must have been about eighteen or nineteen years old, a junior reporter on the *Gazette* in Montreal but still emerging from a confused, erratic adolescence. I had managed to almost deliberately fail my last year of high school, forfeiting an eight-year scholarship that had seemed to ensure my education through university at a private Jesuit college. I was moody, solitary, and on the brink of serious alcoholism. At a particularly low moment, I looked desperately to the army as a way to put some order and discipline into my life.

After several days in the recruiting centre on Sherbrooke Street, across from the McGill campus, I began to have doubts, particularly about spending the next three to five years among the comic-book readers who were my fellow candidates. But I persisted through the medical and aptitude tests, and it was only a friendly and perceptive psychologist who saved me at the last moment.

"If you're serious, get into officers' training," he said. "And if you're not, get out of here."

I didn't think it was necessary to mention this when the woman from the PCO asked me if there was any reason why I would be disqualified from serving on the Somalia inquiry. And fortunately, among the 150,000 documents that the inquiry eventually examined, there was not a trace of my forty-year-old withdrawn army application.

I remained intrigued by the selection process for the inquiry, as was everyone else who knew me. "Why you?" was the common reaction. At first, I laughed and said I was just as puzzled as they were. Later, when it was confirmed that my fellow commissioners were two judges, I said that many inquiries were composed of non-experts as well as experts and I was the representative on the inquiry of the "ordinary Canadian." Secretly I thought, "Why not?" I had spent most of my life as a political journalist. I had some inkling of the way large organizations worked. Political intrigue had always fascinated me.

It was an important assignment. The opportunity to get to the bottom of the Somalia story was irresistible for a journalist such as myself. Here was a chance to be part of something that could influence an important area of national life for years to come. And I was flattered to be asked.

Hazel and I talked it over and I accepted. At the outset, after discussing this with the PCO, I continued as dean at Western. My normal research term in the autumn of 1995 enabled me to devote most of my time to the commission. At the end of the year, as our work intensified and became more protracted, the university appointed an acting dean and I accepted reduced responsibility. In the spring of 1996, I took early retirement and devoted all my time to the inquiry.

———

As a political journalist working in Winnipeg in the 1950s, one of my first startling discoveries was that no one is really in charge. Most people are superficially cynical about politics but believe, on a much more basic level, that there is some sort of sense and logic at the heart of the system. The idea of chaos is simply too frightening.

And experience, at least in most countries, tells us constantly that the system works. Water comes out of taps. Jobs produce money; money buys the food that never fails to arrive in the stores when we need it. Garbage is collected and sewage treated. We recognize unconsciously that none of this could happen without some sort of plan. But the fact is that the plan is within us. It starts at the bottom of the system as each one of us arranges and manages our affairs with varying degrees of competence.

We collaborate with our neighbours to respect property divisions, to help one another, and, on a widening scale, to organize clubs, churches, and local political associations. Higher levels of government are the end result of these many small associations, but they become increasingly erratic. The large bureaucracies that they require take on lives of their own; in their struggle for survival and to protect their own workers, these complex organizations can lose touch with their reason for being.

What saves our political systems from total irrelevance and disaster, at the very top, is a rediscovery of the human values that exist at the bottom. Democracy or dictatorship, all systems of government exist at the highest level as shifting alliances of relatively few individuals. This is comforting in the sense that it bestows human qualities, for good and ill, on the impersonal machinery of bureaucracy; but it is terrifying to understand suddenly, as I did in Winnipeg, that important political decisions were often made by people as ignorant, confused, and uncertain as myself.

Manitoba was a small province in terms of population and the *Winnipeg Tribune* a modest daily newspaper with limited editorial resources. When reporters such as myself were assigned to cover political meetings in rural areas, we were expected to find our own transportation. One of the best methods, I discovered, was to offer to drive the speaker of the evening in his car from Winnipeg to his destination and back again. This was how, at the age of twenty-two, I would find myself spending hours with the leader of the province's Opposition party, Duff Roblin, trading personal experiences and, inevitably, political opinions. When he was elected premier shortly after, I was shocked to find myself, from time to time, being asked for my reaction to some proposed line of political action. He was at the top of the system. He was supposed to know what he was doing.

As my career as a political journalist lengthened into decades, moving from Winnipeg to Montreal to Ottawa, I was constantly reminded of this paradox – the human relations and human frailty at the top of our system of government that are both reassuring and terrifying.

A few days before Brian Mulroney failed to win his first leadership convention, I found myself with a television crew in a luxurious chalet in the Eastern Townships of Quebec. When we had finished filming our story, Mulroney asked me to go upstairs with him to listen to the speech that he had prepared for the convention. He read the whole thing to me as I sat on the side of a bed, then asked me what I thought of it. I thought it sounded fine, at least in that setting. But a few days later, in the convention hall, I knew it was all wrong after only a few lines. It was another illustration of the fact that you couldn't plan everything in advance, no matter how carefully you tried. There were still the imponderables of time, place, and personality that rescued politics from predictability. All this was somewhere in my thoughts in the days after that first telephone call from the Privy Council Office.

In order to avoid any possibility of a leak to the news media, Ottawa wouldn't tell me who the other Somalia commissioners were going to be. This remained the case even after the three of us had accepted our appointments. On the night before the defence minister announced the inquiry in Parliament, the phone rang again and the same woman from the PCO, in a worried voice, asked me if I had written anything in the previous year or so about the events in Somalia. The minister wanted to know urgently. I assured her that the question was the first one that I had asked myself weeks earlier. I had written nothing, mainly because the military is not one of my usual subjects. She was relieved, but I was astonished that such an obvious concern apparently had not occurred to anyone in Ottawa until the very last moment.

Later, after it was announced that Judge Gilles Létourneau of the Federal Court of Appeal would chair the inquiry and that the other two members would be myself and Anne-Marie Doyle, a senior civil servant then in Europe as the Canadian ambassador to the Organization for Economic Development in Paris, there was a political and media storm when it was revealed that Doyle was a close friend of Robert Fowler, the former deputy minister of defence and a potentially significant witness. She gave up the appointment soon after and was eventually replaced by Judge Robert Rutherford from Toronto.

Many people suspected the government of ulterior motives in ambassador Doyle's appointment, but my own experience indicated a much simpler explanation. Since she was in many respects an ideal candidate, with a reputation for brilliance in Ottawa and knowledgeable about the Defence Department, it was likely that someone in the PCO either had overlooked her connection to Robert Fowler or, even more likely, estimated mistakenly that it would not become a sufficiently major issue to derail the appointment. Stupid errors of judgement are made constantly by all of us in our private lives and business affairs. Usually the consequences are minor. In politics, mistakes can be exposed and quickly magnified, with enormous consequences – one of the reasons why secrecy is such a pervasive and paradoxical practice even of democratic governments.

WARNING SIGNALS

October to December 1995

By the beginning of October we had settled into our offices in Ottawa, constructed a room in the same building for our public hearings, hired staff, collected thousands of documents, held initial hearings on issues and procedure, located and interviewed dozens of potential witnesses, and mapped out our approach to the first part of our investigation. Having decided to cover events in chronological order, we started with the pre-deployment phase when the Canadian Airborne Regiment was selected and trained for the Somalia mission. At that early stage, we envisioned this phase being followed by hearings into the deployment of the regiment in Somalia. The third and final phase would focus on post-deployment developments in Canada as the military and the government responded to some of the shocking events that had occurred in the field.

Between October 2 and December 20, 1995, we heard thirty-five witnesses, some of the more important of whom occupied the stand for three or four days. At that stage, we were holding public hearings on average four days a week, three weeks out of four. The rest of the time was taken up with contacting and preparing witnesses, conducting research, reading innumerable documents, and handling the administrative work of the inquiry. Our lawyers and investigators had to interview all potential witnesses, usually with the witnesses' lawyers in attendance, verify and distribute transcripts of these interviews, and then get ready to examine selected witnesses in our hearings in a way that would help us and the public to understand the whole story. This required a great deal of preparation. The public hearings represented only the visible tip of a veritable iceberg of work undertaken by the inquiry.

As our hearings progressed, we learned that the history of this élite regiment involved earlier instances of disciplinary problems that often remained unresolved. In discussing these, we began to encounter the infamous "wall of silence" that had frustrated earlier military investigations. As we drew closer to the December 1992 deployment of the Airborne to Somalia, and worked our way up the chain of command, the number of lawyers involved in the process started to escalate.

The government originally had assumed that military lawyers would represent all soldiers before the inquiry, but it quickly became evident that the attempts of individuals to defend themselves would sometimes involve criticism of others and the military in general. Military lawyers gave ground reluctantly, even when their conflicts of interest between defending the military as an institution and defending its individual members became glaring, but more and more senior officers asked to have the private lawyers that they were entitled to, at public expense. The practice spread rapidly to lower ranks. As dozens of lawyers became involved, each with a right to cross-examine witnesses whose testimony affected their clients, you could sense the process slowing down and becoming more expensive. Our own contacts with government lawyers and senior military officers were becoming more difficult as we grew concerned about the slow delivery of documents to the inquiry.

Despite this, by Christmas 1995 we had started to get a clear picture of the Airborne's historic problems, its difficulties in getting organized to go to Somalia, the effects of the unprecedented change in its leadership on the eve of its departure, and what appeared to be a chronic inability on the part of its senior officers to perceive and deal with problems within the regiment.

In early December, we had also carried out our intention to visit Somalia veterans and other members of the former Canadian Airborne Regiment at bases across Canada. We were encouraged by the support we received from many soldiers.

Full television coverage of the hearings and almost daily press reports were giving Canadians their first close look at the military high command. Letters to the editors of newspapers indicated that it was an eye-opener for many.

Wednesday, November 15, 1995
Ottawa

Last weekend, in London, I was filling the car with gas when the man at the next pump said, "I remember seeing you on television."

I gave my stock response: "You must have a good memory. It's been fifteen years since I was on Global News."

"No, I remember that," he said. "But I saw you the other night. You're on the Somalia inquiry. That must be a tough job."

People who stop me on the street to talk about the inquiry often express sympathy. They have been appalled by the stories about the torture and killing of sixteen-year-old Shidane Arone. Although we are months away from discussing this event in our hearings, most Canadians have already seen, on television and in newspapers, pictures of a Canadian soldier posing proudly with their bloody victim. The images are so contrary to the national ideal of the dedicated Canadian peacekeeper, embodying the quintessential Canadian virtues of moderation and good sense, that Canadians still haven't come to terms with them. Was the murder of Arone just an aberration, a freakish event, or was it a symptom of some widespread sickness in the Canadian military and, by extension, Canadian government and society? Did this mean that we were all responsible, to some extent, for the awful beating that the screaming, pleading teenager absorbed before he died in the dugout in the Canadian camp that night?

Canadians have mixed feelings about our inquiry. They want to know, but are afraid of, the truth. Their dominant reaction is still one of horror, because the images are still vivid and fresh in their minds. Horror and disgust. Overlaid on the blood-smeared television images of Arone are the piss and vomit of the Airborne regiment's initiation and hazing ceremonies at Camp Petawawa on the Ottawa River northwest of the capital.

Selected fragments of these videotapes were broadcast on Canadian networks earlier this year. The national reaction was so strong, coming on top of the grief over the Arone murder, that it completely overwhelmed the proud history of the regiment and its many achievements. Although soldiers and veterans protested, right up to the chief of the defence staff, there was strong public support for the defence minister's decision to disband the regiment.

Before my appointment to the inquiry, I had missed seeing the Petawawa images on television. One day last summer, before our main hearings started, I took the videotapes from the library of the inquiry offices here in downtown Ottawa, closed the venetian blinds in my office, and watched them from beginning to end. It took almost three hours.

I began with the worst one, the tape of the hazing ceremony of the 1er Commando in the summer of 1992. It depicted the progressive disintegration of the initiation from good-natured college-fraternity hijinks to a sprawling, shapeless, sodden sequence of small degrading cruelties with undercurrents of racism and bestiality.

The videotape was physically difficult to watch because the soldier with the camera was either too drunk or too inexperienced to take steady images. For almost an hour, the pictures veered and jolted across the screen, adding to the unreality of the whole scene. When I began to feel nauseous, it was hard to tell whether I was suffering from a kind of seasickness or whether it was the sight of soldiers smearing themselves with human excrement, pissing on chunks of bread and stuffing them into one another's mouths, and pissing on one another that was making me sick.

There was one black soldier among the shaven-headed initiates. He was led around on all fours at the end of a leash with "I Love KKK" smeared in white on his back. Among all the revolting images, this was probably the one that sealed the regiment's fate. That and the later picture of the same soldier tied to a tree, beside one of his white companions, his body covered with white powder. On the confused soundtrack, other soldiers could be heard screaming something about Michael Jackson and White Power, and inviting others to come and see the nigger. There was also a sequence of simulated buggery by one of the soldiers crouched over the back of the black soldier like a dog over a bitch.

These were the images in the minds of people who stopped me in the street to commiserate with me on the job that I had been given. "It must be so difficult," they would say. "It must be tough. I don't envy you." They would never talk about the videos specifically, as if even mentioning them was too threatening. They made me feel as if I were working in a garbage dump, as if the taint of the videos was on me. They felt sorry that I, as one of them, had to be exposed to that mess; they even seemed to feel a bit guilty about making me do this on their behalf.

By this time, I had started to move beyond the images on the videotapes and to become fascinated with the conditions that had brought them into being. When people expressed sympathy for me, I would talk about how interesting I was finding the work on the inquiry. This would puzzle them until, I suspect, they remembered that I was a journalist and perhaps expected to take a somewhat unhealthy interest in the macabre.

Sunday, November 19, 1995
En route London–Ottawa

Several months after I first screened the tapes, the black soldier appeared before us in our hearing room in Ottawa's Vanguard Building. He was over six feet tall, slender, ramrod-straight, his uniform immaculate, creases pressed to a knife edge. He bore the improbable name of Christopher Robin, presumably an entirely accidental association with the little hero of Winnie-the-Pooh because this Christopher Robin had been born and raised in the heart of French-speaking Quebec, in the depressed asbestos-mining centre of Thetford Mines, and he pronounced Robin as Roh-behn, the second syllable accented and nasal. Apart from his colour, he was a typical member of the famed Royal 22e Régiment, the Van Doos, that contributed volunteers to the Canadian Airborne Regiment along with two English-speaking regiments, the Royal Canadian Regiment and the Princess Patricia's Canadian Light Infantry.

It was soon apparent that Corporal Robin saw himself as absolutely typical of the Van Doos, racial heritage notwithstanding. He politely but resolutely denied that the hazing ceremony contained any element of racism. The initiation rituals were just fun, he insisted. There was nothing sinister about them.

Of course Christopher Robin was still in the army and obviously determined to stay there. He admitted at one point in his cross-examination that his main purpose was to defend the reputation of the disgraced and disbanded regiment. His loyalty was to his comrades, not to the processes of our inquiry. In his efforts to be a good soldier, he was quite prepared to be a stubborn witness.

Tuesday, November 21, 1995
Ottawa

Perhaps it wasn't as simple as that. Corporal Robin's testimony recalled for me an episode in the 1960s when I hosted a nightly television program of news and current affairs for the CBC in Montreal. During one of those five seasons, my co-host was a beautiful, vivacious, and intelligent black woman.

Mairuth Hodge was about my own age and had grown up in Montreal's small English-speaking black community. When she joined our television program, most of us – researchers, story editors, and producers – were fairly typical of our generation. Our political views ranged from Marxist to mild socialist. Reacting against the conservatism of our parents' generation, we were anti-establishment and conscientiously radical in our attitudes. We were critical of the racial prejudice and intolerance that had produced discrimination in Montreal society against Jews, French Canadians, and various ethnic and racial minorities from native people to Irish Catholics.

Our views were what would later become known as politically correct. But to Mairuth, they were puzzling. She had grown up believing in racial equality and believing that she had experienced it. At first, she reacted conservatively and even critically to the progressive dogmas of the 1960s. They didn't seem to express her own experience.

I remember thinking that, in a way, Mairuth was almost whiter in her attitudes than we were, at least on the surface. We were fashionably and rather smugly in favour of Black Power; Mairuth seemed to see it as a threat to the comfortable world that she had known.

Our program meetings at the CBC were like daily seminars on current events. Political opinions flickered constantly through our discussions. During that year we watched Mairuth rapidly catch up with current black North American dogmas; day by day, she became blacker. She adopted some of the vocabulary of black American leaders. By the end of the season, she was talking about going to Africa to discover more about her heritage, and soon she did this. Eventually she became an articulate spokesperson for her community and a symbol of its growing importance as she was appointed to the Canadian delegation to the United Nations and to the board of the CBC.

I thought of Mairuth as I listened to the young black corporal politely but steadfastly denying that the indignities he suffered during his commando's initiation ceremony at Petawawa had anything to do with racism. Even more than Mairuth, he had grown up in an entirely white community. The French-speaking black population of Thetford Mines must have been much smaller proportionately even than Montreal's black population. Perhaps Christopher Robin, like the young Mairuth, actually believed, or had persuaded himself to believe, that he belonged in the white community. Perhaps his decision to join the Van Doos was the ultimate expression of this belief.

This would have made it impossible for him to recognize and admit racism in his fellow soldiers. For Robin, to identify the slogans painted on his body, and the white powder that they threw over his black skin, as expressions of racism would have destroyed the whole basis of his world. How could he continue to serve with comrades who really believed in White Power, the slogan that they shouted in English as they urinated on him and one another? How could he accept people as friends who called him "nigger" if he believed that they really meant it?

So his brief responses weren't, at least in my opinion, just a reflection of his desire to defend his regiment. He couldn't afford to admit to even a suggestion of racist motivation in his fellow soldiers. His armour had to be impenetrable. One flaw, one serious imperfection, and the whole structure would fall down, leaving him with no choice but to leave the army.

So he took it all as a joke, just high spirits. Yes, he admitted, he was sometimes called a nigger – *mon nègre* – by his comrades, but it was just a nickname, the way you might call someone Red or Whitey. There was no harm in it, he said proudly, defiantly, as if we were at fault, as if the racism were in our minds, not in his comrades'.

I asked him about the broadcast of the hazing videotapes on national television earlier in the year. Had his parents and family members watched these broadcasts? Had they seen the "racist" scenes that all the networks had excerpted from the tape for their newscasts? Yes, they had watched, he said, subdued. They had asked him about the events. He had explained it all to them, as he had explained it to us.

He left the witness stand without giving an inch of ground. There was a certain kind of heroism in this. His defiance of all of us has remained with me, superimposed on the sickening scenes of the hazing ritual.

The Canadian Airborne Regiment was doomed as soon as someone released that videotape to a television journalist. But why was the tape made in the first place? Did anyone really want a souvenir of this debauch? Did no one realize how dangerous such a record would be? On the soundtrack of the tape, soldiers' voices are heard several times urging others to pose "for posterity." No one seemed to think twice about it until the images came to life again on national television.

I haven't finished the story about the man at the gas pump who recognized me. He turned out to be a veteran of the Airborne, a former paratrooper who had served in Korea. If most Canadians had been disgusted by the hazing videotapes, this man was furious.

"I hope you get all those bastards," he said. "They destroyed my regiment."

He went on to talk about the paratroopers who were his comrades in Korea and later, in London, Ontario, where he had been based with the Royal Canadian Regiment. He told me about the Korean orphan that his regiment had adopted. For years, money was collected among the veterans in Canada to support him, to pay for schooling, and eventually to help him complete university. In later years, he had been brought to Canada to visit the regiment that had helped him.

"That's the kind of soldiers we were," said the veteran, "not like those bastards."

Monday, November 27, 1995
Ottawa

Most Canadians of my generation have neither served in the military nor thought about it much. The anti-war sentiment of the 1960s, in reaction to the Cold War of the 1950s, was particularly strong in Canada. While the Americans multiplied the number of nuclear missiles in their submarines and underground silos, we tied ourselves in political knots over the arming of a few aircraft in Europe with tactical nuclear weapons and the prospect of having nuclear anti-aircraft missiles on Canadian soil. We took a perverse delight in welcoming American draft-dodgers during the Vietnam War. Unlike the Australians, we refused to consider sending fighting troops to Vietnam, although we were happy to sell war materials to the United States.

When Prime Minister Pierre Elliott Trudeau started to reduce military spending, it reflected widespread Canadian disdain for any form of militarism. Our Forces probably would have declined even more quickly had not Canadian soldiers discovered a new and politically acceptable vocation in peacekeeping. Here was the correct military role for Canada – uncontroversial, unobjectionable, unspectacular, gentlemanly, and not nearly as expensive as maintaining a full national defence establishment.

In any case, the Americans were always there to protect us from the Soviet menace. Benefiting without charge from the United States' nuclear arsenal enabled us to afford the more genteel and high-minded role of international arbiter. This policy neatly blended hypocrisy with self-interest.

Having never thought much about the army, I'm discovering, during this expedition into its murkier depths, that I start out with a mixture of respect and condescension. I don't really understand why we need a conventional army at all, particularly since the end of the Cold War, but it's also a grand and somewhat awesome mystery to me.

Perhaps because of my Jesuit education, I find myself attracted to the uniforms, hierarchy, and ritual of the military. I would glimpse this from time to time when I was invited, as a dean of journalism, to address officers at the former National Defence College in Kingston or the Canadian Forces Staff College in Toronto. In Kingston, I would usually arrive the evening before my lecture. As I drove through the gates, I felt as if I were entering a cloistered world. I would be billeted in an enormous old-fashioned room within the fortifications, above the cosy wood-panelled mess. This, and the quadrangle surrounded by stone buildings, reinforced the sense of monastic isolation, of lives subordinated to some higher purpose.

My Jesuit education had made the notion of dedicated self-sacrifice and service familiar to me. Even as a member now and former elder of the United Church of Canada, I still harbour a slight suspicion that married clergy are not quite on the same level as celibate priests. When I encounter a military general these days, I may even be subconsciously aware that the Jesuits who taught me in Montreal belonged to an order also headed by a general.

The military itself cultivates this notion of a select, ordained brotherhood. In the early days of our hearings, when we listened to briefings about the Armed Forces and the Canadian Airborne Regiment, we were frequently reminded that the military is the only career where danger of death is part of the job description. Although this is not exactly accurate – there were times in Bosnia when journalists were being killed at least as frequently as soldiers – it is part of the mystique that binds soldiers together and isolates them from civilian life.

Members of military forces are taught to kill. Killing is an essential part of the trade. In this respect, it is unlike journalism or coal mining or deep-sea fishing or other dangerous occupations, although the vast majority of Canadian soldiers since the Second World War have never killed another person in action and probably have seen less violence than the average big-city police officer.

Most of us outgrew a fascination with uniforms and badges when we left the Boy Scouts. Even clergy in our society have abandoned most vestiges of distinctive dress. Nuns who wore medieval regalia only a few decades ago now dress like contemporary women, live in apartments with their sisters, and hold down day jobs. Only members of the military still cling to barrack life, at least in the lower ranks, and wear uniforms that make them immediately identifiable, distinctive, and more or less superior to their comrades. Inferior ranks are expected to make obeisance to their superiors.

In my home town of London, Ontario, they tore down the empty barracks of the Royal Canadian Regiment about a year ago. Some of the soldiers who went to Somalia once lived in those three-storey white buildings surrounding the parade square. In the spring of 1995, as I mulled over the invitation to join the inquiry, I would walk my dog across the empty square, a few blocks from my home, and peer through the uncurtained ground-floor windows of the deserted rooms.

Places where large numbers of people have lived exert a strong hold on us. As I moved along the walls of the barracks I could almost hear the voices of soldiers echoing in the empty rooms, the commands ringing out over the parade square.

Thursday, November 30, 1995
Ottawa airport and en route to London

The army is an enormous bureaucracy with its own complex protocol. We began to glimpse this a few days ago when a young lieutenant-colonel appeared before us. Now the commanding officer of the Princess Patricia's Canadian Light Infantry in Winnipeg, in 1992 he was on the staff of the Special Service Force headquarters at Petawawa, Ontario, on the same base as the Canadian Airborne Regiment. Maj. John Turner appeared before us as the epitome of the successful career officer: lean, fit, his short ash-blond hair combed straight back. Only his voice belied his collegiate appearance. It could shift in an instant from politely understated to fiercely authoritarian.

At Petawawa in the summer and fall of 1992, Major Turner was placed between Brig.-Gen. Ernest Beno, the commander of the Special Service Force, and Lt.-Col. Paul Morneault, the recently appointed commanding officer of the Airborne regiment.

Colonel Morneault is emerging as one of the tragic figures of the Somalia affair. Early in our hearings, he appeared with his lawyer to listen to a few days of testimony before returning to Europe to await his turn. Morneault is currently posted to NATO headquarters in Brussels, the kind of assignment that an older officer might welcome as a prelude to retirement but one that represents, in Morneault's case, the premature curtailment of a promising career. Sitting beside his lawyer in his colonel's uniform, the badge of the Airborne proudly on his chest – the regiment that he had wanted to command so badly and that had been taken from him so abruptly – he was a dark-haired, brooding presence, shaking his head regretfully but almost imperceptibly as testimony against him was given by one of his fellow officers.

Morneault had been entrusted with command of the Airborne with some hesitation, as we were told by witnesses. But his career path had pointed him toward this command at this particular time and, in any case, it was the turn of the Van Doos, his regiment. Although command of the Airborne wasn't rigidly rotated among the three contributing regiments, there was a tradition of sharing the top job that was generally respected.

On paper, Morneault had all the qualities necessary to be an efficient and respected commander. In particular, he had a talent for administration, and this, strangely enough, turned out to be a liability when he joined the Airborne.

His immediate task was to prepare the regiment for duty overseas. Early in 1992, the Western Sahara had seemed the most likely destination, but, by that summer, news coverage of civil unrest and starving refugees in Somalia had drawn the urgent attention of the United Nations. The Airborne, restless after a long period of inaction and cancelled assignments, received a warning order early in September. It was to be ready within thirty days to leave for Operation Cordon in Somalia, where it would be part of a United Nations mission to bring humanitarian relief to the refugees.

One of the regiment's first tasks was to make an inventory of equipment and personnel required for the mission. Traditionally this job had been done by army clerks working under the direction of senior officers. But Morneault's flair for administration gave him a personal interest in this task, particularly as it promised to be an opportunity to employ his skill with computers, still unusual in an officer of his rank.

At that time, the Canadian military possessed nothing in the way of standard computer software for this task. Most of the junior officers working under Morneault were computer illiterate. The colonel set out to create his own computerized table of equipment and to instruct clerks in the process. This was a serious error of judgement in the eyes of his superior officers. While the soldiers of the Airborne moved into the field to commence training for Somalia, their commanding officer was sitting in his office glued to a computer keyboard. Anyone who remembers the horrible fascination of programming early computers can understand and sympathize with him.

General Beno, meanwhile, was often out in the field. He noted every instance of a missed or botched training assignment by the Airborne and fumed over the absence of Colonel Morneault. This frustration was communicated to his staff officer, Major Turner, who transmitted it to Capt. Jeffrey Kyle, a younger officer from Turner's own regiment who was in charge of operations in Morneault's headquarters. Kyle kept Turner informed of all Morneault's decisions, many of them contrary to Beno's wishes.

It caused a little flurry in our hearings when I referred to Kyle as "the headquarters mole" in Morneault's office, but, perhaps unwittingly, his reports served to reinforce Beno's misgivings about the way the colonel was preparing his regiment for action.

Toward the end of this process, Morneault seemed to sense the looming disaster and to regard his young officer as one source of his problems. In the officers' mess one evening, according to witnesses that we have heard, he turned on Kyle and accused him of betraying him, an accusation that the captain denied. By then, it was too late to save Morneault. General Beno was already trying to discover how a general could take the unusual step of relieving a colonel of his command. There appeared to be no precedent, at least in Canada's peacetime forces, for this type of extraordinary action. Not only would such a decision effectively terminate Morneault's promising career, but it could jeopardize the morale and readiness of the regiment. Although the date for the regiment's departure was being delayed by events in Somalia and at the United Nations' headquarters in New York, the order to move was expected week by week.

Wednesday, December 6, 1995
En route to Winnipeg

Well, I was wrong. When Judge Gilles Létourneau first suggested visiting the army bases, I thought it was a good idea in principle, but I was concerned that we would run headlong into the wall of silence that we've been hearing about constantly.

Perhaps my media background has made me unduly sceptical. I could see the public relations value of being seen to approach the soldiers directly, to move out of our hearings in Ottawa and go "into the field," but I was worried that it could backfire if the soldiers merely listened to us politely, or even in obviously hostile silence.

When I saw the agenda proposed for each visit, I was even more concerned. After the chair's address to the troops, a question period was planned, then an informal lunch with the soldiers. After that, the three of us would make ourselves available for private consultation.

The sessions with the soldiers would be closed to the media, but there would be a brief press conference at each base. What if the soldiers didn't ask questions? What if no one came to the private sessions? I was concerned that the media would interpret this outcome as a rejection of the inquiry and that this would make our work more difficult.

I underestimated the Canadian soldier.

At Valcartier, Quebec, we met about three hundred soldiers in a large, drafty assembly hall. It soon became clear that the officers at the base had gone to some trouble to bring together their Somali veterans as well as others who had served with the Airborne. In the audience I recognized Cpl. Christopher Robin, who had testified before us a few weeks previously.

As soon as Judge Létourneau had delivered his remarks, the questions started. The session was off-the-record, but I can say that it soon became evident that the soldiers were taking a strong interest in what we were doing and were generally supportive. The questions covered a wide range of issues dealing with the inquiry itself, events in Somalia, and their coverage by media.

At the stand-up lunch that followed, I hardly had time to grab a few sandwiches. Many of the bilingual soldiers talked in English to me; others put up with my French. They obviously wanted to talk, and some of their revelations were interesting.

But the biggest surprise came after lunch when we moved into a small office for the private interviews. Many soldiers eventually talked to us, delaying our departure until we almost missed our flight.

The soldiers generally came into the room in self-selected groups of three or four, although some came alone. Often there was a spokesperson for the group. Some had made notes for themselves in the small notebooks that all soldiers seem to carry.

These French-speaking Van Doos were intelligent and animated. I know it's trite to compare "emotional" Quebeckers with "stolid" Anglo-Saxons, but the contrast was startling between these lively, animated men and the more reserved but equally forceful soldiers of the Royal Canadian Regiment that we met yesterday at Petawawa, Ontario.

There, our reception was the same, perhaps even more welcoming. In the movie theatre on the base, we addressed about four hundred soldiers. Almost a hundred of them were forced to stand for lack of seats. Again, the questions started immediately after Judge Létourneau's address. The discussions continued throughout lunch and, again, I barely had a chance to eat a few sandwiches and I never did get to the coffee. Later, there were so many soldiers waiting to talk privately to us that, after the first hour, we moved into three rooms and conducted separate interviews. Even then, after talking with about the same number of soldiers as at Valcartier, we were told that fifteen to twenty more had been turned away.

All of us were surprised by this response, no one more than I. What had happened to the fabled wall of silence? Why were the soldiers now opening up to us, not only in private but in many cases indicating their willingness to testify?

Tuesday, December 14, 1995
En route Ottawa–London

It was during the visit to the army bases last week that I began to understand that the army really is a different kind of organization. The recruiting slogans used to say, "There's no life like it."

The first morning, in Valcartier, I was struck by the sight of about three hundred soldiers sitting in front of us in a stark, drafty auditorium, all dressed identically. It gave new meaning to the word "uniform."

Most of us strive throughout our lives to differentiate ourselves from others. Even in a world of mass-produced products, we insist on differences of shape and colour to set us and our possessions apart. Cars, for example. The mechanical requirements of cars over the years have imposed a uniformity of efficient design with little variation in the basic pattern. If price and utility were our only concerns, the Volkswagen years ago would have driven every other vehicle off the market. But we want design and colour and other incidentals to express our individuality. We want it so intensely that almost all the advertising for cars is aimed at these apparently trivial details.

The army is different. The soldiers that we addressed at Valcartier, Petawawa, Winnipeg, and Edmonton would have been instantly recognizable as soldiers to a Roman centurion. Hundreds of human beings deliberately submerging their individuality by dressing identically and moving uniformly to commands seem to remove themselves from everyday experience and to exist on some different level, not quite human. Together they created a primitive, threatening impression.

As we left the stage of the auditorium at Valcartier, a command was given and all the soldiers stiffened in their seats, bent arms rigid at their sides, eyes straight ahead. It was like walking between rows of robots.

It's hard for me to imagine the kind of individual who seeks out this uniformity. Because they deliberately erase their individuality, soldiers seem to invite us to regard them as so many identical units. I'm sure this is misleading, of course, and that their reasons for enlisting are as varied as the diverse personalities and physical types that the uniforms try to conceal.

In our hearings so far, and in our conversations with soldiers, we have glimpsed some of these motives. There is probably more idealism than we like to admit in this cynical age. There are soldiers and young officers for whom military service is a calling, a public service that gives purpose to their lives. Some come from families where there is a military tradition. Despite being relieved of his command of the Airborne and shunted aside as inept, Colonel Morneault proudly identified himself at our hearings as a former "army brat" and listed the parents, grandparents, in-laws, and brother who have also served in the Armed Forces.

There are those who join the army because it represents a reasonably safe job in a world of diminishing job security. At the far end of the scale are the misfits and adventurers who are attracted by the idea of joining the warrior class. These "wild horses" can be broken and trained to become extraordinary soldiers, according to one school of thought; to other officers, they represent an unpredictable and uncontrollable element, particularly dangerous in a peacetime army.

These soldiers represented only a minority of the regiment's annual intake, but it was they who kept the tattoo parlour in Petawawa busy and flew the Confederate flag from their Harley-Davidsons. These were the soldiers who seemed to be particularly attracted to the Airborne regiment and by its élite reputation, transforming it in their own minds into a kind of military Hell's Angels with distinctive insignia, flags, tattoos, and degrading initiation ceremonies.

Deep within the Airborne there seems to have existed a core of these self-identified rebels who sought an even greater degree of uniformity and exclusivity within the military. It was as persistent as a virus that has acquired immunity to all the usual forms of therapy. And the Airborne, not to mention the entire Canadian Forces hierarchy, never was able either to eradicate or fully control it.

The reason for its persistence, it seems to me, is an ambivalence toward extremism that pervades the military. On one hand, soldiers are trained to be cogs in a machine that functions reliably on command; on the other hand, this requires an extraordinary kind of commitment that sets these individuals apart.

"This is the only profession," soldiers have said to us, "where you commit yourself to kill and perhaps be killed on command." You cannot expect a trained German shepherd guard dog to behave like a Pekingese, they say. But this attitude contains the seeds of permissiveness for occasionally erratic, violent behaviour, perhaps even encourages such behaviour, which seems to be at odds with the unquestioning discipline that an army requires.

The Airborne never seemed to resolve this dilemma, hence the conflicting attitudes toward the characterization of the regiment as "élite." Some officers and soldiers disowned this term; it obviously made them uncomfortable. Others proudly, even defiantly, embraced it. Perhaps it was characteristic of us as a people that our crack regiment was unsure of its basic identity, and that this uncertainty was among the root causes of its eventual disintegration.

It's hard to decide what to make of the so-called "rebel flag" – the Confederate flag that became an unofficial and at times illegal symbol of Two Commando. Was it simply a harmless rallying point for the commando, as many of its officers have contended, or did it symbolize racism and defiance of authority?

Originally it was presented to Two Commando by American soldiers after a joint exercise in the United States. It became the emblem of the Princess Patricia's hockey team when the regiment was stationed in Germany. The team was called "The Rebels."

Over the years, successive commanding officers of the Airborne regiment tried to ban the flag. Why? And why were they unsuccessful?

As testimony unfolds before our inquiry, it is becoming clearer that the flag attracted adherents at different levels. To most soldiers of Two Commando it probably was just a normal part of their unit's identity, akin to the Quebec flag that was sometimes displayed by 1er Commando. The few white supremacists in the regiment would have been more aware of its origins in the United States, the flag of a nation defeated in its attempt to defend slavery.

Whatever the reasons for its display, it seemed to appear at critical moments and became associated with outbreaks of lawlessness. In early October 1992, when a party at the Kyrenia Club at Base Petawawa erupted into the parade square, the flag was flown when soldiers threw stolen incendiaries at military police who were trying to control them. Later that night, the sergeant who had been in charge of the police effort had his car torched on the parade square. Only one soldier confessed and was punished for the pyrotechnics incident; no one was ever charged for the arson.

A few days later, an unannounced and apparently illegal search of the Two Commando barracks turned up more than thirty Confederate flags.

Colonel Morneault himself, when he assumed command in the summer of 1992, ruled that public display of the Confederate flag was not allowed. It could not be hung outside barracks or even displayed inside windows. But display on inside walls or its use as a bedspread was allowed. Morneault explained that the army had no right to regulate the decor of soldiers' private quarters on base, just as it had no authority over off-base living quarters.

It's becoming apparent to me that the Confederate flag was a symbol, true enough, but of the inability of the army to come to grips with discipline problems in the Airborne. There was a persistent reluctance to identify it as part of a serious problem, just as the problem of discipline itself was shoved under the carpet year after year, along with a growing list of unsolved crimes by soldiers.

I used the term "virus" to describe the regiment's recurring strain of defiance of authority – a virus of rebellion that seemed immune to treatment and whose immunity grew stronger as it survived a series of challenges. Colonel Morneault preferred to call it a "cancer" that would remain in remission for months and years before exploding. In the end, it was shown to have the potential to destroy the entire regiment, but no one ever seriously tried to eradicate it. Various conventional treatments were prescribed, but nothing that addressed the seriousness of the threat, even after years of recurring crises.

PREPARING FOR SOMALIA

January to February 1996

After the Christmas break, we resumed our public hearings on January 16, 1996, and continued through to February 22. Having covered the history of the Airborne regiment, we were now dealing with events in the summer and autumn of 1992, when the Airborne was selected and trained for service in Somalia. These hearings led us rapidly up the chain of command, and as the military ranks became more elevated, more time was required for their examination and cross-examination. In six weeks of hearings, we heard ten witnesses, most of them testifying from two to four days.

We were trying to discover why the Airborne had been selected for Somalia despite its history of disciplinary problems. Were there alternatives? Was the Airborne properly prepared for the Somalia mission? In particular, we were concerned about the replacement of its commander, Lt.-Col. Paul Morneault, by Lt.-Col. Carol Mathieu only weeks before the regiment deployed for Somalia. What were the reasons behind this unusual move?

Illustrious names began to appear before us. Retired major-general Lewis MacKenzie spent several days on the stand explaining his role in preparing and dispatching the Airborne to Somalia, as did retired general John de Chastelain, the former chief of the defence staff and a former Canadian ambassador in Washington. This phase of hearings ended with testimony from de Chastelain's civilian counterpart at National Defence Headquarters, the former deputy minister of defence Robert Fowler, by then the Canadian ambassador at the United Nations.

Thursday, January 25, 1996
Ottawa

The inquiry moved up a level this week with testimony from the first senior officer directly involved in the events we are investigating. Lt.-Col. Paul Morneault was appointed to lead the Airborne regiment in the summer of 1992, about four months before he was ignominiously relieved of command.

Colonel Morneault's "firing," to use his own term, was a desperate attempt to fix things at the last minute, a gamble that an effective replacement commander would be able to control the regiment properly in the field, but its flaws were quickly magnified when it found itself under pressure in Somalia.

Morneault, predictably, blamed the disaster in Somalia on his removal. He said that he was just coming to grips with the regiment's discipline problems when he was ordered to step aside. His dismissal sent a message to the soldiers, he claimed, that they could defy authority and get away with it.

About the same time, the authorities sent an unpopular sergeant in the Airborne back to his home regiment. The sergeant had been unfortunate enough to be on duty early in October when the party in the Kyrenia Club went out of control. His efforts to deal with this resulted in the torching of his car.

Morneault told us this week that both these events confirmed the immunity of what he called an undisciplined "cabal" within the regiment and sowed the seeds of the eventual disaster in Somalia.

But things are never as simple as that. Few issues are black and white, few heroes aren't flawed. Morneault emerged during four days of testimony as a paradoxical combination of bureaucrat, idealist, and warrior.

I was surprised to learn, when he introduced himself on the stand, that he was an anglophone despite his French-Canadian name. He was the son of an American mother, and he learned most of his French the hard way, as a junior officer with the Van Doos. This must have marked him out early in his career as an unorthodox soldier. He rose quickly, but despite the promotions his relationships with some of his superiors were frequently strained. He acquired a reputation for being stubborn or, as some put it, "pig-headed." He used the description "pit bull" when he talked about his approach to discipline problems in the regiment.

But, on the stand, there were several occasions when I thought he would break down emotionally. His dismissal from command, even three years later, had left him puzzled, frustrated, and wounded.

Anyone who has lived through a tough organizational struggle knows how difficult it is not to become paranoid and how easy it is to demonize opponents. Colonel Morneault accused his superior, Gen. Ernest Beno, of a catalogue of malevolencies.

Was Beno anti-French? Was he anti–Van Doos? Was he by nature tyrannical? Was Morneault "just the latest in a long series of victims?" "The answer," concluded Morneault, "was all of these."

Meanwhile, Morneault's former superior, the general, spent the four days of his testimony sitting in the audience, directly in Morneault's line of vision. Sometimes it's difficult to focus on the legal aspects of the testimony as one senses the emotional currents crackling across the room.

Next week, General Beno has his chance. The problems definitely grow more intriguing as we slowly clamber up the chain of command. And we're not even in Somalia yet. Some of the paper crossing my desk already indicates that the final phase of our hearings later this year, when we deal with alleged cover-ups, will be the most sensational.

Friday, January 26, 1996
En route Ottawa–London

I was invited to dinner last week by an old friend, who had taken early retirement from the civil service, and his younger wife (a civil servant), who is still moving ahead. She was curious to know why I had been appointed. Had I known the minister of defence? Did I have connections in the party? She was obviously hinting that the appointment had come as some sort of favour or reward.

I said quite honestly that I had no idea, that the call had taken me completely by surprise. That surprised her.

"What do you know?" she said. "The system actually worked the way it's supposed to."

Tuesday, January 30, 1996
Ottawa

I continue to be amazed by the conservatism of the military in many areas.

Despite cutbacks, the Defence Department is still a major item in the federal budget, and its more than 80,000 personnel the largest single payroll in the country. Perhaps the very size of this bureaucracy has made it hard to change attitudes and procedures.

Racism provides a striking example. In my own world, media organizations have struggled for more than a decade with problems of hiring recruits from minority communities, changing racial attitudes of their staffs, and providing better coverage of our increasingly diversified community. News media haven't always succeeded in this effort, but there are many indications of effort.

Many of our police forces have followed the same path and made slow progress. But the army has done little, as we've heard, and in some cases it has lost ground. For instance, there are fewer blacks and native people in the Canadian Forces today, proportionately, than there were a few decades ago. I don't have statistics on this, but this impression is shared by most of the soldiers I've talked with in the past few months.

It's quite evident that diversifying the racial make-up of the Forces has not been a high priority.

This attitude was reflected in the casual approach to the preparation of our soldiers for service in Somalia. "Cultural" or "sensitivity" training consisted of a single lecture by a Somali-Canadian haphazardly recruited for this task in Ottawa. The lecture was restricted to officers who were supposed to pass on the information to their soldiers. Very little made its way down the ranks.

There's no assurance that greater cultural sensitivity would have prevented some of the disasters in Somalia, but it might have. As our experience there showed, time and money invested in this type of preparation would have been more valuable than additional military equipment.

Wednesday, January 31, 1996
Ottawa

The hero of Sarajevo, retired major-general Lewis MacKenzie, strode into our hearing room today followed by a retinue of TV cameras and journalists. Although it has been four years since he became a media personality as the commander of United Nations (UN) forces in the besieged city, General MacKenzie still displays the unmistakable aura of the TV personality. His skin looks as if it has been burnished under studio lights; his greying hair seems to have a kind of windblown energy; his handsome profile is angular, lined, yet youthful. No wonder that he became a favourite spokesperson for UN peacekeeping, so prominent internationally that his views created alarm in political circles back in Ottawa. That, he explained to us, was the reason for his early retirement. Not that he was saying anything that contradicted Canadian government policy at the time, he told us, but he was saying it so forcefully that it might make it awkward for Canada to alter that policy in the future.

So he resigned from the army he had first entered as a thirteen-year-old cadet and became a professional communicator, writing, commenting, and making speeches on peacekeeping and international affairs. In this respect, his appearance before the inquiry probably was good for his business, although his position was dangerous – not the hero of Sarajevo, on this occasion, but one of the contributors to the mess in Somalia.

One of the less fortunate developments in General MacKenzie's series of providential career moves was his appointment in the summer of 1992 to Land Force Central Command in Toronto. Arriving in his new post in September, after a summer of car racing and guest appearances at various military bases, he was plunged into the first phase of the sorry series of events that eventually destroyed the Airborne regiment. Barely was he behind his desk when he received a call from General Beno at Petawawa with the first worrying news about his subordinate, Colonel Morneault. Beno claimed that Morneault was already falling behind in his training of the regiment. MacKenzie must have sensed trouble because he advised Beno that if drastic changes had to be made in the regiment, it would be better to do them sooner rather than later.

As the weeks passed, the news from Beno became more distressing. According to Beno, training was lagging even further behind. He was being forced to provide Morneault with more and more specific direction. By the beginning of October, it was painfully clear that the problem was becoming critical. Either Beno would have to decide that Morneault was at least adequate or alternatives would have to be explored.

Thursday, February 1, 1996
Ottawa

Possible options included cancelling the mission or substituting another regiment. The first was politically impossible, the second impractical. To admit that Canada's élite paratroopers, our designated rapid-response unit theoretically ready to fight anywhere at a week's notice, was incapable of getting its act together would have been disastrous, a national disgrace. Prime Minister Brian Mulroney would not have gracefully accepted being unable to meet his commitment to the American president; Defence Minister Kim Campbell's career would have come to an early end; and heads would have rolled at National Defence Headquarters.

As for keeping the Airborne at home and sending another unit, there simply wasn't another regiment available. As General MacKenzie told us yesterday, you could put the whole Canadian army in Toronto's Maple Leaf Gardens and still have a thousand seats left over. Despite years of cutbacks in military spending, Canadians still haven't accepted our defence limitations. Most of us don't know how thin our military ranks are, and almost no one cares. Our aging air force has become little more than a token of past glory; our navy barely has the capacity to monitor foreign fishing fleets off our own coasts; and the army's shrinking establishment was one of the hidden reasons for the Somalia disaster.

The Airborne was picked for Somalia because it was the only unit available. As General Beno told us this week, in many ways the Airborne wasn't a rational choice. It had been so stripped down in the preceding year that it no longer had armour or even vehicles. In order to train for the mission, it had to borrow armoured personnel carriers from another regiment, the Royal Canadian Dragoons. It only kept a machine-gun platoon in operation by hiding its existence from budget-cutting senior officers.

It would have made far more sense to assign one of our regular regiments to Somalia, but they were all occupied in other parts of the world. By moving the Airborne out of Canada, our leaders left our own country dangerously short of soldiers. It would have been very awkward if we suddenly had had to face something such as the Oka crisis. At the time of the Airborne commitment, military planners were keeping a wary eye on the shores of Lake Huron, where native Canadians were agitating for the return of territory confiscated during the Second World War.

In 1992–93, we were far more exposed to military risk than all but a few Canadians realized. In the 1995 referendum, there was speculation about the role of the Canadian army in the event of Quebec separation. Bloc Québécois leader Lucien Bouchard was criticized for writing a letter to Canadian soldiers stationed in Quebec in which he anticipated a "yes" result. In reality, the threat of force on either side has a hollow ring unless Canada is prepared to bring most of its forces home from overseas. How awkward it would have been, if the vote had gone the other way, to have had to summon our soldiers from the former Yugoslavia to prepare for the defence of our own federation.

Suitable or not, despite equipment shortages and persistent discipline problems, it was either the Airborne or nothing in 1992 when Prime Minister Mulroney made his expansive gesture of support to Washington. It was this lack of resources that narrowed the room for manoeuvre as senior officers confronted a crisis in the Airborne only weeks before departure.

Monday, February 12, 1996
Ottawa

Back in Ottawa again after a week at Western wrestling with budgets and faculty problems.

This morning, when the inquiry resumed, I was asking questions again, watching someone dodge and weave on the stand, fighting for reputation. Although I joke about applying for a job on the Supreme Court after this is over, I'm beginning to develop a taste for the intellectual games that lawyers play. I notice that I'm getting better at the examination process, but the pleasure that this provides is tinged with doubt. Winning a battle of wits in the inquiry doesn't necessarily further the exposure of truth. Sometimes the competitive game becomes an end in itself.

Today we were continuing the cross-examination of a colonel. Only a few months ago, I would have been impressed by a colonel. Now I wait impatiently for the parade of generals to resume.

Thursday, February 15, 1996
En route Ottawa–London

The pace is definitely picking up. The procession of service officers through our hearing room was overshadowed today by word that some of the soldiers who were in Somalia have started to provide new information.

The critical focus at this moment is not on the murder of Shidane Arone, which has dominated the headlines and which is directly responsible for our inquiry, but the earlier shooting of two Somalis on March 4, 1993.

According to my understanding of the incident until today, the two men were looters apprehended in the act of sneaking into the Canadian camp at Belet Huen. One of them was killed; the other wounded.

Soon after the incident, however, Maj. Barry Armstrong, a doctor from the Airborne's medical staff, indicated that the wounds inflicted on the Somalis were inconsistent with the official version of events. Suspicions were heightened by the long delay between the incident and the dispatch of military police from Canada to investigate it. But, so far, officials have stuck by their original story.

Now our lawyers are telling us that at least one soldier, possibly two, are testifying in interviews that the Somalis were outside the perimeter wire of the Canadian camp on the night they were shot, that they were just squatting there and only began to move away when they became aware of Canadian soldiers nearby. If this proves to be true, then we're dealing with a new case of suspected murder.

I can't say that this news doesn't cause a stir among our lawyers and the commissioners, and I become aware of the complications this will create.

Already, for instance, our lawyers are becoming concerned about the presence of government lawyers at the interviews where these soldiers are offering new evidence. The government position has always been that its lawyers represent not only the Department of National Defence but all officers and soldiers who don't elect to be represented by their own lawyers.

For officers who may be under scrutiny at the inquiry, the solution is simple. As soon as we serve them with a Section 13 notice, warning them that the inquiry may make a negative finding in their case, and providing some description of our concerns, these officers are entitled to engage their own lawyers at government expense. The reason, of course, is that if they are found guilty of serious misconduct, the government itself could become their prosecutor. It would be impossible for the government to defend its own interests and the conflicting personal interests of these officers at the same time.

Ordinary soldiers who have already been subjected to disciplinary measures because of their actions in Somalia are not the main focus of our inquiry and so have not been given Section 13 notices. Only one soldier so far has been granted the right to be represented by his own lawyer.

So the soldiers who are now coming forward with new and incriminating evidence are still represented by government lawyers who also represent the Department of National Defence. These lawyers presumably are there to protect the interests of their primary client, the government, and not the interests of the soldiers. The conflict of interest is glaring, and it's an issue that has been simmering below the surface of the inquiry for some time. This new turn of events threatens to bring it into the open in a way that could force a rethinking of the entire role of government counsel.

At the moment, lawyers on our staff and the two judges who are my fellow commissioners seem to feel that this new development will complicate our work considerably and perhaps prolong it even more.

There has been some criticism in the media recently that we're "spinning our wheels" and that the inquiry is spending too much money. The most recent estimate is about $8 million. My own comment, at this stage, was that if anyone still had doubts about the importance or relevance of what we are doing, evidence of a second serious incident should put these doubts to rest. In the long term, it may not have much effect on the main recommendations of our inquiry about changes in military structures and methods, but over the short term it will confirm rumours of cover-up and evasion.

My main concern now is that we are still several months away from putting these soldiers on the stand to testify. It will be the beginning of April before we are ready to start hearing about events in Somalia. On the one hand, that makes me nervous. These men are still within the military establishment and subject to all kinds of pressure. On the other hand, once it is known that the wall of silence has started to come down, the floodgates might open. There is already a fairly lengthy list of new evidence accumulating for the in-Somalia phase of our hearings, and we suspect that more remains to be discovered.

One of the security guards at Ottawa airport recognized me today. A surprising number of people are following the full hearings on CPAC, the public affairs channel seen on cable television, including some veterans who have been calling to complain about the disrespectful way in which our women lawyers are questioning senior officers. I joked with the security guard about the hearings being a sure cure for insomnia, but she insisted that she found them engrossing.

"Well, there's better stuff to come," I said.

———

At the hearing yesterday, a staff member handed me an envelope during the lunch hour. It was from one of our simultaneous translators telling me that my friend Vic Wilczur had died at 3 A.M. Two days earlier, I had made my last visit to Ottawa Civic Hospital. Vic was too exhausted and ill to talk to me, but he knew I was there.

We had first encountered one another as young journalists in our twenties, in Montreal and Winnipeg. With his tall, stooping posture, loping walk, thick glasses, and low, almost guttural way of speaking, Vic was a distinctive character. In Winnipeg, as the "chief" of a news bureau with only one employee, himself, Vic slept in the office for a few months to save money. Eventually he moved into a small, dark apartment in an ancient building across the street from the CNR station. In the summer, he wore sandals on his bare feet, something that attracted attention in Winnipeg in the 1950s. Later, he worked as an information officer for cabinet ministers in Ottawa and for Edward Schreyer when he was governor general.

He was always full of ideas. Recently he claimed that the Canadian army had enlisted jailbirds in the 1950s to fight in Korea. He said that judges were encouraged to offer prospective convicts the alternative of military service, and he related this somehow to the Airborne's attraction for a small number of white supremacists and right-wing fanatics.

The cancer treatments had left Vic looking less than human. As I sat there, he would raise his emaciated arms and rub his face, a common enough gesture but one that seemed at odds with his condition, as if the imminent approach of death demanded something more dramatic than rubbing the side of one's nose or screwing knuckles into one's eyes.

When I stood up to say goodbye and good luck – I couldn't think of anything else to say – he silently mouthed something I couldn't understand and held out his hand for me to shake. I grasped it for the last time.

Thursday, February 22, 1996
En route Ottawa–London

We've finished the first phase of our hearings, investigating the history of the Airborne regiment, why it was chosen for Somalia, the problems that bedevilled it in Canada, and that ultimately made it the first regiment in Canadian history to be disbanded in disgrace.

For five months, we've watched videotapes of degrading and disgusting initiation rites, listened to ordinary soldiers describe their experiences in the regiment, talked with soldiers and officers at bases across Canada, and crawled laboriously up the chain of command from master corporals and sergeants to the most senior generals in National Defence Headquarters (NDHQ).

These past few days, we've been listening to the handful of men who control the professional lives of Canada's soldiers. Although I'd been looking forward to this, the actual experience was anti-climactic.

Just as there was a wall of silence that surrounded events at Petawawa before the Airborne's departure for Somalia, an equally impenetrable barrier seems to surround the upper levels of National Defence Headquarters in Ottawa. Although the Airborne's base at Petawawa was only a two-hour drive from the capital, it might just as well have been on another planet for all the news that reached the executive levels of NDHQ.

At Petawawa, when officers were faced with the wall of silence in Two Commando of the Airborne, they marched the soldiers into the field for a week, isolated them from the outside world, and threatened to keep them at home when the rest of the regiment went overseas if they wouldn't talk. Sometimes I wished we could have done the same to the senior officers

who met us with something even more frustrating than silence
– an almost impenetrable flood of words.

Why didn't senior officers at NDHQ know that the replacement of Col. Paul Morneault as commander of the Airborne
was related to his failure to break through the wall of silence
among his men? Why didn't they ask? Reasons for their ignorance were given to us, but none for their apparent lack of
curiosity.

THE GOING GETS TOUGHER

April to June 1996

This was supposed to be the in-theatre phase of our public hearings. As testimony resumed on April 1, we heard witnesses describing the many positive achievements of the Airborne in Somalia. We were concerned that these had been overshadowed by the publicity about the murder of Shidane Arone and other disturbing events, and that our inevitably strong focus on these incidents would make it look as if we also had lost sight of the good work of many Canadian soldiers. So, for the first week of April, we let men and women who had served in Somalia talk about their success in enabling relief supplies to reach starving Somalis, in providing medical treatment for Somalis, and in repairing schools for their children. Canadians also had worked hard to restore some semblance of civic administration and policing to a society that had been decimated by civil war. These activities undoubtedly made the Canadian-administered Belet Huen Humanitarian Relief Sector a model for regions controlled by other participants in the U.S.-led intervention.

All this "good news" was intended to lead us into hearings on the controversial events in Somalia. Instead, reports about the alteration and destruction of Somalia-related documents at National Defence Headquarters forced us to change course.

The military itself was becoming alarmed about missing documents. Under orders from Gen. Jean Boyle, chief of the defence staff, Canada's entire military force was diverted from its normal duties on April 8 to search for Somalia documents that might still be in its possession, despite our year-old order for the production of all these documents.

Our decision to interrupt our examination of the Somalia mission to hold hearings on missing or altered documents delayed our progress by five months. We wouldn't return to events in Somalia until the following September. But we felt that we had no choice. The documents that were being reported as altered, missing, or destroyed were *our* documents, covered by our order of April 1995 for production of documents. They were vital to our inquiry. Our own credibility required us to examine this issue.

So instead of hearing about events in Somalia in 1993, when the Conservatives were in power, we held hearings on the activities of the Media Liaison Office at National Defence Headquarters from 1993 to 1995, which brought us into the Liberal era of the current prime minister and to actions of the current chief of the defence staff, General Boyle. No one had foreseen this development when we were appointed.

Another indication of more difficult days ahead occurred at this time when our chair, Judge Gilles Létourneau, was accused of bias by one of our witnesses. As commander of the Special Service Force at Petawawa in 1992, Brig.-Gen. Ernest Beno had been the Airborne commander's immediate superior when the regiment was being prepared for Somalia. His legal action to disqualify Judge Létourneau was the first of many attempts by senior officers to delay or invalidate the inquiry.

Monday, April 1, 1996
Ottawa

Today we began the second and final phase of our public hearings, after a month's recess. There are already signs that the first part of our hearings, with forty-five witnesses on the stand, has been only a calm prelude to the stormy times ahead.

The first thunderbolt struck last week when the CBC carried a report from the information commissioner, John Grace, criticizing the military for altering documents about Somalia requested by the CBC under Access to Information. Grace didn't mention any names in his report, but one of those under suspicion, Col. Geoffrey Haswell, immediately went to the *Globe and Mail* to announce that he was under suspicion and to insist that he had been merely following orders.

Whose orders? Grace's report, although carefully written in the usual official style, was interpreted by the media as leaving open the possibility that responsibility for tampering with documents could involve the very highest levels of the military, perhaps even the new chief of the defence staff, Gen. Jean Boyle, and his predecessor, Gen. John de Chastelain. In the *Globe* interview, Colonel Haswell indicated that he was ready to implicate his superiors. Because General Boyle at the time was in charge of the unit with responsibility for handling all information about the Somalia affair, it looks as if it might be difficult for him to extricate himself from this mess.

One of the most puzzling questions at this point is why Boyle accepted the promotion to chief of the defence staff in January if he knew, as he must have, that these allegations were going to surface? And if he knew this, did he inform Defence Minister David Collenette when his promotion was being discussed?

But this is only part of Boyle's problem. In two weeks, we will commence to hear evidence on missing documents. Although we have so far collected more than 80,000 documents, some of the most critical, including documents from regimental headquarters in Somalia and from National Defence Headquarters in Ottawa, are still unavailable.

Boyle's and the military's strategy at this point may be simply to deny and deny. Even if he is accused by Colonel Haswell of ordering the alteration of documents, he can deny it. He and other senior officers may simply offer no explanation except technical or clerical error for the disappearance of documents. Without documentary evidence of wilful destruction of evidence, it will be hard to pin down responsibility. But even if he evades legal responsibility, it's hard to imagine that the scandal won't deal a serious blow to Boyle's career.

Meanwhile, this week, we're giving the military an opportunity to talk about its successes in Somalia before we return to the failures that brought our inquiry into being. Today we viewed several hours of videotape showing conditions in Somalia before the military intervention in 1993, and how the country and its people looked to the Canadian soldiers who arrived there in December 1992.

Tuesday, April 2, 1996
Ottawa

More videos, photos, and soldiers' recollections of Somalia today. It was certainly hot and dusty. After several hours of screening videotapes in our hearing room, I could almost feel the grit on my skin. The soldiers were unable to bathe during their first weeks in Somalia. They lived at first in shallow dugouts by the airfield at Baledogle, later in tents at Belet Huen. There must have been times when the heat and dust made them long for the clean snows of Petawawa.

Many of them had flown directly from the subzero temperatures of an Ottawa Valley December into the desert heat of dry season in Somalia where temperatures exceeded 40°C during the day. With barely a pause at the airfield outside the capital city of Mogadishu, just enough time to receive ammunition and check weapons, they were transferred to Hercules aircraft for the forty-five-minute trip to the gravel airstrip at Baledogle in the direction of the Ethiopian border.

We watched videos of the first Airborne soldiers running down the ramps of Hercules aircraft with guns at the ready, prepared to fight their way into Somalia. On hand to welcome them were the American soldiers who had arrived earlier and a few Somali spectators. Apparently still not certain what dangers lay ahead, the Canadian soldiers scraped shallow pits in the sandy soil near the airfield, pitched canvas shelters, and cleaned their weapons in preparation for an attack that never came.

Farther north in Belet Huen a few days later, soldiers arriving directly from Canada were still running from the Hercules transports as if they might be fired on, much to the amazement

of Somalis who had already congregated outside the barbed-
wire enclosure of the airfield. In the cool early-morning hours
of a desert dawn, the first Canadian soldiers formed up and
marched through Belet Huen with flags flying to their encamp-
ment on the other side of town.

The camp itself, as seen on the videos, is puzzling. During
their final exercise in Petawawa before deploying to Somalia,
the Airborne soldiers had constructed a single triangular camp
as suggested in some of the standard peacekeeping manuals. At
that time, the probable destination was Bossasso, a settlement
on the north coast of Somalia. The broad base of the camp was
designed to face the seacoast with the point on the inland side.

Belet Huen, hundreds of kilometres from the coast, required
an adaptation of this design, but it's hard to understand why
Col. Carol Mathieu, who had replaced Col. Paul Morneault,
decided to build a series of camps along the road outside the
town. Each of the three commandos constructed its own camp,
as did the service commando, the engineers' commando, and
the headquarters commando. Within a short time, the large
tracts of arid scrub between the camps started to fill up with
the huts of squatters and refugees.

Even to my untrained eye, the camps appeared to be impossible to defend. Each commando was isolated from the others
and from the headquarters compound at the end of the road.
Nor was there any common-ground plan evident among the
various camps. From the air, each appeared to have a different
arrangement of tents, vehicle parking areas, entrances, and
storage compounds.

Many kilometres of wire were required to surround all these
encampments, as well as platoons of sentries, far more than a

single camp would have needed. Fields of fire encompassed not only civilians in the intervening spaces but the territory of adjacent campsites. Defending the camp of one commando from intruders would have involved firing directly into the camp of another commando.

I'm looking forward to hearing explanations for this layout. Apparently one justification is that it helped to maintain the "integrity" of the different commandos. This made sense only if one understood that the history of the Airborne regiment reflected in its own crazy way the history of Canada. Even our crack national regiment had been unable to overcome our national differences. In Petawawa, each of the three commandos, the English-speaking Two and Three Commandos from the Patricias and the Royal Canadian Regiment and the French-speaking 1er Commando from the Royal 22e, had lived, trained, and partied as an independent unit. Even the selection of the regiment's commanding officer was dominated by political considerations of language and loyalty to one of the three home regiments. What was more logical than to see these Canadian absurdities reflected in the landscape of Somalia – a Canadian regiment scattered across the desert in little independent knots, each one jealously guarding its independence, collectively unable to defend themselves?

Partly as a result of this fragmentation, the Airborne couldn't even provide properly for its own security. Infiltration and thievery became a constant problem, frustrating the efforts of soldiers and officers, exasperating them and eventually contributing to the killings.

Among our witnesses today was John Main, a large, soft-spoken Irishman who worked in Belet Huen for the International

Red Cross from the summer of 1992 until the spring of 1993. He described how the Red Cross was operating feeding stations in the area before the Canadian soldiers started to arrive in December 1992.

By that time, the worst of the starvation was under control. Main explained, for example, that one pocket of refugees went hungry because they refused to accept food at a feeding station operated by refugees from another clan. Sufficient food was reaching Belet Huen to allow the Red Cross to pay its local volunteers with more food than they required, encouraging them to sell their surplus food in local markets to help re-establish the local economy. This explained why Canadian soldiers were later shocked to see Red Cross supplies for sale in markets at Belet Huen. The soldiers assumed that this food had been stolen by the warlords from the Red Cross. In fact, as Main testified, looting of food supplies in the Belet Huen area was only a minor nuisance by the time the Canadians arrived and consisted mainly of sporadic attempts by children to leap aboard moving food convoys in order to throw down a few sacks of beans or rice to their friends.

Nor was personal security a major problem for Main and the other Red Cross workers. The landlords of buildings that the Red Cross had rented in Belet Huen for offices, warehouses, and living compounds supplied guards to protect their property. These were unarmed watchmen similar to those I have seen sitting at night outside office buildings, wealthy homes, and middle-class residential compounds in Nairobi in neighbouring Kenya. Main testified that these unarmed guards were sufficient to maintain security for the Red Cross in Belet Huen. During his year there, he had no personal goods stolen, which must have made Belet Huen more secure than Nairobi and the cities of many other African nations, and certainly more secure than the Canadian camp down the road.

What these unarmed watchmen were able to accomplish for the Red Cross in Belet Huen was apparently beyond the ability of hundreds of heavily armed Canadian soldiers in their compounds just outside the city.

By the time the Canadian soldiers arrived, Belet Huen was one of the most peaceful regions in Somalia. There was nothing for the Canadian soldiers to do except maintain this peace and maintain the security of their own camps. But even this was beyond the capability of the Airborne, or at least part of it. And the Somalis must have sensed this. They seemed to take a perverse delight in testing the overextended perimeters of the Canadian camps. Inside, bored and frustrated soldiers and officers allowed themselves to be goaded into retaliation.

Within a few weeks, as our lawyers have told us, that's the story that will start to unfold before us in detail. We already know that the facts are more appalling than Canadians realize, even more shocking than the stories that have been reported.

Will this trigger a new surge of outrage against the military, or do Canadians already feel overwhelmed and surfeited by events in Somalia? Although I now know the details of revelations that will be made over the next few months, I'm not certain what the public reaction will be.

Wednesday, April 3, 1996
Ottawa

While we were listening today to young non-commissioned officers testify proudly to the achievements of their men in

Somalia, their commander-in-chief was sending an unprecedented message to them and their comrades. Earlier in the day,
Gen. Jean Boyle, the chief of the defence staff, had videotaped
his message for distribution throughout the military. A photo-
copy of the text was waiting in my office when our hearings
adjourned.

Reacting to reports of missing and altered Somalia documentation, General Boyle denied any involvement. "I never
participated in any effort to interfere with the work of the
Somalia Inquiry Commission," he said.

Boyle also stated that he had never seen any evidence of an
"institutional conspiracy to subvert the purposes of the Somalia
Inquiry." But he admitted that there are "gaps in the documentation" and stated that "individuals will have to explain these
gaps." Then he took the unusual step of ordering the military
to drop everything next Tuesday in an all-out effort to find the
missing documents – "to stand down all but essential operations . . . to conduct a thorough search of all their files."

From the officer who last year was in charge of the military's
effort to collect information for us, this new directive is
surprising. For almost a year now, we've been asking for documents from the military. The response has been slow, reluctant,
and incomplete. General Boyle has been fully aware of this.

In the meantime, our own chair is under attack by lawyers
for Gen. Ernest Beno, one of the senior officers liable to be sin-
gled out by us for criticism. Judge Létourneau angered Beno
several months ago when he accused him, during one of our
hearings, of "fiddling" with the truth. Subsequently, after a
fact-finding visit to an army base in Calgary, the judge was
accused by a reserve officer of making negative comments
about Beno in casual conversation.

Judge Létourneau immediately denied this, but Beno's attorneys aren't letting go. Even the reputation of an outstanding judge of the Federal Court isn't safe as senior officers battle to preserve their reputations.

Today we were asked if we could set aside time in two weeks for a special hearing on General Beno's request that Judge Létourneau should step down as chair.

Tuesday, April 9, 1996
London

Today was "D" day – Missing Documents Day. The media predictably treated it as a circus. First thing in the morning, Peter Gzowski, host of CBC Radio's "Morningside," announced that he couldn't do the show because his entire staff was busy looking for missing documents. The *Ottawa Sun* published a list of ten ridiculous places where documents might be found. Journalists drew up lists of imaginary, inane objects that might be uncovered during the search.

No matter what the result, it's hard to see how the military can win on this one. If they don't find the documents, it looks as if the whole thing has been an expensive waste of time. Someone estimated the worth of one day of the military's time at $16 million. If they do find some, they will have to explain why they didn't find them before.

Almost everything the military does now seems to go awry. Even General Boyle's video message to the troops was badly produced. I noticed immediately, when I saw it on the news that night, that the general was fiddling nervously with a pen in his left hand. Sure enough, the next day almost every newspaper report was describing the general as visibly nervous, frequently citing his fidgeting with the pen as proof. It's hard to believe that the military's public affairs directorate was stupid enough to approve a video like that.

Thursday, April 11, 1996
En route Ottawa–London

At a meeting of the commission in Ottawa, preparing for next week's hearings, we were told that the military had suddenly found the hard disk containing computerized logs for the National Defence Operations Centre. Is it credible that the whereabouts of such a basic element of the information system would remain unknown for almost a year, would elude a military police investigation during this time, would remain hidden despite specific orders from our inquiry to produce such documentation, and then would pop up a few days before we hear evidence about missing documentation?

This morning, the military had still not responded to repeated requests from us to provide a witness for next Monday's hearing to describe their efforts to procure documents for us and to explain some of their failures. Word arrived only this afternoon that a colonel had been designated. This means that the interview by our lawyers, which all witnesses have to undergo before appearing at our hearings, will be done in a hurry over the weekend, and we commissioners will have little time to prepare.

What does this stonewalling signify? The government and the military have assured us constantly that their only desire is to assist us in every possible way, to help us to get to the bottom of the story so that they can put the whole mess behind them as quickly as possible. This has been the public posture of all senior military officers. But the reality is quite different. Documentation has taken months and months to arrive after we have requested it, files have been mixed up, and the military has done little to assist us in sorting out the confusion. We have had to create our own computerized directories of information, to organize the military's records for them and to identify gaps in information that the military probably has been aware of for a long time.

Is this due to an unbelievable level of disorganization or to a deliberate effort to slow us down? Last Saturday, the *Globe and Mail* ran a story, obviously fed to it by someone in the military, in which the unnamed source speculated that most of the "missing documents" were in fact meaningless computer glitches. A quick check of our own records revealed that most of the documents that we have listed as missing are real and that the gaps are significant.

Some of our lawyers think that the military is now in a state of panic. Others continue to believe that there is some sort of master plan behind its apparent confusion and that we can expect a clever and unforeseen defence to be presented to us next week. If that's wrong, then next week will reveal a level of bureaucratic disarray that will go a long way toward explaining the tragedy of Somalia.

The media are now comparing all of this to Watergate, where the initial crime was eventually overshadowed by the attempted cover-up. The comparison doesn't seem far-fetched.

We've certainly got the public's attention at this point. We were the *Maclean's* cover story this week: a photo of General Boyle and the headline "What Did He Know?"

Sunday, April 14, 1996
London

On Friday morning, I taught my last class at the University of Western Ontario. It's hard to believe that I have been at the university for fifteen years. The "historic moment" went by quickly. I told the students this was my last class, they grinned uncertainly, and that was it.

Yesterday I chaired a panel discussion at a conference at Western on peacekeeping and foreign aid. The panel included Paul Koring of the *Globe*'s Ottawa bureau. During a coffee break, chatting carefully with Paul, I said that I didn't feel that the attempt to unseat our chair, Judge Létourneau, would be successful. I repeated several times that I was not speaking for quotation. Koring said that lawyers for various parties before the inquiry were predicting that Judge Létourneau would be forced to step down. He told me that he knew for certain that the Privy Council Office was already taking preliminary steps to find a replacement for the judge. I found this a little hard to believe.

Monday, April 15, 1996
Ottawa

In Paul Koring's *Globe* story this morning, a "source close to the inquiry" is reported as saying that one of the commissioners is sure that the charges against Judge Létourneau are not serious. I guess that's me.

————

As soon as I arrived at the inquiry's offices on Slater Street, our lawyers were telling us that new documentation had continued to be delivered to our offices up to and including this weekend. General Boyle himself, arriving for an interview with our lawyers on Saturday prior to his scheduled appearance later this week, suddenly produced documents that our lawyers had never seen before. Apparently the documents contradict some of his earlier statements.

Our staff say that the general looked tired and haggard. Speculation is growing that he will not be able to survive the revelations of the next few weeks. But we're all going to have to wait a little longer for the facts to emerge. Our lawyers have asked for several days' delay while they examine the new documents and distribute the relevant ones to other lawyers. This time, ironically, it was the government lawyers in the hearing room who objected to the delay, after almost a year of foot-dragging in producing the documents that we requested last April. The level of political posturing increases daily.

The nationwide search for documents, ridiculed by the media, has produced another startling result. The original Somalia logbooks of Two Commando apparently were discovered last week in a locked filing cabinet somewhere in the base at Petawawa. We had photocopies of some but not all of these logbooks in our files, but why the complete set of original logbooks have languished in Petawawa since the Airborne returned from Somalia three years ago remains unexplained. Col. Jean Leclerc said on the stand this afternoon that

confusion over the disbanding of the regiment might have
accounted for it.

I think we all had some sympathy for Colonel Leclerc today.
At the start of this whole process, he was appointed by General
Boyle to direct the Somalia Inquiry Liaison Team (SILT), a group
within National Defence Headquarters created to assist us in
collecting documentation. In this job, Leclerc was caught
between our escalating demands and the increasing delays in
the production of documents. Whatever decisions might have
been made to conceal or tamper with documents probably
occurred at a higher level, although we won't know that for certain until next week when we start calling witnesses on the
whole question of documentation.

Thursday, April 18, 1996
En route London–Ottawa

Tomorrow morning at 9:30 A.M. we will hear the motion for
our chair's disqualification. We may also hear the latest report
from our own lawyers on the state of documentation, now that
they've had time to review the items turned up by the nationwide search. There may be a tendency for the news media to
pay more attention to this report than to the motion against
Judge Létourneau. We're not above a little media manipulation
ourselves.

The motion against Judge Létourneau has contributed to a
public debate about the usefulness of this type of inquiry. Some
years ago, the media used to focus on the cost of royal commissions and the futility of many of their recommendations. It
was the kind of routine exposé that showed up in newspapers

on a dull news day. Although there's still discussion of the cost, as lawyers' fees drive them to astronomical levels, more attention has been paid recently to the obstacles being placed in the path of these inquiries. The Krever inquiry examining the state of Canada's blood-supply system is the latest example. Here again, government creates an inquiry only to find itself in the position of a litigant opposed to certain aspects of the inquiry.

The motion to unseat Judge Létourneau, and much of the debate during our hearings, shows how difficult it is to conduct an aggressive public inquiry while taking care not to unfairly damage reputations in the process.

I've discovered that public inquiries exist in something of a no-man's-land when it comes to procedure. For example, our hearings are conducted, in some ways, like a court. We enter the hearing room with the solemnity of judges, and bow before taking our places. Witnesses testify under oath. But in some important ways, our procedures are much less rigid than those of a court. It's common, for instance, for lawyers to ask leading questions of witnesses in a way that would not be tolerated in a trial.

This leeway is meant to provide a forceful instrument for the discovery of information. Although in our case my two fellow commissioners are judges, our role is not judicial but inquisitorial. We are supposed to ask tough questions. We are supposed to be persistent in getting at the facts.

Sometimes it's impossible to do this without confronting a witness directly with inconsistencies in his or her testimony. Confused by General Beno's testimony a few months ago, Judge Létourneau angrily accused him of "fiddling" with the facts. Now this is one of the incidents being used to show that he lacks the impartiality required to give Beno a fair hearing.

It's necessary to protect witnesses from reckless accusations, but it's also important to allow commissioners to question witnesses aggressively. The difficulty in maintaining this
balance grows as the number of lawyers involved in our hearings increases. By the end of last week, more than thirty military personnel had come under sufficient suspicion to warrant
having access to their own lawyers. With dozens of lawyers
watching our proceedings, the chances of this type of legal
challenge increase exponentially – as does the cost of our
inquiry.

Although I hate to suggest another inquiry, it might be time
to create one to review the public inquiries legislation and to
explore more efficient, economical, and effective ways of
investigating wrongdoing by instruments of the government
itself.

Friday, April 19, 1996
En route Ottawa–London

Before the hearing today, Judge Létourneau was clearly preoccupied by the allegations made against him. But by the end
of the day, there was a sense that the tide had started to turn in
his favour.

An article in the *Globe and Mail*, favourable to the judge,
was taken as a good omen. It had been written by Hugh
Winsor, a *Globe* veteran of almost a quarter-century and a
good friend of mine. Hugh had called me at home in London
yesterday, looking for some personal "colour" about the judge.
As he stated in his article today, Judge Létourneau, despite the

important positions that he has filled in Quebec and Ottawa, as vice-dean of Laval's Law School, a senior official in the Quebec Justice Department under the Lévesque government, and head of the federal Law Reform Commission, is almost unknown to the Canadian public.

Hugh had found almost nothing in the *Globe* files. So, when he called me, I tried to provide him with some personal details interspersed with information that had a more editorial aspect. I mentioned the judge's interest in hunting, his interest in rifles, which was evident when armaments were discussed before the inquiry. Hugh already had learned about the judge's lifelong love of hockey, as an adult player until recently and as the author of an official report on violence in amateur hockey in Quebec. These details helped to alter the picture of Létourneau that Hugh apparently had started out with, that of an austere and aloof intellectual. I was able to confirm that the judge was quite the opposite – a down-to-earth individual with a marked zest for life. I mentioned his interest in good food and wine, and his reputation as an amateur chef. I knew this was the kind of material that Hugh needed, and I tried to use it to illustrate Létourneau's positive role in the inquiry.

The visits to the military bases, for instance, had been his idea. With the soldiers, Létourneau had been direct and natural, gaining their confidence as a straight-shooter. The success of these visits, in terms of the numbers of soldiers who had talked to us and the quality of the information they provided, might have worried some senior officers. Ironically, as Hugh pointed out, it was during one of these visits that Létourneau allegedly had run into trouble.

Tuesday, April 23, 1996
Ottawa

Yesterday I cleaned out my office at the university. It was almost fifteen years ago that my wife, Hazel, and the administrative officer of the graduate school, Lynn Larmour, selected the straw-coloured, textured wall covering and the brown floral-pattern drapes. Hazel and I found an old wooden office desk at an antique dealer in London. It was said to have come from Hamilton's City Hall. It wasn't particularly distinctive, just a sturdy, leather-topped pedestal desk, but it was cheaper, and far more interesting, than any of the modern desks in the office furniture catalogue.

We framed some prints from my great-grandfather's news-magazine of the 1860s and 1870s, the *Canadian Illustrated News*, to decorate the walls. Yesterday morning they left square pale patches on the darkened surface.

Many other things reminded me of the passage of time. Boxes of files from the Royal Commission on Newspapers that I had carted down from Ottawa in 1981. Shelves of obscure and forgotten books on events in Quebec in the 1960s. Filing cabinets that disclosed memos, minutes of meetings, letters to faculty, remnants of old issues and battles that had seemed of overwhelming importance at the time.

This kind of thing has to be done quickly, like surgery in the eighteenth century, before anesthetics. It took me only three hours to clear away the accumulated debris of fifteen years, the longest period that I had ever spent in a single job and place. It was surprisingly emotional, a little like moving out of a house after a marriage breaks up. Today I cancelled my planned attendance at a meeting in Toronto next Friday to discuss the ongoing fund-raising campaign for the school. I realized that my time at Western is actually just about over.

This morning I read and marked student essays for the last time.

On the plane to Ottawa this evening, during a rough flight, I read material relating to witnesses who will be appearing before us over the next two days. At issue is the disappearance or alteration of Somalia documents in the public affairs directorate at National Defence Headquarters. Among the witnesses are the officers and bureaucrats who were trying to manage media coverage as the Somalia affair began to explode.

As I read the material, I felt more at home with the evidence. This was my world I was entering, the domain of media management, manipulation of information and "damage control" – the world where appearances are created to mask reality. Over the next few weeks, the inquiry will be on territory familiar to me. Although no one could have foreseen this at the outset, this phase of the inquiry adds logic, retroactively, to my original selection as a commissioner. This is where I should be particularly useful.

When I checked into the hotel this evening, there was a letter waiting for me. The brown envelope bearing the title "National Defence" contained a one-paragraph message: "Dear Sir: If you really want to get to the bottom of the Somalia cover up within the Department of Defence you need to recall [I've had to delete the name here for legal reasons]. He was privy to and helped to orchestrate everything. You are on the right track. These civil and military servants are careerists. They do not care about the soldiers they are empowered to lead or the country to which they were to serve. A Friend."

Thursday, April 25, 1996
Ottawa

I've often wondered what judges do when they retire "to their chambers." Our retreat is a conference room adjacent to the miniature auditorium-TV studio where we hold our hearings. Often the three of us spend lunch hours and coffee breaks with lawyers or other members of our staff discussing strategy, responses to requests or motions by lawyers for other parties, and organizational problems within the inquiry. Today the conversation turned to hockey. It was one of those days – they usually happen toward the end of the week – when we seemed to want to talk about anything but the inquiry.

The two judges, Létourneau and Rutherford, sometimes have conversations under the generic title "Who's Doing What to Whom in the Legal Profession." I suppose it's just my exaggerated impression that every one of our thousands of Canadian lawyers knows all the others, but Gilles and Bob can happily spend hours, or so it seems, trading new developments and old stories about other lawyers. Journalists are the same when we get together.

The mood in our "chambers" depends a great deal on what has happened in the hearing room. Today, for instance, I managed to force a telling admission from our witness, Roberto Gonzalez, former director general of public affairs at NDHQ. It was Gonzalez who masterminded a shake-up in public affairs that included changing the title of a category of documents that has now become controversial: "Response to Queries" was changed to "Media Response Lines."

This esoteric sample of bureaucratic wordplay has assumed immense significance because of the persistence of a CBC reporter, Michael McAuliffe. It was he who asked the Department of National Defence in 1993 for copies of all Responses to Queries produced by National Defence in the previous six months, during the events in Somalia.

Responses to Queries were explanations of military actions or policies created in order to answer questions from journalists. They were produced by public affairs officers working under Gonzalez, a former army major who had previously been in charge of the Defence Department's parliamentary affairs branch.

Two actions were taken in response to McAuliffe's request. Some of the Response to Queries documents were altered, and the entire Response to Queries system was renamed Media Response Lines. The first action reduced the amount of embarrassing information given to McAuliffe; the second made it unlikely that he would get any more in future. From then on, when he asked for copies of Responses to Queries, he would be told they no longer existed.

But it has been difficult to find an example of an alteration in a Response to Queries that was significant. Most of the deleted pages include relatively innocuous background information. As our lawyer questioned Gonzalez, I skimmed through the RTQs, as everyone now calls them, in our evidence books. All three of us should read these before hearings, but the amount of documentation is overwhelming. It is almost impossible for us to keep track of it all, and we rely heavily on our lawyers to guide us to important evidence during the hearings. This time, however, I found a discrepancy between an original RTQ and the doctored version that had been supplied to McAuliffe. In this case, there was clearly a tampering with the document to delete a reference that was critical of military conduct in Somalia.

I forced an acknowledgement of this from Gonzalez, and the change was significant enough to destroy his stand that only cosmetic and unimportant changes had been made in the RTQs.

I'm beginning to understand lawyers' fascination with courtroom debate, the contest of wills and intellect between a determined counsel and a reluctant or evasive witness. Right after I had scored my point, we recessed for ten minutes and I walked into our conference room feeling the same sort of "high" that elates an athlete in the locker room after a successful game. These moments give all of us a feeling that progress has been made, that another piece of the puzzle has fallen into place. In this case, the whole structure is slowly but surely threatening the credibility of the current chief of the defence staff, Gen. Jean Boyle, who was Gonzalez's superior officer at the time.

It now looks as if we might spend up to a month examining the question of missing and altered documentation, and that the military might have a new chief of the defence staff before we're finished. This has become the most interesting and vital part of the inquiry, but it isn't at all what we were planning to do at this time, even a month ago. It's as if the inquiry has taken on a life of its own.

Monday, April 29, 1996
Ottawa

It struck me again today that the inquiry is almost a living thing. In a world where everything is tightly managed and controlled by big governments or big corporations, the inquiry, once set in motion, starts to move wherever the evidence takes it. This is what makes it so unusual, gripping, and valuable.

A great deal is being written at the moment about the futility of public inquiries. The Krever inquiry into the nation's blood supply is now tied up in legal knots by the very government that created it. No matter how legitimate the government's concern might be, it appears contradictory to the average citizen and breeds scepticism. Nor do the vast amounts of money consumed by these inquiries encourage the belief that they benefit the public. Lawyers are seen to be the main beneficiaries.

Even considering all that, this kind of inquiry is one of our few institutions that has a chance of doing what it is supposed to do, without being influenced by any of the big players in our society. This requires, to begin with, a determined and independent chair, and we're fortunate in having that in Gilles Létourneau. Judge Rutherford is just as uncompromising in his quest for factual information. As a veteran with a distinguished war record, he is even more affected than Gilles or myself by stories of misconduct by soldiers.

An independent inquiry is a double-edged sword for the government that creates it. At first, it protects the government from charges of inaction on a pressing issue. The minister can always say that he is waiting for the inquiry to report while, in the meantime, saying and doing very little. But then, once the inquiry is in motion, the government has no control over its procedure and outcome.

In this case, although the inquiry was created to investigate events that occurred under the previous Conservative government, we have now veered toward events that occurred under the current government, and the political future of the present minister of defence may be linked to the fate of the chief of the defence staff whom he appointed.

Today the chief lawyer for the government opposed a motion by one of the soldiers' counsels for release of military police interviews of Defence Department officials implicated in the alteration or destruction of documents. When we ruled against the government's position, and for the release of the documents, the government's lawyer, Peter Vita, asked for a stay in our hearings so that he could consult his superiors. This raised the possibility of a further delay, although we won't know Vita's final position until we reconvene tomorrow morning.

While the government was raising these objections in our hearings, the minister of defence was insisting, during Question Period in the House of Commons, that he wished the inquiry to do its job in the most thorough fashion and to deal with all allegations of cover-up. The contradiction between the government's public position and the efforts of government lawyers to protect the Defence Department and some of its senior officers and civilian officials becomes more glaring day by day.

One of the paradoxes of the current situation is that we wouldn't be investigating cover-ups right now if the Defence Department had done its job properly. It's because we still don't have all the documentation we requested a year ago, and because attempts were made to destroy some documents within National Defence Headquarters, as recently as last fall, that we are now embroiled in a detailed inquiry into the whole cover-up question, a phase of our work that we didn't anticipate addressing until almost the very end.

Watching Judge Létourneau handle the objections and motions that constantly arise is an education in itself. I've been struck by his quickness in going to the heart of an issue, and his ability to marshal arguments in support of his decisions. Of course to an outsider such as myself, some of this process appears more wondrous than it really is. This is the judge's own field. Even so, I learn much from him every day about logical argument and the careful consideration of evidence. I've reached the point of making a few useful suggestions myself as we draft our decisions. Judge Rutherford doesn't say a great deal, but when he does, he speaks with the authority of experience and always with common sense.

It has been years since I've seen someone work with a pen. During the lunch hour today, as we ate our take-out salads in the conference room next to the hearing room, Gilles wrote in longhand the opinion that he had to deliver in our hearing that afternoon, after consulting with the secretary of the inquiry, Stan Cohen, and with Judge Rutherford and myself.

Writing out his judgment takes time, but the process itself seems to assist him in reaching his conclusions. He continues to develop his thoughts when his script is being typed into the computer, then revises the first printout by hand.

Over lunch we continued to discuss the wording of his decision. Paragraphs were occasionally moved or deleted. Words were changed here and there. At one point in this free-flowing process, I said something about slowly losing my awe of the majesty of the law, having long ago lost most of my illusions about the solemnity of the political process. Most professions tend to lose their impressive and carefully cultivated air of mystery when you draw close, as when, watching a surgeon operate, you realize that this is just carpentry of a very precise and elaborate kind.

At 6 P.M. I went to the Booth Building on the Sparks Street Mall for a radio interview about the future of the CBC. Michael

Coulton interviewed me from Toronto for about twenty-five minutes, for a "clip" or two that might occupy ten or fifteen seconds in his report. When I walked into the eighth-floor newsroom of CBC Radio, the first person I saw was Michael McAuliffe, the CBC reporter whose investigations of National Defence Headquarters had produced revelations of document tampering and led directly to our current hearings. Ironically, because McAuliffe is now being referred to regularly by witnesses, and because he may be called to testify, he has been taken off coverage of our hearings for the time being, losing the chance to report on the very story that he created.

I looked around the cramped and cluttered CBC office, with its tiny studio and control room at one end, and thought how modest are the resources provided to most journalists. Newspapers this week have been remarking on the salaries earned by a few prominent television journalists. In Canada, television anchors for major networks or the largest local stations are paid from $100,000 to $300,000 a year, perhaps one-tenth of what the top American anchors earn. TVO's Steve Paikin earns $132,000 annually, according to a recent report. But most radio and television journalists, and all but a few print journalists, earn far less than $100,000, and often work in offices that a self-respecting secretary would reject. Almost never do they have the research or editorial support that one would expect in an industry whose main raw material and chief product is information, and whose reputation depends on the reliability of that information.

Despite this, individual journalists – such as Michael McAuliffe – can still make a difference. The members of the public affairs directorate at National Defence probably outnumbered him twenty-to-one, at least, but his single-minded determination was enough ultimately to discredit the twenty, and perhaps to bring down a chief of the defence staff too. On Sunday, the *Toronto Star*'s lead editorial called for the immediate resignation of General Boyle because of evidence heard by us up to now.

Tuesday, April 30, 1996
Ottawa

Nella came into the office as usual about 9:15 A.M. to empty the wastebasket. She's Haitian, I would guess in her twenties, wearing jeans and a loose cotton top. We often exchange a few words, usually about the weather. She hates the Ottawa winter.

This morning, when she entered, I was signing a birthday card for Cymbria, my oldest grandchild, who will be fourteen on Saturday. The card bore a painting of beluga whales and the best I could think of, after a lifetime of using words, was to wish her a "whale of a day." A small oblong box on the desk contained the simple necklace of tiny freshwater pearls, jade and some sort of carved iridescent shell that I had bought yesterday. On impulse, I showed it to Nella and asked if she had any children.

No, she said, firmly. She wasn't going to have children until she found the right man. I mentioned a niece in Ottawa who is a single mother, living in a one-bedroom apartment with her six-year-old son. Nella mentioned a thirteen-year-old niece who had died recently in Haiti from cancer. I said, "Thirteen?" in disbelief. Yes, they had amputated her leg, but she had hurt the other, and the doctors had discovered cancer everywhere.

From there the conversation moved quickly to sickness, death, and immortality, then to the reason for life. It's a curious thing, I said to Nella, that the only important question is the one we can't answer: Why are we here? She looked heavenward and said something about God knowing. This was a strange conversation to be having at 9:30 A.M. on a Tuesday with my desk littered with paper, the computer terminal staring at me expectantly, and the necklace lying in its box in front of me. I suppose I wanted to end it when I tried to laugh and make a joke about dying being necessary, otherwise where would we put all the people. Nella didn't laugh.

Half an hour later, I returned to "Somalia" to hear the lawyer for the government eating crow in the hearing room, accepting yesterday's ruling on the distribution of tapes and transcripts to other lawyers. Overnight, we were told privately, the word had come down that the minister's position would prevail over the lawyer's arguments for delay and possible derailment of our inquiry. Behind the decision was the imponderable force of public opinion. So far at least, the government doesn't want to appear to be creating obstacles for us.

Yesterday's witness returned to the stand and, under questioning, linked General Boyle even more closely to the process of altering and destroying documents that had occurred at NDHQ in 1993. The noose seems to be slipping over his head and tightening slowly.

Friday, May 2, 1996
En route Ottawa–London

We're all fascinated by the possibility of spectacular crimes committed by important and influential people. News media congregate at our hearings when generals and deputy ministers take the stand. Almost unnoticed yet often more important are the Nancy Fourniers.

Nancy Fournier was in the news months ago when the *Globe* first broke the story about document tampering at National Defence Headquarters. Most of the details of her story were known before she made her appearance before us today. But hearing her tell it was quite different than reading about it. It all sounded so ordinary and matter-of-fact that you had to make an effort to remember from time to time that if colonels and generals and perhaps even a cabinet minister should be forced to resign as this story unfolds, Nancy Fournier is probably as responsible as anyone.

I had pictured her as an older, tiny, spinsterish office worker. I don't know why. She turned out to be a brunette in her forties perhaps, slightly plump, with a pleasant, engaging smile. Our lawyers had warned us that she was very nervous about testifying, but there was little sign of this during the more than five hours she was on the stand. Perhaps it had something to do with the skilful yet considerate questioning by our own counsel, Barbara McIsaac, who has served her own time in government offices and understands what it is like to keep family and career going simultaneously.

Fournier has been a clerk at National Defence Headquarters for the past seventeen years, one of many who work in the Canadian "Pentagon" on the east bank of Ottawa's Rideau Canal. During all that time, she has worked in the public affairs directorate, assisting a succession of officers whose job it is to project a positive image of the Canadian Armed Forces through the news media. Her domain for much of this time was the nerve centre, the Media Liaison Office, an enclosure where officers equipped with phones, tape recorders, and video equipment jousted daily with journalists.

It was always a delicate symbiosis, each party needing, but wary of the other. Some journalists, truly ignorant of military affairs, were happy to trade junkets overseas for glowing reports about Canada's gallant peacekeepers, but there were always a few reporters who wanted to look beneath the surface, who kept asking awkward questions. Michael McAuliffe was one of these, a sharp-featured, tense reporter for CBC Radio whose beat was NDHQ and who began to work it like a ferret in the spring of 1993 when the horrifying events in Somalia started to emerge. At first it was only a trickle of bad news, but the military couldn't seem to staunch the flow. Within a few months, journalists were buzzing around the Somalia story like flies around a festering wound, and the military was starting to panic.

McAuliffe had sources, some of them disgruntled former officers, who guided him toward sensitive areas at NDHQ. He began to cultivate some of the officers in the Media Liaison Office. Still trying to sound him out, to see if he might play ball if carefully handled, they invited him to tour the office, to meet the staff and to see how they operated. Apparently it was during this visit that McAuliffe first became aware of the Responses to Queries.

McAuliffe had the bright idea of asking the office to give him all the RTQs relating to Somalia. No one had ever asked for them before. He happened to make the request just as the Defence Department, worried by media coverage of Somalia, was trying to get a better handle on its media liaison services. Someone in the Media Liaison Office got another bright idea: Give McAuliffe what he wanted, but carefully, in order to avoid forcing him to make an official Access to Information request. So the RTQs were sorted, culled and edited, and then given to McAuliffe as if they were complete and intact.

It was Nancy Fournier who did this, following instructions from her superiors. Some months later, it was Nancy Fournier who again edited these RTQs when McAuliffe, perhaps tipped off by one of his sources, used Access to Information to request these RTQs and others. It was Nancy Fournier who was told to destroy Somalia documents in her files after our inquiry had ordered them to be produced. And finally, crucially, it was Nancy Fournier who put off performing this act of destruction until after Labour Day in September 1995. She dawdled and dithered until a young navy lieutenant in the Media Liaison Office, Al Wong, asked her what she was doing. When she told him, he immediately ordered her to stop and went to his superiors for instructions. So Nancy Fournier carefully removed all the documents that she had put into the "fire bag" for destruction and replaced them in her binders while her superiors decided what to do.

Shortly after that, it was those binders that provided much of the evidence of document tampering that began to shake the entire structure of the Department of National Defence, and the quake continues to grow in intensity. It was Nancy Fournier's reluctance to destroy the files that she had so carefully built up over the years that fatally weakened the chain of conspiracy.

But Nancy Fournier today seemed anything but proud of what she had done. She was still torn between loyalty to the department and old colleagues and the desire to do the right thing. She didn't want to be on the stand at all, you could tell. She just wanted to get back to her computer terminal and her friends in the Media Liaison Office, but she had destroyed that

world as surely as if she had planted an anti-personnel mine in
the centre of the office.

Sunday, May 5, 1996
En route London–Ottawa

On Friday night, back home in London, I settled down in front
of the television set to watch *The Pelican Brief*. The film opens
with the murder of two justices of the U.S. Supreme Court. As
an exercise in legal detection, and to impress her law professor
who also happens to be her lover, a female law student devel-
ops a theory to explain the murders. It involves a wealthy oil-
man, a pelican sanctuary, and an environmental group in a
high-stakes struggle, and there are connections to the White
House. The president himself may be involved. Within a few
days, the professor-lover has been murdered, killers are pursu-
ing the law student, and a black journalist is about to break the
whole story Watergate-style.

This wasn't the first American film I had seen based on the
idea that there is corruption at the highest levels of the U.S.
government. It's a distinct genre. Another recent film, *Clear
and Present Danger*, starred Harrison Ford and involved a
Colombian druglord. I remember thinking at the time that a
succession of films such as this must promote the idea among
Americans that their entire political system, up to and including the White House, is corrupt.

In *The Pelican Brief*, an improbable theory by an unknown
law student sets in motion a wave of terror that soon litters the
screen with bodies. In the Somalia affair, a clerk at National

Defence Headquarters sets in motion a chain of events that now reaches the chief of the defence staff. Has she faced personal danger? Has she had to go into hiding and dodge hired assassins?

Exactly the contrary. As a result of her actions, junior officers in the Media Liaison Office invited her out for coffee and urged her to go to the *Globe and Mail* as the "Deep Throat" of National Defence Headquarters. When she refused, the officers went to their colonel and confessed that some of them had been talking to the *Globe*. When an internal investigation was launched, the colonel called Nancy Fournier into his office, waved his arms at her and tried to tell her what to say to the investigators. He was singularly unsuccessful.

In our hearings, Fournier has described herself self-deprecatingly as "only a Clerk Four." After her preliminary interviews, our lawyers told us that she was very upset by all the fuss and might break down on the stand. But today, in the face of an aggressive, harrying cross-examination, Fournier let us glimpse her true mettle. She handled the lawyers without batting an eye, calmly turning aside all their courtroom tricks.

When the litter of wrecked military careers is finally swept out of National Defence Headquarters, Fournier will probably still be working at her computer terminal, quietly keeping an eye on things.

The heroine of *The Pelican Brief* risked her life to bring down a president. Nancy Fournier went to lunch with her husband, another civil servant, and decided she didn't need the *Globe and Mail* to do what she had to do. She had a better way to make sure that the little conspiracy in the Media Liaison Office self-destructed. She made sure that all the evidence was intact when the investigators arrived. I thought to myself: This is the way we do it here. No guns. No mysterious disappearances. A clerk can help to bring down a chief of the defence staff and the worst thing she has to face is a courtroom interrogation by smart lawyers.

Tuesday, May 7, 1996
Ottawa

Navy Lieut. Joel Brayman of the Media Liaison Office was on the stand. I was busily noting down his testimony in my black notebook when I heard his voice break. I looked up quickly as Barbara McIsaac, our lawyer, suggested that as it was almost four, our usual time to adjourn, we should end the hearing until tomorrow morning. So we rose, bowed, and left. Once the door of the hearing room had closed behind us, I asked Judge Létourneau if the witness had choked up. Judge Rutherford, who sits closest to the witness stand, confirmed that he had.

"There were tears running down his cheeks," he said.

Throughout the day, Lieutenant Brayman had been unshakable, even under some of the most intensive questioning of our hearings. At one point, Barbara McIsaac took the unusual step of asking for a ten-minute adjournment so that he could consult documents and think carefully about his answers – a signal that she was finding him unresponsive and inconsistent. Because he was dealing with media liaison matters, and making them unnecessarily confusing, in my view, I had been persistent myself in trying to pin him down.

His demeanour and tone of voice never changed. His black naval uniform, short black hair, wire-rimmed glasses, and thin parson's nose made him look as humourless as his voice sounded. His sudden breakdown was completely unheralded.

I had to struggle to remember exactly what he was saying at the time. He had been describing a difficult episode in the Media Liaison Office in the fall of 1995 when the scheme to alter documents provided to CBC reporter Michael McAuliffe was starting to unravel. Officers were beginning to worry about repercussions. Brayman himself had started to keep a daily record of events for his own protection. He referred to it frequently today. It showed that at one point he had visited the office of one of his superiors, Cmdr. Douglas Caie, to discuss strategy.

"I went to see him because I was concerned," he said, or something close to that, "and because he had been a good friend. . . ."

Then he stopped, cried silently, and we adjourned.

What had touched him at that moment? I wondered as I walked back to the hotel on Cooper Street. Was it only tension after hours of answering lawyers' questions on the stand? Or, more likely, had the recollection of his friendship with Commander Caie brought him to tears?

We tend to forget that the people before us are more than witnesses. I've become so immersed in the whole history of document alteration and destruction that witnesses, to me, have become nothing but instruments for the production of information. If they help me to understand, I like them; if they conceal information or try to confuse me, I become annoyed. I don't want to let the human aspects of the story get in the way. They're not important to our inquiry.

But they were important at the time to the people involved in the crisis that overtook the public affairs directorate at National Defence Headquarters in the wake of the Somalia mission. Some of the officers and clerks had worked together for years. There must have been friendships, alliances, and rivalries that we know nothing about. And there must have been conspiracies and betrayals as the cover-up began to disintegrate.

Some of Joel Brayman's testimony today placed Commander Caie in a bad light. Nancy Fournier yesterday repeated negative remarks about Brayman by his boss, Col. Geoffrey Haswell.

Perhaps Brayman suddenly remembered a happier time when the team in the Media Liaison Office was working smoothly to project a good image of Canada's military. Now this same office had become the source of the most serious threat in years to the good reputation of the Armed Forces. The whole experience must have seemed like a nightmare to those who were involved. Joel Brayman perhaps remembered today what it had been like, and how it had all fallen apart.

Thursday, May 9, 1996
En route Ottawa–London

Navy Lieut. Joel Brayman was back on the stand today, cool and methodical in his answers after his momentary lapse yesterday. But his story became even more dramatic as he described the decision that he and several of his colleagues made last September – to tell Michael McAuliffe that, a year and a half earlier, he had received documents from their office that had been deliberately altered. Brayman said that he did this because he had become convinced that one of his superiors, Colonel Haswell, had decided to pin the whole thing on him. Against all rules and regulations, he went to McAuliffe, as he told us, to make sure that the real truth about events in NDHQ would be made public.

"I realized that my career would never be the same after that," he said, showing a trace of the emotion that had shaken him yesterday.

It was a Canadian version of "Deep Throat" or the Pentagon Papers, perhaps less dramatic but just as earth-shaking for those involved. The participants met in the cafeteria at NDHQ. Later, at a downtown Ottawa restaurant, Brayman told McAuliffe all about the altered documents. McAuliffe promised not to use the story until there were further developments, but, from then on, the facts in McAuliffe's possession were like a time bomb ticking just outside the walls of NDHQ. In the weeks that followed, McAuliffe would phone Brayman occasionally to say that he was getting close to publication. Brayman would provide him with more information and urge him to wait.

Brayman had used McAuliffe to protect himself from enemies within his own department. Now McAuliffe was using Brayman, and the threat of publication, to pry more and more information out of him.

I wondered if the events in Somalia had fostered Brayman's belief that senior officers could shift blame for fiascos onto subordinates such as himself. He had seen the system operating in Somalia from a privileged vantage point in the Media Liaison Office. Was this what it had taught him? When he went to McAuliffe to spill the beans, he knew that the department had already started an internal investigation. He obviously didn't trust it.

At the end of the afternoon, with Watergate and the Pentagon Papers still in mind, I searched the bookcase in my office for my copy of Lt.-Gen. W. R. Peers's book on the My Lai massacre. It was twenty-eight years ago this spring that American soldiers slaughtered 347 civilians at My Lai in Vietnam. General Peers, a combat veteran of three wars who commanded an infantry division in Vietnam, headed the official inquiry into the incident. He described this episode as "an illegal operation in violation of military regulations and human rights, starting with the planning and continuing through the brutal, destructive acts of many of the men who were involved, and culminating in aborted efforts to investigate and, finally, the suppression of the truth." I suspect, even at this stage, that our own report will echo this, though on a smaller scale.

General Peers placed responsibility squarely on the leadership of the U.S. army in Vietnam. The men of Charlie Company who rampaged through My Lai "were average American soldiers," he wrote. "If other units with the same kind of men did not commit atrocities of this order, there must have been overriding causes." The decisive factor was leadership, or the lack of it. The Peers inquiry found that American forces were badly trained in the laws of war, badly prepared for their role in Vietnam, badly educated about the Vietnamese people, and badly led by commissioned and non-commissioned officers.

In a personal note to Gen. William Westmoreland, the American chief of staff at the time, General Peers laid down principles of leadership, among them that:

"Commanders at all echelons are responsible for the actions and welfare of all of the men under them. A commander cannot delegate such responsibility to his subordinates nor can he shrug it off by indicating a lack of knowledge. It is his duty to ferret out potential and actual trouble areas and to be on the spot to take corrective action."

It's already evident that the behaviour of the entire command structure of the Canadian Forces in Somalia failed to meet that standard.

At My Lai, admittedly, there were hundreds of innocent victims. The longer and generally benevolent Canadian occupation of Belet Huen in Somalia produced three Somali deaths. Only one has been officially recognized as murder; the circumstances of the others should become clearer in a few months.

But My Lai occurred under the stress of war. American soldiers were being killed every day by an enemy that was almost invisible. Vietnamese soldiers could hide their weapons and rudimentary black uniforms and disappear instantly into the rural population. Women and children were known to assist them. Land mines had caused heavy casualties among the soldiers of Charlie Company. None of this excused the massacre, but it did explain the pent-up anger of the soldiers.

At Belet Huen, conditions were relatively peaceful. Not a single Canadian soldier died at the hands of Somalis. The only Canadian fatality at Belet Huen was shot accidentally by one of his comrades. The only provocation that Canadian soldiers had to contend with was minor thievery.

Seen in this light, the murder or murders by the Canadian soldiers, and the mistreatment of Somalis detained as suspected thieves, seem even less explicable than the massacre at My Lai. The absence of leadership was perhaps even more glaring.

Sunday, May 12, 1996
En route London–Ottawa

As if echoing my thoughts last Friday night, the *Globe and Mail*
on Saturday published an article in its "Focus" section entitled,
"Where have all the leaders gone?" The writer, as is often the
case in the *Globe* these days, was not a professional journalist.
His name was Bob Evans and he was identified as "a Toronto
business consultant and former Canadian Armed Forces officer."

Evans used our inquiry and two others, the inquiries into the
national blood supply and the Westray mine disaster in Nova
Scotia, to reveal a common theme: "an unwillingness or inability of leaders to accept responsibility for what happened." In
our own inquiry, Evans observed "beribboned senior leaders in
the military" who "display selective amnesia, lose documents,
declare ignorance of events that demonstrably took place under
their noses and employ the worst of bureaucratic double-
speak." He said this represented a "crisis in our society" and
that this "arises from the observable fact that we no longer
know what leadership is." In Evans's opinion, "to be a leader"
is about "accepting full responsibility for every lapse, failing
and screw-up that occurs under your jurisdiction."

"It means being blamed for something over which you had
no control whatsoever," he concluded. "Stripped of all its trap-
pings, leadership is the exercise of moral courage."

After months of listening to senior military officers and
civilian defence officials trying to evade responsibility by claiming ignorance of events under their command, Bob Evans's cri-
tique seemed at first to hit the nail right on the head. But, like
most angry polemics, its impact was strongest at first reading.
Then came the more difficult questions. His description of the

disease was accurate, but his explanation of the cause was less satisfying. To say that the problem is a lack of "moral courage" isn't really to say very much. How do you measure moral courage?

I'm not sure that our report will be more successful than Evans's short essay in defining causes. I'm sure that we'll describe accurately and in detail the disease and its symptoms, and for this reason alone perhaps there is merit in his suggestion that our report, and those of the Westray and Krever inquiries, "become required reading at Royal Military College, in all business, public administration and professional faculties and in every cabinet office across the land." And I'm sure we'll propose changes in military regulations and procedure designed to avoid a repetition of the Somalia fiasco. But I doubt that we'll produce, or even know how to describe, the kind of moral reform that Bob Evans wants.

Evans's theme is repeated constantly these days. At least in developed countries such as Canada, there is a widespread uneasiness and concern, a sense that things in general are getting worse rather than better. It isn't yet an apocalyptic, end-of-the-world feeling, but it's becoming that. Newspapers have carried a number of articles attributing this to the approaching end of the century. Some historians have detected similar millennial crises at the close of earlier centuries.

Whatever the cause, it's true that humanity appears to be undergoing a crisis of confidence. In the nuclear age, large-scale wars no longer provide a cycle of dedication to glorious ideals, opportunities for heroism and sacrifice, and a postwar period of renewal and rebuilding. The technological advances of recent times seem to have created almost as many problems as they have resolved. Certainly our lives in many cases have become easier and longer, but for what purpose? To create an over-populated world slowly sinking in its own waste?

Television may have something to do with this pessimism. I'm beginning to have some real doubts that the traditional values and practices of journalism, the ones that I have believed in for most of my life, have worked effectively in the world of television journalism.

When independently owned daily newspapers were the main carriers of news and opinion in their communities, newspapers had a muck-raking role to play as the moral consciences of their communities. Some editors and journalists did this seriously and prompted important reforms. Many others practised a debased form of journalism designed to create a furore mainly to generate sales. In any event, people took newspaper stories with a grain of salt. Journalists were sometimes feared, often despised, and rarely respected.

Television transformed journalism into a profession with immense authority and influence. It could be argued that a few TV journalists have wielded more power than most politicians. But the ideals of journalism remained locked in an imaginary nineteenth-century newsroom where irascible editors sit at roll-top desks. The flaws, distortions, and sensationalism of old-time journalism have been magnified by television journalism, and have wreaked unintended havoc as a result.

Some studies have shown that daily television newscasts, based on the traditional journalistic principle that "good news is not news," have contributed to a feeling of pessimism and powerlessness among millions of people. These people have been convinced by television that the world is becoming more violent and uncontrollable and that nothing can be done about it – least of all by the politicians who are shown on television, in the news and in television drama, as being cynical and corrupt.

Monday, May 13, 1996
Ottawa

There's a lawyer who sits in our hearing room almost every day. He rarely intervenes. The officer he represents has seldom been mentioned in testimony. I heard today that this lawyer so far has billed the government about $200,000 for his services.

I understand that the top rate for lawyers involved in this type of federal inquiry is $2,000 a day. The problem lies not so much in the rate, although it seems inordinately high, particularly during a time of cutbacks everywhere else and fierce competition among lawyers, as in the amount of time billed. In effect, it's up to the lawyers to be reasonable about this, and some clearly aren't.

This particular form of excess wasn't unexpected. As public servants, the military officers have the right to hire lawyers at government expense if they are likely to be accused of wrongdoing. Early in our inquiry, the government met with our officials to devise some method of controlling legal fees. An eminent lawyer was appointed to act as an adjudicator. This man was assigned to inspect the billings submitted by lawyers in order to assess their claims. He would bring an expert eye to bear on the amount of work they claimed they had done. He would decide not so much whether they had appeared at our hearings on the days they claimed, but whether they needed to be there. His judgement would carry professional weight.

That was the system, but it has fallen apart completely. The lawyer I just mentioned, for example, threatened to sue the government if it didn't pay his bills without question. Apparently that was enough to make the government back off.

Strictly speaking, this has nothing to do with us. It's a matter for the lawyers and the government to regulate, although our involvement in appointing an adjudicator was a sign of our concern. We're worried about the public reaction to our final accounting. Although we won't include these lawyers' fees in our total cost, they will be a matter of public record. Someone, someday, will add them to our own costs to produce what most people will regard as a horrendous total.* There are now at least seventeen private lawyers representing as many individual clients before our inquiry. On an average day, the number in attendance will be anywhere from six to ten. Some of the others, presumably, are interviewing their clients, conducting research, and performing other billable activities.

Most of the lawyers come only when required in their client's interests. But there are a few who sit there day after day, saying nothing, doing nothing, and earning $200 an hour.

No one seems to be able to control this peculiar form of extortion. Perhaps it's because we're relying on lawyers to control lawyers that we've been unsuccessful.

When health care costs threatened to escalate exponentially, society moved to take the administration of medical care out of the hands of doctors. The Ontario government recently had to intervene to bring legal aid costs under control. Perhaps it's time to extend this kind of mandatory supervision to cases such as ours.

---

* This is exactly what Defence Minister Doug Young did a year later.

Tuesday, May 14, 1996
Ottawa

The long agony of navy Lieut. Joel Brayman is almost over. He began his testimony last week with the evident desire to portray himself as the one who blew the whistle on the destruction and alteration of documents at NDHQ. But his testimony became so evasive and inconsistent, under intense cross-examination, that it began to look as if his motive was to save his own career when he sensed that the scandal was about to become public.

As Lieutenant Brayman continued to encounter heavy weather today, one of the military's lawyers also ran into trouble. Brayman told us he contacted Lt.-Col. Kim Carter last September to discuss the alteration and attempted destruction of documents that had been occurring in the Directorate of Public Affairs. As he told his story to us, Kim Carter herself, a slender lawyer-officer with a short, military haircut and clipped British accent, was in the hearing room acting as his counsel. Toward the end of the morning, it became clear that Lieutenant Brayman's version of their conversation last September was significantly different from the version that Colonel Carter had given some time later to the military police. This means that she will have to be summoned as a witness within the next few weeks. Suddenly, the lawyer has become a participant in the events under examination and in conflict with her own client.

When she refused to step aside voluntarily, we ordered her to give up her role as counsel for this phase of the hearings and to await her call as a witness. The television cameras followed the unusual spectacle of a military lawyer being expelled from her position at the counsel table.

Watching all this from his seat in the hearing room was
Michael McAuliffe, who was awarded the prestigious Michener
Award for public service journalism last week. Commissioners
and lawyers, I'm sure, have now lost sight of McAuliffe's role
as we try to unravel the complexities of the story, but without
McAuliffe there might well have been no inquiry at all. This
great, awkward, expensive, and unwieldy mechanism that I'm
now part of is very much a journalist's creation.

When I think about that, when I watch McAuliffe, I feel less
pessimistic about the future of journalism. No matter what
happens to newspapers, or the various new technologies that
are changing the definition of journalism at the moment, journalists will always represent a court of last resort for the victims
of "the system."

As a society, we have to be careful to protect the ability of
journalists to fulfil this role. In a sense, the journalist, despite
all the limitations imposed by media ownership, self-interest,
and lack of resources, is the only "loose cannon" in the system
that politicians, bureaucrats, and businesspeople cannot always
control. Cynicism about the news media is often understand-
able, but a weakening of the media's ability to respond to cries
for help, to receive information confidentially, to investigate on
our behalf, would endanger everyone.

Thursday, May 16, 1996
En route Ottawa–London

Every morning, when the three of us enter the hearing room,
lawyers, spectators, and our own officials rise. We bow to the
court as a sign of respect for the process. Our registrar

announces in English and French that the session is about to begin. One of our lawyers reads out the names of the lawyers who are present. A witness takes the stand and is sworn. These formal rituals lend our proceedings an air of dignity and high purpose.

Beneath all this, particularly on days such as this, lurks a more primitive spirit. This is a hunt, after all, even if the objectives are truth and justice.

A public inquiry such as this is not a trial. We repeat this over and over. We are inquisitorial, not adversarial. We are not trying to assign guilt, we are not sentencing anyone to punishment. Our assignment is simply to investigate and make public the whole Somalia story.

This is all true, strictly speaking, but everyone also understands that it is a fiction. Reputations in fact can be destroyed in these hearings; careers can be ruined. In extreme cases, criminal prosecutions may arise from evidence that we unearth in our search for the truth. Everyone knows that this process has victims.

Today was one of those days when the scent was in the wind. You could feel the excitement growing in the hearing room.

None of us know exactly where the trail will lead, but one of the possible casualties at the end of this phase, as everyone appreciates, is the current chief of the defence staff, Gen. Jean Boyle. And beyond him is the minister of defence, David Collenette, who brought the inquiry into being. For if General Boyle falls, the minister who appointed him will be severely damaged.

Initially, it was assumed that we would focus on events that occurred in Somalia during the term of the previous Tory government. This seemed to be one instance where a government could do the right thing – appoint an inquiry – without having to worry about the outcome. But the failure of the military to properly handle the production of documents for the inquiry has shifted our focus, for now, from the 1993 events in Somalia to events in Ottawa in 1994 and 1995, when the Liberals were in power.

General Boyle had no military role in Somalia. When the soldiers were in Belet Huen, he was in Ottawa helping to run the Directorate of Public Affairs, where, as we now know, documents were altered and orders were given to destroy vital documents. As the Somalia crisis escalated, he was placed in charge of the Somalia Working Group at National Defence Headquarters to supervise the release of Somalia-related information. Some have referred to this as "damage control." His conduct in both these roles may have involved him in the cover-up of Somalia events that is now the centre of our attention.

Navy Lieut. Al Wong took the stand today. A public affairs officer recalled from the reserves in British Columbia to help deal with the Somalia crisis at NDHQ in 1993, Lieutenant Wong had constant access to General Boyle and other senior officers. This made the quiet-spoken, somewhat reserved officer the target of intensive questioning by our lawyers and ourselves.

He agreed with me, at one point, that Boyle was a hands-on administrator closely in touch with all activities within the Somalia Working Group. Then a memo signed by the general enabled us to bring him closer to the doctored documents. It is out of these small admissions and discoveries that the larger picture is constructed. If it can be shown that Boyle was aware of this exercise in disinformation in 1993, he will probably have to resign. No chief of the defence staff could withstand exposure of his role in a deliberate attempt to mislead the public. In this case, the doctoring of documents quickly led to offences against the Access to Information law.

You can feel the excitement among the pack of lawyers at times like this. And because of the close media attention, and the fact that our hearings are carried live or after a short delay on CPAC, the public affairs channel, there is a sense of the national audience drawing a little closer to our hearings, breathing a little more tightly.

Friday, May 31, 1996
En route Ottawa–London

The week has been filled with phone calls and interviews about the Conrad Black take-over of the Southam newspaper group. I find myself repeating the same things over and over to the *Toronto Star*, Canadian Press (CP), CKGM in Montreal, and "As It Happens" and "Morningside" on CBC Radio.

Adapting to these changes is difficult for journalists of my generation. On "Morningside," I briefly recalled getting my first job as a CP copy boy at the age of seventeen. The office was on Hospital Street in what later became known fashionably as Old Montreal. On the early shift, I would take the streetcar from the west end of the city, where I lived, to the harbour downtown to pick up the shipping reports on the way to the bureau. The streets and stone buildings, some of them several centuries old, seemed to me to resemble the London thorough-fares of Dickens's time. I could almost imagine sailing ships and early steamers tied up to the wharves. I remember the dusty light of the city sifting across the crumbling stone façades of the buildings.

The CP bureau on Hospital Street was equally romanticized in my eyes. News copy from around the world slowly unrolled from the teletype machines. I sorted it and spiked it on large hooks attached to a board for the editors to pick up, read, select, edit, and process for their Canadian services. The editors, thin, nervous types as I remember them, wrote on typewriters and handed their work to teletype operators, older men paunchy from years of sitting before keyboards. From time to time, I would go to a café downstairs for Cokes, coffee, and sandwiches for the editors. Everyone including myself smoked constantly.

During the day there would be several visits to the *Montreal Star* newsroom a few blocks away on St. James Street to pick up the "blacks," flimsy carbon copies of stories written by local reporters. I remember wood and glass partitions, ancient upright typewriters, editors in shirt sleeves. The building was so old and inflammable that the journalists had to congregate in the washroom to smoke.

On the night shift, I would walk twice to the *Gazette*, the last trip near midnight, through the deserted streets, on the lookout for drunks and other lurking dangers. In the mailroom at the *Gazette* I would wait for the presses to start with the men and women who sold newspapers on the downtown sidewalks, a quarrelsome, unfriendly, and vaguely threatening bunch. The building would shake as the presses gathered speed, and the papers would start to spew out into the mailroom and everyone jostled and shoved one another for priority, as if the papers were in desperately short supply.

On Saturday afternoon, the editors and teletype operators at CP would play cribbage. I was allowed to sit at the main desk, scanning the copy coming in and alerting the editors to anything important. I could even compose routine messages to keep the traffic flowing.

One red-letter day when the bureau was short-staffed, I was dispatched to the harbour to meet an incoming ship bringing home a victorious Canadian hockey team from the world championship in Europe. I boarded the huge liner clutching my notebook, found the players and interviewed them, and ran back to the office to type my story. Then I saw my by-line on the page when I ripped up the copy a few minutes later. Sports editors across the country were seeing it. Soon thousands of people would be reading my words and my name.

The editors took time to correct my stories and to explain the changes. The bureau chief held classes every week for myself and two other copy boys. He gave us newspaper stories to rewrite and showed us our mistakes – when he wasn't chasing his secretary around his office. Everyone called her "The Potato" and her screams could be heard from time to time before she stomped out of the office swearing. Today this would be called sexual harassment, but I remember it as a kind of ritual in which the secretary, although the pursued, was also the dominant participant. The bureau chief, a frequent and steady drinker, chased her as a matter of form. It was the expected thing to do. "The Potato" used these occasions to show him who was boss. The rest of us regarded it as entertainment.

This afternoon, at Rideau Hall, thoughts like this were shifting in and out of focus as Governor General Roméo LeBlanc presented two new journalism awards sponsored by the Canadian Journalism Foundation. During the reception afterwards I talked with Dalton Camp. He was hobbling about on a damaged foot from kicking something. "Or someone?" I suggested. Almost forty years ago, when I was covering the election campaign he managed for Manitoba Conservatives, Dalton sat on a high stool before a drafting table in a Winnipeg hotel room and instructed me in the art of political organization. Of course his remarks had what we would now call a definite "spin," but they were filled with astute observations about politicians, the media, and the political process.

Before the ceremony, Knowlton Nash, the chair of the foundation, and I met the governor general in one of Rideau Hall's ornate reception rooms. Roméo LeBlanc eased himself a little stiffly onto a sofa. In the early 1960s, a much younger LeBlanc had scrambled nimbly into the back seat of an open convertible that awaited us at the tail end of a cavalcade welcoming Prime Minister John Diefenbaker to a small Ontario town. With "the Chief" in front, we headed down the main street, convertibles carrying the press behind the dignitaries' vehicles.

Soon I noticed that the crowds lining the sidewalk were doing more than cheering and clapping for the prime minister. They were laughing, and they seemed to be laughing harder as our car approached and passed. Squirming around, I saw Roméo, in a dark, almost clerical suit, perched atop the back seat of the convertible, bestowing a papal blessing on small-town Protestant Ontario.

This afternoon he chatted about Canadian history to me and Vince Carlin, a CBC news executive currently involved in a project to produce a twenty-six-part video history of Canada. Knowledge and understanding of our history, said the governor general, would reduce many of the divisions that separate us. Someone asked, Which histories?

Pierre O'Neil joined us. Now a public relations counsellor for Bombardier in Montreal, he was Prime Minister Pierre

Elliott Trudeau's press attaché when I was in the Press Gallery. These were the early days of planned manipulation of the press, television in particular, for political advantage. Political staff were beginning to ration television access to the prime minister, and using the promise of access to bargain with television journalists for acceptable coverage. I remember Pierre was disturbed by some of the tactics that his own office was using; now they are standard practice.

Monday, June 3, 1996
Ottawa

About twenty minutes before I was due to go down the two flights of back stairs for the usual 10 A.M. start to our hearings – we can't use the elevators from the eleventh to the ninth floor because of the media congregating outside the hearing room, waiting to pounce – the phone rang. The caller identified himself as a Foreign Affairs officer, and he was calling from his office in the Pearson Building. He was still furious about the testimony last week by Ruth Cardinal, the former director general of public affairs at National Defence Headquarters. Cardinal had said that there was nothing wrong with the department's new practice, in 1994, of giving its Media Response Lines a shelf life of seventy-two hours and then discarding them. This would ensure that media response lines were always up-to-date, she said. What she didn't mention was that it would make it impossible for journalists or other researchers to obtain these documents, as Michael McAuliffe had done in 1993 and 1994, under Access to Information.

"What nonsense!" said my caller. "It's our job every morning to scan the news media and other sources and prepare Q&As for the minister so that he can answer questions in the House. And we make press lines to help with his answers to the media. And of course these documents are kept.

"The producer of the document always keeps a copy. You want to make sure your ass is covered. And the department keeps copies for reference, so that they can see what we've said in the past on a certain issue.

"What the hell has happened to our public service?" he asked suddenly, his voice rising. "I thought to myself when I was watching [Cardinal] on television: What the hell has happened to Canada? Is this the country of Lester Pearson? Well, I don't recognize it.

"Ottawa is run by three hundred pricks," he concluded. "These are the people who rise to the top of the system. These are the marks of success – evasiveness, avoiding responsibility – that are rewarded by promotion.

"How could this happen?"

———————

Ruth Cardinal was on the stand all day. Her version of events in the public affairs directorate last fall becomes more bizarre by the hour. She said that by late September 1994, Michael McAuliffe was calling her at home to tell her about his latest conversations with members of her department. They no longer bothered to check with her before contacting him.

Col. Geoff Haswell, her immediate subordinate, was calling McAuliffe to deny stories that his junior officers were spreading about him. Lieut. Joel Brayman was calling McAuliffe because he was afraid that Haswell was out to get him. The deputy minister's staff officer was receiving calls from McAuliffe demanding answers and threatening to broadcast even more damaging disclosures on the CBC.

It's a rule in public affairs, in a crisis, to begin by controlling leaks. Centralizing the flow of information so that the organization speaks with one voice is a basic principle. In this crisis, the public affairs directorate itself was shattering under pressure. Yes, admitted Cardinal, things were out of control.

In all the confusion, adherence to our own legal order for the production of Somalia documents was forgotten. The directorate was still focusing on damage control. Its officer had violated the Access to Information law in 1994. Cardinal and other senior officers were trying to decide how to handle McAuliffe's inevitable exposure of this illegality. Cardinal admitted that she had completely overlooked the fact that, in the meantime, her directorate was continuing to lag behind in its production of documents for us. Also at issue was the directorate's failure to notify us that there had been an attempt to destroy some of these documents.

A slight, blonde woman with a "lazy eye" that gives her a hesitant, oblique air, Ruth Cardinal was visibly wearing down as we approached 4 P.M. But she had another bombshell to drop before she concluded her testimony for the day. Under questioning by Arthur Cogan, Colonel Haswell's lawyer, Cardinal said that she had discussed her evidence with General Boyle, then chief of the defence staff, only last month, after she knew that she would have to appear before us. At mid-morning, one day, she had been summoned by phone from her current job in the Privy Council Office to meet Boyle in his office at NDHQ over the lunch hour. She told us that the interview lasted ten minutes. Boyle had asked if she had told him about the new media-response system when it was introduced, a subject that our own lawyers plan to raise with him.

Arthur Cogan quickly pointed out that, whether Cardinal said that she had told him or not, the information would assist Boyle in shaping his own testimony.

My understanding is that witnesses talking among themselves isn't necessarily illegal, but it's certainly unwise when you're a senior officer asking a subordinate what she is going to say when she appears before an inquiry. In this case, since both Boyle and Cardinal are represented by the same government lawyer, it would have been a simple matter for Boyle to acquire this information through his own counsel.

Why had he called her to his office? Why did he deliberately open himself to the suspicion that he might be trying to influence others' testimony, or at the very least to use the status of his office to benefit his own case?

Day by day, the stories become more incredible. Sometimes I walk out of the committee room shaking my head in disbelief – once I'm safely out of camera range.

Tuesday, June 4, 1996
Ottawa

As Ruth Cardinal concluded her testimony this afternoon, she answered a question that will loom large during the next few weeks.

Under discussion was the letter that General Boyle had signed in 1994 as the Defence Department complied with the Access to Information request by Michael McAuliffe for sixty-eight Responses to Queries (RTQs) prepared by the department's public affairs branch. As everyone now knows, those RTQs had been tampered with. They were altered to conform with the versions that had been given to McAuliffe informally in 1993. If the RTQs had not been altered then, McAuliffe would have discovered that his 1993 documents were not what the department had said they were.

Giving altered documents to McAuliffe informally might have been unwise, but it was not illegal. Providing him with altered documents through Access to Information was. So one of the key questions in this phase of the inquiry is: Did General Boyle know that the documents had been altered when he signed the covering letter dispatching them to the Access to Information co-ordinator? Another is: Even if General Boyle did not know, or claims that he didn't know, is he responsible?

Ruth Cardinal gave an unequivocal answer to this: Yes. Whether or not Boyle had taken the time to read the documents, they had been prepared under his command and he was responsible. The question that will follow over the next few weeks is: Can a general continue as chief of the defence staff if he acknowledges responsibility for an illegal act that occurred under his direct command?

This afternoon, lawyer turned witness when Lt.-Col. Kim Carter took the stand. Ejected from her role as a government lawyer because the evidence showed that she was a participant in some of the events that we are examining, she found herself on the stand today warding off questions about the propriety of her own conduct.

There is no doubt that she learned of the "double set" of RTQs given to McAuliffe last September, and that she was told about the attempted destruction of documents. Our questions to her were about her subsequent conduct. What did she tell her superiors?

As a lawyer and an officer, she had a double obligation to bring the attempted destruction immediately to the attention of the government and of the inquiry. Because the documents were not destroyed and were eventually turned over to us, Colonel Carter claimed that there was no problem. I tried to get her to distinguish between an attempted crime and one successfully committed.

"If I attempt to rob a bank and I'm stopped in the process," I asked, "haven't I committed a crime?"

She explained that the destruction of documents had not been intended to foil the commission but to prevent McAuliffe from getting his hands on them.

I asked whether the intent was important. If I attempt to rob a bank and then explain, after I'm caught, that my intent was only to feed my family, is that a defence?

I never did receive a simple answer.

Over the past few days, we've seen senior officials in both the public affairs branch and now the legal branch of the Armed Forces constantly forgetting details of events and conversations that occurred only a few months ago, admitting to failures to assume responsibility when confronted with evidence of wrongdoing, evidently trying to protect the department's reputation as their first priority, completely losing sight of the real purpose of their offices, and generally behaving in ways that are unprofessional, unwise, and ultimately destructive even of the limited interests that they are trying to protect.

Colonel Carter said that she had supplied one of her superior officers with only limited information about the alleged destruction of documents.

"It seems to me," I said, "that limited information would be the most alarming kind of information for a senior officer to receive. We are all children of Watergate. The linking of the inquiry and the destruction of documents in any form should have been enough to send up the rockets right away."

I'm sure that many Canadians are drawing the same conclusions.

Damaging as the events in Somalia and the notorious hazing rituals of the Airborne regiment were, they were not nearly as destructive to the military's reputation as the subsequent activities within National Defence Headquarters. Day by day, the problems of leadership emerge more dramatically.

Saturday, June 8, 1996
London

Home for the weekend, after a long seven-hour drive from Ottawa to London on Thursday night, the domestic routine is welcome. Cleaning the car. Cutting the grass. Taking my mother out to a Swiss Chalet dinner from her nursing home. As I wrestled her stroke-paralysed left leg into the car, collapsing her wheelchair and loading it into the trunk, I placed her purse on the roof of the car and, of course, forgot all about it. My mother, with no short-term memory at all, noticed the absence of her purse before I did, when we were already in the restaurant. There was no money in the purse, no credit cards, perhaps not even any identification. But being even more forgetful than my mother was quite an accomplishment.

At the other nursing home in the afternoon, I played cribbage with my mother-in-law and "skunked" her twice. Sometimes I let her win, but she's so competitive, so suspicious that I'm cheating, and so slyly triumphant when she does win, that I have trouble keeping my own competitive instincts under control. Today, with good cards, I decided recklessly to make a clean sweep of both games. She cheered up when Hazel and I promised to take her out for fish and chips tomorrow evening at a small restaurant near the nursing home. Weekends like this help to keep the Somalia saga in some sort of perspective. The rough edges smooth out and patterns become more evident.

By the end of the past week, it was becoming possible to foresee the conclusion of this phase of the hearings. Particularly revealing was the testimony of Gen. Jim Fox, a three-star former commander of the army who was brought out of retirement last year to act as a special adviser to the department on Somalia. In this role, he was responsible, according to his orders from the chief of the defence staff, for helping the department to formulate a "position" before the inquiry and for helping our inquiry to obtain all the documents we required from the department. The job description contained an inherent contradiction. General Fox was being asked to serve two masters, the department and the inquiry. His critical test came last September when he was told by Lt.-Col. Kim Carter about the attempted destruction of Somalia documents in the public affairs directorate and the falsification of a response to the CBC in 1994 under Access to Information. Fox should have informed us immediately of the attempt to destroy documents that were covered by our order to produce all Somalia-related documents the previous April. He didn't.

When he was asked about this, General Fox said that he had never made the connection between the attempted destruction of documents and our order. He explained that he was thinking only of the offence against the Access to Information law. However, he also had done nothing immediately to bring that offence to the attention of the information commissioner who is charged with overseeing compliance with Access to Information. Our order was the only apparent reason to destroy the documents. If our inquiry had never been created and our order never given, no one would ever have discovered the 1994 falsification of documents requested by the CBC. There would have been no need to destroy any documents.

But this was not clear to General Fox at the time.

During the hearings, when illogic is presented as logical, and irrational behaviour as reasonable, you start to lose your bearings. You almost expect Alice and the White Rabbit to run into the hearing room and take the oath. Sometimes it is only days later that you come back to earth. Common sense is restored.

It is now apparent that General Fox's testimony, and similar testimony from others, may prevent us from linking these matters directly to General Boyle. Bit by bit, Boyle is being surrounded by a protective wall of ignorance erected by the officers who served under him, and many who still are.

When Boyle appears before us, probably in August, I think that he will claim ignorance of the attempt to destroy documents and the falsification of records. He will not evade responsibility. In fact, he will make a virtue out of accepting responsibility, but he will argue that his ignorance of events mitigates this. He may be criticized, but General Boyle will tough it out. It will likely be at least mid-1997 before our report is issued. Who knows what will have occurred by then? There may very well be a new defence minister. The issue will seem less urgent when this portion of our inquiry has been superseded by more revelations about events in Somalia. Boyle's own career at National Defence will have had more time to become established.

Sunday, June 9, 1996
London

This afternoon I've been reviewing the draft of a speech that our secretary, Stan Cohen, will make in a few weeks to the Canadian Club in Ottawa. Cohen has cited a 1993 decision by the chief justice of the British Columbia Supreme Court, which deals with the difficult role of commissioners of a public inquiry such as ours.

The judgment in B.C. contains the reminder that "unlike judges, commissions do not sit to hear both sides and determine an issue between parties. In the nature of things," the decision continues, "commissioners often cannot perform their function with that degree of impartiality which is inherent in the role of a judge. It is not uncommon for them to start with a view that there is a problem to be investigated and solved, and to thus approach the task with a degree of seeming partiality which would be unacceptable in a judge conducting a trial."

I can testify to the truth of this carefully phrased judicial opinion. Although I had written nothing about the events in Somalia before my appointment, I was certainly aware of Shidane Arone's murder and the subsequent charges laid by military police. The infamous hazing videos had already been shown and discussed in the media. If there was not strong evidence of serious wrongdoing, our inquiry would not have been appointed.

Having said that, we have to make certain that all the facts are presented to us, and that we listen to all interpretations of these facts. And we have to appear to be listening. Lawyers for the government and various parties can grimace and roll their eyes at some witnesses, but we have to remain unmoved. The wife of one of our recent witnesses has already complained in writing about the disrespectful behaviour of lawyers at the back of the hearing room. Any hint of this kind of behaviour from us would be dangerous and would be quickly attacked by lawyers whose clients are on the defensive.

The process of making up our minds about the evidence is a continuing, cumulative one. We don't sit there for a year listening impassively and then suddenly reach a decision. In fact, there already exists an informal consensus among us on some of the evidence that we have heard in the pre-Somalia phase, and background parts of that section of the report are being drafted.

When we question witnesses these days, it must be evident that we are speaking with considerably more experience and knowledge than we had last summer, and that some of our questions are based on certain assumptions. At the same time, it's vital that we don't appear to have closed minds on any aspect of what we are investigating. Witnesses have to be listened to respectfully.

This demands a certain amount of self-control when military officers contradict one another about important events, as some of them have been doing. In these cases, someone is telling the truth and someone is lying, but we can't let on which one we believe. When officers and Defence Department bureaucrats forget almost all the details of important conversations that they had only a few months ago, we can register some degree of scepticism but we can't badger them.

These moments are among the most frustrating of the inquiry. At times you know that a witness is lying, either because of previous testimony or because the witness's testimony is simply incredible, but you can't confront him or her directly. Sometimes I've even felt that a witness was laughing at me as he or she lied, daring me to do something about it.

In a television interview, in years gone by, I would have known how to indicate disbelief without stating it, either by a careful choice of words or body language. Here I can't afford to do that, not with lawyers waiting to pounce at the slightest hint of bias.

Tuesday, June 11, 1996
En route Ottawa–London

In Ottawa we spent the day discussing the next phase of our inquiry with some of our technical advisers – in this case a former general and a former colonel who are acting as consultants. I suppose one could regard them as mercenaries, in a very broad sense. They are selling their military expertise. In this case, however, the "enemy" forces are some of their old comrades in the service.

Their rationale, which is valid, is that they are still working for the good of the Armed Forces. If we do our job properly, that will be true. The inquiry will be seen to have been a useful if painful exercise for the military.

Since the hearings last week, I've become increasingly concerned that senior officers and bureaucrats don't share this
view. The evidence of General Fox is still in my mind. Perhaps
he was placed in an impossible position by his superiors –
instructed to help his colleagues to develop a good defensive
position in the face of the inquiry, and then to help us to penetrate that defence.

The Somalia Inquiry Liaison Team (SILT) that the military
created to assist us has suffered from the same conflicts as its
special adviser, General Fox. We have tended to regard it as the
clearing house for documents that we need. The military, it
seems apparent, has regarded it as the mechanism to control
information that we receive. Proof of the dominant tendency in
SILT can be seen in our continuing difficulty in getting the military documents that we require.

It's now about fourteen months since we issued our order for
all Somalia-related documents, and there are still significant
gaps in the records. We've been focusing on hard drives from
computers at NDHQ. One vital hard drive apparently was lost
for months until it suddenly showed up recently in an overlooked corner of NDHQ. Another appears to have had files
erased. Of course we always receive plausible explanations:
hardware and software failures, untrained operators, various
"housecleaning" and "tidying up" efforts.

At our meeting today we discussed the danger of losing control of the documentation process and simultaneously losing
credibility. I said that General Fox's testimony had increased
scepticism about the role of SILT in helping us. I believe that the
delays are not the result of technical problems, nor personnel
difficulties, nor lack of time. Not after fourteen months. It's

arguable that the delays have been part of a careful plan to slow us down and to sabotage our process.

The problem is complicated by the friendly working relationships that have developed over the past year between some members of our staff and the military. The officers selected to deal with us are, for the most part, approachable and apparently eager to assist us. Perhaps they have been selected for these attributes. Over a period of time, as our deadlines have passed, we have reluctantly accepted their excuses while we pressed again and again for deliveries. We ourselves have become corrupted by this process. Having accepted their failures bit by bit, we find ourselves if not defending them, then at least explaining and justifying them.

"We've been doing things according to Hoyle," I said, "but they haven't been playing by the rules. It's time we stopped fooling around and got serious about this."

In the end, we agreed that we would make some sort of clear statement on documentation, or the lack of it, at the end of this phase of our hearings in August. Perhaps our intention to do this will serve as a warning to SILT that the rules are changing.

———

During these discussions today, I realized anew how fortunate we are to have Gilles Létourneau as chair. As I wrote a few months ago, he has a keen sense of the independence of the judiciary, as well as a brilliantly logical mind. His talent for organization, developed in the Quebec civil service, has helped to keep our large and inherently makeshift organization on track. The nature of a royal commission is temporary. Staff must be recruited quickly. Structures must be improvised and adapted to suit demands that are not always apparent at the outset. Gilles dominates the organization not only because of his abilities but also because of the example he sets of dedication and hard work. His strong ethical sense sets the tone for the entire group. As we study the attributes of effective military leadership, his own role among us provides a kind of unstated standard.

He's intellectual but not bookish. A stocky, fair-haired man who looks more Nordic than Gallic, he has a strong physical presence. He has a passion for hunting and could hardly wait, last fall, for the deer season to open. In argument, he is combative. Behind his reasoned positions you can often sense an emotional commitment, and flashes of temper when he is opposed.

Sunday, June 16, 1996
En route London–Ottawa

Just after take-off, before my seatmate considerately moved to an empty place across the aisle, he confided to me that he has been following the inquiry on CPAC, often staying up late at night to catch the next instalment. Although we're far from rivalling the ratings of the recent O. J. Simpson trial, we seem to have slowly accumulated a cult following. Members and former members of the military form our core audience, but, as time goes on, more and more "ordinary Canadians" are watching the procession of military officers moving across their screens at odd hours of the day and night, catching our hearings live or rebroadcast.

Like my former seatmate, almost all viewers who identify themselves to me support what we are doing. I can't recall a single negative comment from anyone who has been following us on television. All of them seem to have grasped the importance of the inquiry. All are appalled by the evasions and contradictions in the testimony of senior military officers. All offer words of encouragement. There are many comments about the amount of time that the inquiry is taking to complete its work, but these are never offered in a critical or sarcastic tone. At least so far, the people who talk with me seem to feel that the job we are doing is necessary. In fact, a strong thread running through the comments I get is sympathy, for myself and the other commissioners who are being exposed to this unpleasant mess month after month.

My reading on the flight today is an article in yesterday's *Globe* by Paul Koring of the paper's Ottawa bureau. Koring has been covering our hearings regularly. During our recess last week, he took the time to reflect on different Canadian and American approaches to accountability by the military.

His article was inspired by the American reaction to the April 3 crash of a U.S. military aircraft near Dubrovnik, killing all crew and passengers, including Secretary of Commerce Ron Brown. Since then, as Koring stated, an American general and two colonels have been relieved of their duties for failing to ensure that their subordinates obeyed orders. Koring compared this with the reaction to the killing of Shidane Arone more than three years ago: "... no general has been held accountable, no one has taken responsibility, and no one has had it thrust upon him."

Koring also focused on the *Tailhook* affair a few years ago "in which U.S. naval aviators got drunk and sexually abused other officers and female civilians at a party in Las Vegas. The result: two admirals were fired, 30 other admirals had reprimands placed in their files and the Secretary of the Navy resigned."

"By contrast," Koring continued, "the Canadian three-monkey defence has so far been sufficient to exculpate all senior officers in connection with the hazings.

"At the same time, generals and admirals who planned and oversaw the Somalia operation or were involved in the aftermath have been promoted or rewarded." Then Koring zeroes in on General Boyle: " 'Truth, Duty, Valour' is the military-college motto. The current CDS, Gen. Jean Boyle, invoked it as his guiding principle when he was named to the job in December. There is no precept etched on the portals of the Somalia Inquiry but after hearing from dozens of officers it seems too often to be 'Dissemble, Forget, Pass the Buck.' " At the end of his article, Koring held out some hope that the "Somalia saga may eventually spark a wide-ranging renewal of the Canadian military, as the Vietnam War did for the U.S. forces."

As far as I can tell at this stage, this article captures the consensus that now exists in the minds of Canadians who have taken an interest in what we are doing. At some point during the past year, the military's initial line of defence, the "few bad apples" explanation, has sunk into oblivion. Koring's piece reminded me how completely it has been overwhelmed by the testimony that we have heard.

Over the next year, we have to describe the problems as clearly as possible and offer the beginnings of a solution. Obviously we can't write a comprehensive plan for reform of all aspects of the Canadian Forces, but we can indicate some obvious new directions.

This is what keeps all of us going as we head into another two weeks of hearings before the summer break, and as we contemplate at least five more months after that – the sense that this is a decisive moment in the life of an important public institution.

Tuesday, June 18, 1996
Ottawa

This morning I woke up in the room of my apartment-hotel about 6 A.M. thinking of questions to ask Gen. Brian Vernon.

Shortly after we had been appointed, General Vernon had taken it on himself to send an e-mail to his friends in the high command suggesting that they should get together to plan a co-ordinated response to us. His superiors had promptly closed down this effort, ostensibly because they were worried about public reaction, and ours, if they tried to give us what one general called "the King James version" of events in Somalia. This was the official reason for stopping Vernon's initiative. But was the real reason to protect the efforts that more senior officers already were making to organize a response to the inquiry?

I got out my laptop, sat on the edge of the bed, and typed out a page of questions. Only then could I relax, go for a swim in the pool downstairs, get dressed, eat, and head out for the inquiry.

Our lawyers' examination of General Vernon ended about half an hour into our morning session, and I brought out my sheet of questions.

My list helped me to follow a logical sequence, as lawyers do, but it wasn't as effective as queries that come to me spontaneously as I'm listening to a witness. I wasn't surprised by this. Similarly, my best questions when I was doing television interviews were the ones that came to me on the set, in reaction to something that guests had just said.

Paul Koring's *Globe* article was cited in today's hearing. Many witnesses are now being asked to provide us with definitions of military accountability. General Vernon stated today that ignorance of what subordinates are doing does not eliminate a senior officer's responsibility for what is done under his or her command.

Wednesday, June 19, 1996
London

In the hearing room, the atmosphere is formal. When lawyers and the witness are ready for us, the usher invites us to attend. He precedes us into the room, announces our arrival, and orders everyone to stand.

One of us once absent-mindedly entered the room before the usher. Lawyers, chatting with one another, were not in their proper places. The witness was outside the room. It was as if someone had raised the curtain in a theatre a few minutes too soon. Everyone froze in consternation until we retired. We waited for a few moments behind the door and then made a proper entry.

At the end of a session, we rise, bow to the court, everyone stands, and we march out in single file. We walk down a short hallway to a conference room which serves as our "chambers."

Apart from abstract paintings and prints on the wall from the national art bank, the room is sparsely furnished. There is a

conference table with ten black leather swivel chairs, a sofa and
several armchairs, credenza and coffee table, and a television set
with VCR. At the far end of the room, an expanse of window,
screened by venetian blinds, overlooks a parking lot and garage.
Patches of sky and distant suburban horizon are visible between
nearby office towers. We are facing away from Parliament Hill,
the Ottawa River, the Gatineau Hills, and Ottawa's only
impressive view. Looking south, the downtown cityscape is
bleak. We could be anywhere.

The hearing room itself is artificially lit for the television
cameras. Behind us a wall of curtained windows. We face our
audience and behind it the audio-visual control booth and a
second soundproofed window through which we can see the
simultaneous translators opening and closing their mouths like
fish in an aquarium. Some translators sit stolidly before their
microphones; others weave their hands in the air as they speak,
totally silent to us unless we pick up the headsets on our table.

Day after day, for almost a year, we have sat in the same
places under the same lights. The testimony varies, but the routine is always the same.

We start at 10 A.M., giving the lawyers and ourselves the
early-morning hours to prepare for the session. At 11:30 A.M.,
we break for fifteen minutes. Sometimes I walk to the window
of the conference room and peer through the venetian blinds
like a prisoner looking between strands of barbed wire at the
world outside. We drink tea or coffee from vacuum canisters.
Three muffins are set out in a row, covered by paper napkins.
The chair never eats his, but it is always left there for him.

At 1 P.M., we break for lunch. On the conference table is
salad in plastic containers, a roll and margarine, mineral water
and juice, sometimes a bit of pastry. Tuesdays and Thursdays

the salad is replaced by miso soup and sushi from a Japanese restaurant across the street, the preference of Judge Létourneau and myself. Judge Rutherford has come to enjoy it, or so he says.

Often there is business to discuss, either a formal meeting of the commission with staff present or an informal session with lawyers about some current issue or dispute that might require a ruling. On other days, we eat quietly, chatting about family, friends, activities outside the work of the commission. Over the long months, we slowly get to know one another.

Judge Robert Rutherford, in his early seventies, is the most relaxed and gregarious of us. It is impossible to dislike Bob. His abundant curly grey hair, ruddy complexion, and robust build give him a Dickensian air. I think of him as being quintessentially Upper Canadian, a Torontonian of a fading pattern. His great-grandfather was the first settler to reach the Owen Sound area, travelling by Indian trail in the early 1800s from Galt. Judge Rutherford has a cottage there amid other cottages and a farm owned by his close relatives. The Rutherfords of Owen Sound must be something like the Kennedys of Hyannisport on a smaller scale.

Bob seems to know a vast number and variety of people in Ontario through his legal and military associations over the years. He still holds honorary military positions. An international association to assist Gurkha military veterans in Nepal is one of his philanthropies, with members in the United States and Britain as well as Canada. He always seems to be having dinner with someone in Ottawa. The other evening it was with a friend who had been best man at his wedding, shortly after he returned from overseas service in the Second World War, and then best man again when Bob remarried after the death of his first wife. He showed me a 1995 photograph of the two couples, and an earlier snapshot of Bob and his friend in Holland toward the end of the war. Across the space of almost fifty years, Bob looked at me, instantly identifiable, his expression as open and engaging as it is today.

The three of us share few common interests. Bob and I provide a polite audience for Gilles's enthusiasm for hunting and outdoor activities. Neither of them seems to be as interested in music, novels, and the theatre as I am. Sometimes we talk generally about politics. Gilles and I share a Quebec background, if not language, that provides some common ground. I suspect that Bob's views on Quebec would be quite different from mine, but we never talk in detail about this.

All three of us are quite careful about what we say. Perhaps it couldn't be otherwise, three men thrown together by chance in later life, coming from three different worlds. But occasionally we let down our guard.

The other day, Gilles announced that he was approaching his twenty-fifth anniversary and he confessed that he was more in love with his wife than ever. His older and younger sisters had been married on the same day in a triple ceremony. We talked about wives and children on this occasion. My own four marriages and ten children put me in a somewhat different category from the other two – Bob with two children and Gilles with three. We discussed divorce, changing attitudes toward marriage, our concerns and pride as we watch our own children as adults or, in Gilles's case, moving into adulthood.

Not surprisingly, we talk about the minor aches and ailments that bedevil three men as they grow older, attacks of indigestion or insomnia, intimations of arthritis.

Friendship and respect for one another develop slowly but tangibly. We seem to be lucky in this respect. It's as important in a task such as this as intellectual agreement on points of evidence.

At the end of the day, released from the ninth-floor hearing room, I go to my office on the eleventh, check my e-mail, my voice mail at the university, the documents that are accumulating in my "in" basket, and head for the elevator. In the lobby, I greet the night security guard in his booth. He happens to come, by appropriate coincidence, from Somaliland. I walk about six blocks to the apartment-hotel where I stay. The one-bedroom unit is always the same, no matter on which floor I happen to be that particular week. If I'm not eating with my daughter Michelle, her husband and two children, or my son Nicholas, or my daughter Jane when she returns to Ottawa next fall from studies in Moscow, I buy something frozen, perhaps a few rolls from a nearby bakery, and spend the evening reading documents, writing up this journal, phoning home, and watching television.

The routine is a little gulag-like in its monotony, except that a prisoner usually has a hope of early parole, while our sentence seems to get longer and longer, stretching now into the distant months of mid-1997.

Thursday, June 20, 1996
En route Ottawa–London

Yesterday we received copies of the second military police report on the alteration and attempted destruction of documents.

This second report was made necessary by the discovery last April of Somalia documents that had previously been undetected.

Military police didn't have these documents when they first interviewed General Boyle and when he told them that he had not known at the time about the altered documents given to Michael McAuliffe by the Directorate of Public Affairs, a department under his command. However, new documents found in April bear his notations and signature, and seem to indicate that he had known. This inconsistency had been evident some time ago in documents that we had tabled, and government lawyers had already attempted to excuse the general's lapse of memory. Having it identified as an untrue statement in a military police report brought it sharply to public attention again.

Although the police report was tabled only this morning, all network television newscasts had its highlights last night. CBC followed its news report with a Brian Stewart documentary on Boyle's career that looked suspiciously like the first instalment of an obituary. This morning, the *Globe* ran a story about General Boyle's refusal to be interviewed again by military police, saying that he would remain silent until he appears before our inquiry. While there may be sound legal reasons for this defensive posture, it presents a poor example for soldiers under his command. If the chief of the defence staff refuses to appear before military police investigators to answer questions, why should ordinary soldiers? What sort of leadership is that?

Monday, June 24, 1996
Ottawa

The *Globe* this morning landed a one-two punch as we head into the last week of our hearings before we recess until

August. On the front page, Paul Koring reviewed our progress so far, focusing on the linked fortunes of Defence Minister David Collenette and Gen. Jean Boyle.

"In their worst nightmares," he wrote, "neither could have imagined that the killing of Shidane Arone would eventually cast them beleaguered and together, with their reputations and futures seemingly entwined."

Koring leaves little doubt that these futures are dismal. The events in Somalia have become almost incidental. Instead, the inquiry has devoted itself to "cover-up and accountability . . . document tampering and allegations of interference in the military-justice system . . . shattered morale and the draining of the reservoir of public good will that the Canadian military has always taken for granted."

More cautiously, the *Globe*'s anonymous editorial writer, in the same issue, decides that the "final conclusions of this long-running exercise are beginning to seem a bit beside the point." Citing our new deadline of next March 31, announced by the Privy Council Office last week, the *Globe* asks, "Can the leadership of the military remain in limbo until then? Can the Defence Department sail rudderless for another year?"

The editorial urges us to "press forward and continue" our investigations. Despite this second extension of our mandate and the mounting cost, most people seem to feel that we are doing a useful job as quickly as possible. This high level of approbation depends on our continuing "productivity" – a steady flow of disturbing revelations. This strengthens the general conviction that reform of the military is essential, and that the inquiry is the public agony or catharsis that must precede reform.

As long as we continue on this course, and don't make any major mistakes, we should be able to maintain this public confidence in our work. But nothing in public life should be taken for granted. I'm sure that there are those in the military right now who would love to discredit us. The challenge to Gilles Létourneau's leadership, originating in Calgary and now making its way slowly toward the Federal Court, is an indication of this.

Dr. Ken Calder, assistant deputy minister, policy and communications, resumed his testimony today. He continued to have great difficulty remembering any details at all of important top-level meetings at National Defence Headquarters within the past two months. Once again, Judge Létourneau showed signs of exasperation. He has been using words like "flabbergasted" more frequently during the hearings to describe his reaction to some of the testimony. Today he described Dr. Calder's explanation of some event or other as "handy" – an indication of a high degree of scepticism on the scale of judicial language.

Listening to Calder, I thought to myself that this soft-spoken bureaucrat with the Roman-style haircut, looking a little like a chubby, tired Beatle, didn't really care what the public thought about his testimony. The only audience that he sees in his mind's eye is made up of his fellow bureaucrats. Their opinion is the one that he values.

In the end, one of the few weapons that democratic governments possess to combat this bureaucratic solidarity is an inquiry such as ours, which can sometimes lift a corner of the otherwise impenetrable curtain bureaucrats draw around themselves.

Wednesday, June 26, 1996
Ottawa

One of the strengths of the public inquiry lies in cross-examination by outside lawyers. Our own lawyers, and we as commissioners, can work to bring out the truth, but a clever witness can still prevent disclosure, particularly when documentary evidence is missing. As commissioners, we have to maintain a fine balance by looking critically at testimony and questioning witnesses vigorously on the one hand, while assuring witnesses that everyone is being given a fair chance to be heard on the other. Lawyers representing their clients before us – and there are now more than thirty – are under less restraint. They can go to great lengths to bring out testimony favourable to their clients, or to try to damage the credibility of witnesses whom they regard as hostile.

All the lawyers before us have their own styles. If the law is a science, its practitioners are more like artists, even prima donnas in some cases.

Arthur Cogan is the most striking example of the lawyer-artist among those involved in this stage. As counsel to Col. Geoffrey Haswell, he has been with us for only a few months, but long enough to make himself noteworthy.

I assumed for the first few weeks that Cogan was Irish, perhaps because his name sounded like "Hogan," or perhaps because his style seemed Irish. A tall, rangy man in his fifties with receding and greying curly hair, a loud voice just this side of raucous, Cogan looks and sounds as if he is more at home in the criminal court than a public inquiry. His questions are often long and convoluted. He interrupts witnesses. I get the feeling that he would much rather get up from his table near the back of the hearing room and approach witnesses on foot, until his accusing finger was only a few inches from the tips of their noses.

Another "Irish" trait that I thought I detected in Cogan was his sense of humour. Even in moments of angry conflict with other lawyers, he can always laugh at himself.

But Cogan isn't Irish at all, as I should have guessed. A reference to the "King James version" of the New Testament a few weeks ago moved a Jewish lawyer, Stuart Hendin, to explain why he and Cogan were at a disadvantage in understanding what this meant. Today, annoyed by another lawyer's interruptions of his questioning with points of order, Cogan replied by quoting "an old Yiddish saying," something to the effect that a wise man who answers a fool will soon hear two fools in conversation.

Sometimes raillery between lawyers is a way of letting off steam, cooling tempers, and reminding everyone that this is, for all its serious implications, a sort of highly skilled professional "game." At other times, the raillery becomes nasty and can threaten to disrupt the decorum and ritual that are essential to a judicial exercise.

Thursday, June 27, 1996
En route Ottawa–London

I felt this afternoon as if I had been released from school as we adjourned our hearings until August 12. The routine of daily hearings, week after week, leaves everyone tired and cranky. This afternoon some of the lawyers in the hearing room were sniping at one another even more frequently and spitefully than earlier in the week. One of them, eager to catch a flight to his home outside Ontario before the end of the afternoon, asked another during lunch hour if he could estimate how long his cross-examination would take. The lawyer, still riled by the insulting crossfire during the morning session, refused to tell him.

When they're in this mood, lawyers can deliver the ritualistic phrase "my learned friend" with a sneering intonation that makes it sound almost profane. They deliberately test one another's patience by exploring the outer limits of acceptable cross-examination, like naughty boys playing a game of "I dare you. . . ." When one of them rises to the bait and complains to the chair, the offender becomes righteously indignant that anyone would dare to insinuate that his knowledge of the law and professional ethics is less than perfect.

Judge Létourneau occasionally recesses the hearings for fifteen minutes to let tempers cool; in rare cases, he rebukes the worst offenders. One was lectured yesterday for declaring histrionically that if this was the way he was going to be treated, then he would walk out of the hearings, etc. etc. After a brief recess, Gilles chided him for threatening a boycott, and everyone calmed down.

We all seem to need a break before we start the final prolonged stretch in August, moving quickly to hear General Boyle, end the hearings on documentation, and start finally to investigate events that occurred in Somalia.

There are signs that the government, heading toward an election next year, is becoming unhappy with us. When we were first appointed, events in Somalia, occurring under the Mulroney government, were expected to be our main focus. But the documentation issue changed all that, and for the past few months we've been probing into events that occurred under the Chrétien government. There were rumours today that officials in the Privy Council Office are becoming annoyed. No one knows whether these are accurate, but they may be linked to a puzzling decision by the Justice Department to support the intervention of Brig.-Gen. Robert Meating in the Beno case against Judge Létourneau in the Federal Court of Appeal. At first glance it appears contradictory for the Justice Department, which is part of the government that appointed us, to support the case against Gilles according to which he is alleged to have shown bias against General Beno.

This may be an expression of the government's impatience with us. As I've said, recent revelations about defensive tactics within the Defence Department have made me a little paranoid. I even wonder sometimes about the security of the conference room where we commissioners talk frankly about witnesses during our breaks from the hearings. I know that the rooms have been swept and debugged, but even so. . . .

Next year's election will assume growing importance as we progress. One of my Ottawa contacts told me this week that the federal Conservatives are now contracting for media analysis and other campaign services next year. On "Canada A.M." this morning, during the final "Pundits" session before Parliament's summer break, Somalia was identified by the Opposition spokespersons as one of the government's most visible problems. The Liberal participant in the discussion raised the question of an interim report by our inquiry at the end of our hearings on documentation. These public suggestions are never accidental. Perhaps the government would welcome an opportunity to get rid of General Boyle if our report should provide a rationale.

There's also talk of a cabinet shuffle before the election, perhaps during the next few months. If Collenette were given another post, a new defence minister would find it easier to ask for Boyle's resignation on the grounds that a new minister requires a new team. An interim report from us, which isn't at all likely, would assist this process. Even without it, the appointment of a new minister would be interpreted as preparing the way for Boyle's exit.

This kind of speculation reminds me that many things might have changed by the time we resume hearings in August. An inquiry like this isn't an autopsy, even if it is sometimes referred to as a post-mortem on Somalia. The body politic wriggles on the examination table.

Wednesday, July 3, 1996
Ottawa and London

Yesterday was my sixty-third birthday, celebrated in Ottawa where Hazel and I had driven to meet our daughter Jane, who was returning from a year's graduate study in Russia.

On Monday, Canada Day, we drove from London to Ottawa, arriving in the afternoon. The sidewalks of Elgin Street leading up to Parliament Hill were filled with strollers decked out in nationalistic regalia. Red maple leaves were everywhere, on T-shirts, stencilled on cheeks, on small flags tucked behind ears, into headbands, belts, and boots, on huge flags worn as cloaks or carried on poles above the heads of the crowd.

At dusk we walked with thousands of others toward Confederation Square. The entire Parliament Hill area and surrounding streets were closed to cars and buses. We walked as part of a dense stream of human beings past the Château Laurier and north on Sussex Drive until we came up against barriers at the National Art Gallery. The crowd pressed and surged behind us, and for a few moments there was a tremor of claustrophobia until people backed off and found space for themselves. Shortly after 10 P.M., fireworks started to explode across the dark sky behind the gallery, reflected and multiplied in the panes of its glass tower. Everyone cheered and waved their flags; people sang the national anthem and danced in the street.

For a Canadian of my generation, this display of patriotism was exotic, almost un-Canadian. I remember Dominion Day as a quiet holiday reserved for family picnics. In our neighbourhood in the west end of Montreal, the odd fervent patriot might hang a small red Ensign on the front porch. Modest displays of fireworks flared in backyards before family audiences. We thought of Americans as the flag-wavers of North America; our patriotism was of a more genteel nature.

But this refined patriotism has not always been the norm in Canada. Speeches and newspaper editorials at the time of Confederation and the decades that followed were filled with elaborate proclamations of patriotic fervour. It was during the years of my childhood, particularly after the Second World War, that Canadian patriotism reached a low point. After the war, nationalism was in disrepute everywhere and that suited Canadians. Canada drew closer to the United States until this created a strong counter-movement in the 1960s.

In that year, the success of Expo 67 surprised and impressed Canadians. National self-confidence began to grow, only to be blindsided at the very outset of this rediscovery of patriotism by the burgeoning nationalism of French-speaking Quebec. From then on, Quebec nationalism slowly provoked a growing sense of community in the rest of the country. Every separatist politician in Quebec who stated that English-speaking Canada was not really a nation, at least not compared with *la nation* in Quebec, encouraged this development.

And that's what was happening in Ottawa on this Canada Day. The crowd in the centre of the city, largely English-speaking and estimated at more than 140,000 by newspapers, seemed to be expressing its patriotism in reaction to the scare of the recent Quebec referendum. There was a spirit of defiance in the air, unconsciously directed toward the Quebec side of the Ottawa River.

THE ORDEAL OF GENERAL
JEAN BOYLE

·

August 1996

B y the end of June 1996, we had heard all the witnesses in the
document-tampering phase of our inquiry except the most
important, the current chief of the defence staff, Gen. Jean Boyle.
In his previous appointments at National Defence Headquarters,
General Boyle had been closely involved with supervising the
Media Liaison Office, where document tampering had occurred,
and the Somalia Inquiry Liaison Team (SILT), in charge of co-
ordinating the delivery of documents to the inquiry. His appearance before the inquiry required careful preparation between the
end of June and mid-August, when he took the stand.

General Boyle testified for nine days between August 12 and
28, the longest testimony of any of our witnesses. As expected, it
was the most dramatic two weeks of hearings, closely followed by
many Canadians who watched it live on television. Boyle fought
determinedly to defend his reputation and save his job. By the end
of his ordeal, the news media had decided that he had failed, but
the general, a former fighter pilot, apparently had not given up.

Sunday, August 11, 1996
En route London–Ottawa

The break from the inquiry ended last week when I drove with Hazel from London to Ottawa for two days of meetings with the other commissioners and staff. While I pored over documents and slowly picked up the threads of our investigation, Hazel spent several steamy August days searching for student accommodation with our daughter Jane. In one more year at Carleton University, Jane will earn her master's degree in Russian studies, the last of all the children to complete her university education, several years before my oldest grandchild begins hers.

Last week the other commissioners and I talked about how quickly we seemed to forget about Somalia last month. Judge Létourneau had attended a judicial conference in Strasbourg, stopping with his wife in Paris on the return trip to visit a son who is working there. Judge Rutherford spent the month at his cottage overlooking Georgian Bay. I haven't thought about the two judges as symbolic of Canada until this moment, but I suppose that they are. Gilles Létourneau, from the working-class suburb of Lévis across the St. Lawrence River from Quebec City, recalls generations of Quebec farmers and workers. His stocky, muscular build seems the inheritance of workers rather than the clerical or notarial élite of old Quebec society. His thinking patterns are analytical and logical but surprisingly direct, even blunt for a lawyer educated in Quebec's classical system. Judge Rutherford is the older of the two by two decades. His family's roots are embedded as deeply in the rich farmland of Ontario as are Gilles's in the rocky soil of Quebec's south shore.

Between these two powerful representations of English and French Canada, I might pretend to stand for something in between – a mixture of old Quebec on my father's side, combined through his mother with Swiss or German-American ancestry, Scottish grandparents on my mother's side, Roman Catholic in upbringing but Protestant in practice, recalling the Presbyterianism of my Scots ancestors, haltingly bilingual, never quite certain where I stand in the eternal Canadian dialogue between the Létourneaus and Rutherfords of this nation.

Tomorrow we begin our examination of Gen. Jean Boyle. In my briefcase I have an outline of the questions prepared by the inquiry's lawyers – thirty-five pages in all. The examination and cross-examination are expected to last all this week and part of the following. Then, perhaps, we will finally be ready to march into Somalia.

At our meetings last week, there was a growing sense of urgency. The list of future witnesses is being reviewed and reduced. Schedules of hearings are being constantly revised with an eye on the calendar. In the background, the federal government, creator and perhaps target of the inquiry, looms with an expression of mounting impatience and concern.

The ambivalence of governments toward independent inquiries is currently being illustrated by the Krever inquiry into the national blood-supply system. Under fire for moving slowly to protect Canadians from blood transfusions carrying the AIDS virus, federal and provincial governments used the appointment of the Krever inquiry to cool off an aroused public and to buy time. But as the inquiry moved toward assigning responsibility for the distribution of tainted blood, governments became nervous. Recently they created a federal-provincial committee to examine the national blood supply and to recommend changes, exactly what Judge Horace Krever was asked to do. In effect, the governments seem to be trying to regain the initiative by stealing a march on Judge Krever, trying to render his report obsolete before it is issued.

In our own case, Defence Minister David Collenette a few weeks ago announced that a parliamentary committee will be asked to study the system of military justice, one of the major focuses of our own work. The committee will gather evidence similar to ours, listen to many of the same experts, and undoubtedly make recommendations that will precede and overlap ours. You have to wonder if this is an indication of the minister's disapproval of the direction that we took when we moved our investigation forward into post-Somalia events and closer to the minister's own office.

Regardless of the politics of these developments, this undermining of two independent inquiries shows how easy it is for a government to affect them even as it officially maintains an arm's-length relationship. There seems to be very little public awareness of this. As inquiries become more complex legally, more expensive and time-consuming, people become sceptical and cynical about the process itself. But if independent public inquiries do not remain effective, our system of government loses something valuable, and there isn't anything to replace them.

Another worrisome development is the continuing legal action to prove bias against Judge Létourneau and disqualify him from ruling on the conduct of one of the senior officers, General Beno. This suit, based partly on comments allegedly made by Judge Létourneau during a visit to an army base in Calgary, has the potential to seriously disrupt the inquiry. Having been rejected by the inquiry, the action is now moving toward the Federal Court of Appeal.

A senior officer who wants to intervene in support of General Beno has now become a key player in the action. The media haven't yet picked up on this. Today the federal Justice Department officially supported the right of this officer to intervene before the court. This could be interpreted as showing a lack of confidence on the part of the government in the chair of the inquiry. There is a great deal of speculation about the meaning of this decision. Is it simply a misguided, wrong-headed legal opinion? Or is it a deliberate sign of official discontent with our inquiry?

While the cameras focus on the official proceedings, we're aware of tremors and undercurrents beneath the surface that could bring the whole machinery of the inquiry to a juddering halt.

Monday, August 12, 1996
Ottawa

Gen. Jean Boyle, less than a year after his appointment as chief of the defence staff, took the stand before us this morning to defend his handling of the Somalia crisis.

Although he had nothing to do with the actual mission in Somalia, General Boyle was involved in almost every facet of the effort at National Defence Headquarters to "manage" its aftermath. He was in charge of the Somalia Working Group that was created as the crisis escalated. This was where senior officers and departmental officials exchanged information in an effort to combat the demoralizing effects of continuing revelations about the behaviour of the military in Somalia. Later,

Boyle was in charge of the office responsible for providing our inquiry with the documents we required. This placed him at the centre of revelations about missing documents, reported attempts to destroy documents, and law-breaking by officers who provided false responses to media requests for documents under Access to Information.

Since our inquiry was appointed last year, General Boyle has said nothing about Somalia. He has saved it all for this moment, as he said on the stand today. This is his opportunity to clear his name and, perhaps, to save his job.

Paul Koring, in a front-page story in the *Globe* this morning, concluded: "In Ottawa, both in military and political circles, there is a widespread belief that Gen. Boyle's performance before the inquiry and, more importantly, the public perception of it, will determine whether he keeps his job."

We were all a bit on edge as the session opened this morning. Judge Rutherford complained of having a cold. My stomach was mildly upset. I noticed that Boyle took the Bible in his left hand before responding to the request to "place your right hand on the Bible" and swearing to tell the truth.

The examination by our own counsel began, as usual, on safe ground – questions about his career in the military, details of his appointments at NDHQ, and the structures created there in 1993 to handle the escalating Somalia crisis. The general spoke quietly, methodically, easily recalling names, dates, and other minor details of business.

A handsome officer, his confident, even commanding, presence is marred only by a mouth that is tight-lipped and clenched, creating an impression of severity and defiance. It was this tense expression that conveyed an unfavourable impression to media commentators last spring when Boyle sent a videotaped message to his soldiers announcing the day-long search for missing Somalia documents.

Questions and answers were routine until the last hour of the afternoon when discussion focused on the military's preparation for our inquiry over the past year. At that time when it became evident that Boyle's own actions in relation to Access to Information requests would be under scrutiny, and that he would have to testify about them, he had had to exclude himself from planning sessions where this was being discussed. While this protected him from conflict-of-interest problems, it also meant that the military was "leaderless" as it planned its response in this area. In this respect, his involvement in handling the fall-out from Somalia had compromised him and affected his ability to do his job as chief of the defence staff. The general said that this made him "uncomfortable," but he continued to fulfil the many other responsibilities of Canada's top soldier. This was his first admission of real difficulty – an unresolved conflict that affected his ability to do his job, at least to some degree. It's hard to say how he will emerge from all this. Several times today he took advantage of a difficult question to shift to grounds of his own choosing, paying tribute to the record of soldiers in Somalia, urging the awarding of a "Somalia medal" to veterans of the campaign, speaking through us to the troops under his command and beyond them to the Canadian people and their political leaders.

I expect the media reviews of this first day will be mixed. General Boyle gained some territory but suffered a few flesh wounds in the process.

Tuesday, August 13, 1996
Ottawa

The reviews were positive. "Boyle Breaks Somalia Silence" was the headline on the *Globe*'s front-page story by Paul Koring. The subhead read: "Military will not blame others for debacle, general testifies." Other newspapers, and television newscasts the night before, reported Boyle's profession of relief that he was finally able to state his side of the story, and his initial shouldering of responsibility on behalf of the military. He specifically exempted the media from blame, usually a popular stance with journalists.

This first day showed the effects of Boyle's careful preparation. Having done media training myself, preparing corporate executives for their fifteen seconds of television exposure, I could easily imagine the grooming that Boyle has been receiving from his lawyers and handlers. Yesterday he was able on occasion to draw on his mental portfolio of prepared messages, inserting them into his responses whenever he had an opportunity. This is one of the standard procedures to combat hostile interviewers – nod briefly in the direction of the unfriendly question and then take off in a direction of your own choosing. This is even easier to do at an inquiry than during a television interview. Witnesses are rarely interrupted. There are few time constraints on their answers.

But the unravelling process started this morning, almost as soon as we resumed at 10 A.M. The general took everyone by surprise by confessing that he had learned only last Thursday, when he was briefed for his appearance this week, that computer disks containing intelligence logs from Somalia were still located at a military base in Kingston, Ontario, instead of being in our hands, where they should have been a year ago.

These logs are among the many documents missing from our archives. It's true, as Boyle pointed out, that we have been provided with an enormous amount of material – something in the area of 100,000 documents so far. I've seen speculation on the inquiry's internal e-mail that this may already be a record for Canadian royal commissions. But it's also true that hundreds of documents and sections of documents are still missing, sixteen months after our original order for their production. Among these are some of the operational logs from Somalia, particularly the intelligence logs from Canadian headquarters.

We already knew that these logs had come back to Canada from Somalia with our returning soldiers. They had been brought back under guard, an indication of their importance in the eyes of the military. We also knew that in flagrant violation of our order they had been destroyed at Kingston as recently as last February. Although the logs were shredded, there still existed the computer disks containing the material listed in the logs. Headquarters staff in Ottawa – the team assigned to assist the inquiry in collecting material – had been notified of the existence of these disks four months ago. Last Thursday, General Boyle was told that nothing had been done in the intervening time to turn the logs over to us.

He said that he had immediately ordered an investigation and implied that heads would roll. But this episode did more than any of our questions to illustrate the problems that we have been having in getting documents.

In response to further questions about missing documents, the general could provide only regrets, few explanations. This led Judge Létourneau to initiate a discussion of leadership and accountability. Boyle's answers tended to be long and convoluted. While he had readily accepted responsibility for Somalia on behalf of the military yesterday, personal responsibility was another matter. He started to shift blame downward to his subordinates and associates for not informing him of problems about the assembling of documents, and up the chain of command to his superiors for not acting on the advice that he had given them.

Toward the end of the afternoon, we turned to the question of incomplete documents that had been provided in 1993 to Michael McAuliffe. General Boyle, who said yesterday that he usually liked to brief himself thoroughly, and provided examples of careful reading of basic documents, stated today that he had reluctantly agreed to the informal release of documents to McAuliffe without ever seeing them. Both the chair and I questioned him about what I called this "uncharacteristic" behaviour.

The style adopted by our lawyers is to carefully lay out the evidence and let it speak for itself. Because of this, an intelligent, adroit, and well-briefed witness such as Boyle has many opportunities for obscuring the central issues, and for inserting his own message into his testimony. So this afternoon, Judge Létourneau and I virtually took over the examination. This has its risks. There's nothing improper about it – our mandate as commissioners is to inquire – but we have to be careful that we don't look as if we have made up our minds about any of the issues or witnesses. Even the number of questions we ask can be interpreted as indicating scepticism. At the other extreme, if we don't ask questions, we can be accused of not doing our job properly or, in the case of prominent witnesses, of treating senior officers more gently than lower ranks.

It looks now as if our examination-in-chief of General Boyle may last for another two days before lawyers for other officers can begin to cross-examine. Even more difficult questions lie ahead for the general.

Wednesday, August 14, 1996
Ottawa

By this morning, the media pendulum had swung decisively against General Boyle. On CTV's national news last night, the network's military expert was speculating about his ability to withstand much more.

Watching the general on the stand today, I couldn't help thinking of a wounded bull, its head lowered, waiting for the picadors to charge. The lances sink into its shoulder again and again, but still the bull stands. Every now and then, it raises its head and lunges at its tormentors, still dangerous, but the defiance becomes weaker and less frequent as the blood flows. An overly dramatic image, but there is a *Death in the Afternoon* air about the hearing room as the general fights for his reputation and career.

Just before 10 A.M. every day, the media are allowed into the hearing room to photograph the commissioners and the witness. Sometimes there are only two or three television cameramen and photographers. This week, the space before our table has been filled with jostling cameramen, bright television lights, and photographic flashes. General Boyle endures this for several minutes before ushers herd the media from the room.

Two fixed cameras from CPAC remain to provide live coverage. Most of the newspaper and television correspondents watch the hearings on monitors in the media centre just outside our hearing room. When we recess, they cluster about the exit, waiting to scrum witnesses and lawyers for comments on the session that has just ended.

Today there were no spectacular revelations, just a continual grinding away at Boyle's credibility. He insisted doggedly that at the time he knew nothing important about the provision of altered documents to Michael McAuliffe. He repeated that when the documents were provided informally to McAuliffe, he approved the decision without reading them. When the same altered documents were provided under Access to Information some months later, he looked at them, but the alterations were not apparent to him. He didn't notice them. Then he blamed his subordinates for not informing him.

This morning I received a fax from a retired colonel in British Columbia who watches our proceedings on television and gives me his impressions from time to time. He was appalled by the general's evasion of responsibility. In the navy, he said, there is no such confusion. If a ship runs aground, the captain is held responsible. If the ship goes down, the captain goes with it. Whether General Boyle can maintain his position of accepting responsibility up to a point while pleading ignorance and blaming others beyond that point remains to be seen. His admission today that he broke the spirit of the Access to Information Act, if not the letter of the law, was damning.

It was five minutes before our normal closing time of four o'clock this afternoon when the general asked for a reprieve. We had taken a mid-afternoon break less than an hour before, but he was plainly exhausted and becoming irritable. For the first time since Monday, he looked as if he were starting to buckle under the strain. But the worst is yet to come – the cross-examination next week by lawyers for some of the people whom he has blamed this week.

Thursday, August 15, 1996
Ottawa

As I discovered later this morning, the inquiry office had tried to reach me shortly after 7 A.M. when I was downstairs in the hotel enjoying my daily twenty-minute swim. I didn't get the message. It wasn't until I reached the street corner opposite our building that I encountered Stanley Cohen, the inquiry's secretary, who told me that General Boyle had been given a reprieve for the day. The husband of our senior counsel, Barbara McIsaac, had taken ill during a trip to Sudbury, Ontario, and was scheduled for emergency surgery today. Barbara was already on her way north. After a brief meeting at 10 A.M. with Stan and the other commissioners, I spent the rest of the day reading the transcript of this week's hearings and preparing for their resumption next Tuesday.

Perhaps the unscheduled recess will provide time for others to reflect on the revelations this week. This may not help the general. The first newspaper editorial that I have seen appeared in the *Ottawa Citizen* this morning. Its conclusion: "While the commissioners pursue the rest of the facts, the government's duty is already apparent. If the generals of the Canadian Forces cannot take their responsibilities, Prime Minister Chrétien must order the appointment of others who can.

"That is his responsibility."

This morning, a member of our staff rose early, after a restless night, and placed thoughts on paper. The memo was on my desk when I arrived at 9 A.M. This staff member, who has an extensive military background, had already moved beyond yesterday's admission by General Boyle that he broke "the spirit of the law" to its wider implications. Did this mean, for instance, that a subordinate of Boyle's could now use the same excuse for failure – that the letter of the law or military regulations had been followed even if the spirit of the law had been broken? Would a private now be able to plead the same defence? Our adviser was deeply concerned that the effect of Boyle's statement on military discipline would be disastrous.

My own thoughts yesterday and overnight had to do with the communications policy described by Boyle. This is my own area of expertise. I perceived, in the general's description, the genesis of the problems now threatening to overwhelm him. This afternoon I summarized my line of reasoning in a brief note that I shared with the other commissioners. It may be interesting because it illustrates the way ideas and conclusions start to crystallize as the inquiry progresses:

Possible Line of Questioning for General Boyle
Thursday, August 15, 1996

- Initial mistaken premise: That the military had an "image problem" as a result of Somalia. Blame placed on "a few bad apples." Blame placed on the media.
- Proposal: The image problem can be corrected by better communications.

- Solution: Adopt the techniques of corporate public relations. Decentralize public affairs in the military. Attach a public affairs officer to every group at headquarters in Ottawa. Make sure that consideration of the public affairs impact pervades every decision taken by senior commands.
- Problem: Confusion about the reason for doing this. Officially it is to make the military more accessible and responsive to the media. But it is also designed to control information issuing from the military to the media. These two objectives are often in conflict and when conflict occurs, the "control" objective takes over.
- Another problem: The army is not General Motors. It is not a private corporation deciding how to control private information. It is a public institution; most of the information in the military belongs to the public – unless it involves national security or privacy.
- Another problem: This corporate public affairs strategy had a strong appeal to the military. It sounded strategic. It sounded as if one just had to adopt the correct battle plan and the "image" problem would be defeated.
- Another problem: The plan was being controlled and implemented by people with almost no public affairs experience – Boyle himself, and Roberto Gonzalez, his director general of public affairs. Some of the officers in the Media Liaison Office had taken a short course in public affairs; others didn't even have that.
- Perception: Regardless of the motives for implementing the new communications strategy, it was interpreted by those working for Boyle and Gonzalez as emphasizing control of information. One thing is clear from the testimony of everyone working for Boyle and Gonzalez – they all believed that

they were doing what they were supposed to be doing! They all believed that they were doing what General Boyle wanted them to do . . . to control information and thereby control the public agenda.

- End result: The gradual erosion of transparency and accountability, starting with the irregular and informal release of RTQs to Michael McAuliffe of the CBC and leading inevitably to the offence against Access to Information.

The public affairs policy itself created a public affairs problem. The policy that was designed to cure the military's image problem created in the end a much more severe image problem than the original one, with even more serious consequences for senior leadership.

Friday, August 16, 1996
En route Ottawa–Winnipeg

One theory current among some staff and lawyers associated with the inquiry sees General Boyle as a victim. According to this interpretation, Boyle was moved into the key position of associate assistant defence minister, policy and communications, in the spring of 1993 as events in Somalia were creating a full-blown crisis for the military. One of his first actions in this role was to create the Somalia Working Group, a high-level committee without specific written authority, agendas, or detailed written minutes of its meetings, that acted as a central switchboard at NDHQ for the exchange of all information on Somalia and discussion of counter-strategies. Closely related to this was the reform of communications policies and methods within the Department of National Defence to ensure closer supervision of information supplied to the media.

With Boyle in this position, others were effectively insulated from the developing crisis. If Boyle were unable to handle the crisis, he could be held responsible and jettisoned. But if he were successful, he might then be appointed chief of the defence staff. He would then be in a position to control any further investigation. The system would remain as closed as it had always been.

Sunday, August 18, 1996
En route Winnipeg–London

No matter where I am in Canada, I can never entirely escape the long shadow of the Somalia inquiry. This past weekend in Winnipeg, at the wedding of my youngest daughter Jane (known in the family as "Little Jane" to distinguish her from the older "Big Jane" who has been studying in Russia), people came up to me throughout the day to make brief comments on the inquiry, particularly the events of the past week.

These were not the journalists, politicians, and bureaucrats that I normally encounter in Ottawa. They had caught the inquiry out of the corners of their eyes, as it were, as they watched the television news before an evening baseball game or similar pursuit. Their comments indicated that they regard the whole Somalia affair as a sad story. They have almost lost the capacity to be shocked by it.

The wedding guests in Winnipeg often expressed sympathy for my assignment, as if it must be distasteful, a dirty job. Occasionally there were even expressions of gratitude for the public service that I and the other commissioners are performing – a welcome reminder that not everyone is as cynical about the political process as many of the people I routinely meet in Ottawa.

———————

Winnipeg always stirs powerful memories in me. It is the city where I spent five years as a young journalist almost forty years ago. From our room on the twenty-fifth floor of the Delta Hotel on Portage Avenue I could look down on the parking lot on Smith Street, where the *Tribune* building once stood. The formal wedding pictures were taken on the steps of the Legislative Building, where I learned the elements of political journalism. Later, I showed Hazel the chamber where the legislature meets, and its small Press Gallery perched above the Speaker's throne. It seemed immeasurably larger and grander forty years ago. The nearby office where our desks and typewriters were jammed together has disappeared.

The past kept struggling to intrude throughout the day, but it was Jane who pushed it into the background. The shy little girl who had visited us every summer in London had become, apparently overnight, a slim, poised, elegant young bride who looked like Audrey Hepburn, only prettier in a simple long white gown.

I wasn't going to say anything at the wedding. The speeches by the best man and maid of honour were made on the steps of the groom's parental home after the ceremony in the living room. But when it became evident that Jane's mother would not speak, I climbed a few steps, introduced myself and spoke. I said that separation and divorce are always hard on children. Many times, over the years, trying to cope with my own feelings of guilt, I had told Jane that I would understand if she blamed me, if she felt angry. She would always reassure me. She was fine. There was nothing to worry about.

"And so it was from Jane that I learned about unqualified love," I said.

Tuesday, August 20, 1996
Ottawa

General Boyle must have been working over the weekend. This morning he fought back with a more spirited defence of his conduct than we had seen last week. Perhaps the growing media chorus demanding his resignation, or that the government fire him, has stiffened his resolve. Perhaps he has decided that if he is going to go down, he might as well go down defiantly.

He stuck to his position today that subordinates had let him down, that he had made every reasonable effort to inform himself. While he accepts general responsibility for what happened under his command, he obviously doesn't think that it's a matter serious enough to warrant resignation. And if the government believed that it did, he said, he wouldn't still be in command of the Armed Forces.

So he has decided to try to ride out the storm.

Wednesday, August 21, 1996
Ottawa

More sparring with General Boyle before the examination-in-chief by ourselves and our counsel, Barbara McIsaac, came to an end at 3:55 P.M. He has been on the stand for six days minus five minutes.

Near the end, I asked the general to elaborate on an earlier remark that he had had difficulty at times distinguishing between Jean Boyle and General Boyle, Boyle as a private citizen and Boyle as chief of the defence staff. This was in response to questions about his use of personnel at Defence Headquarters to gather material to assist his appearance before the inquiry, a privilege specifically denied to at least one other subordinate general.

I asked whether he wasn't concerned that accusations levelled at his individual conduct in the Somalia affair hadn't already "contaminated" the professional role that he had to play as chief of the defence staff. I used the example of police officers who are usually suspended from duty until allegations of misconduct are dealt with.

The general said that he certainly had thought of this option, and had discussed it, but that he had decided to remain at his post as long as he had the confidence of the minister of defence. When this quote was played on the news this evening, it was followed by a clip from the minister, David Collenette, reiterating his support.

Many people think that Boyle's testimony before us has damaged him irretrievably. Boyle disagrees. It was evident from his testimony that he sees himself as emerging stronger from this ordeal, having taken his medicine, admitted his failings, weathered the ordeal of the inquiry, and learned his lessons. He seems to believe that this has fitted him to lead the Forces into a new age.

In any case, the general's real ordeal will start tomorrow. After the government lawyers finish their examination, lawyers for some of Boyle's subordinates will have their chance to defend their clients at Boyle's expense.

Friday, August 23, 1996
En route Ottawa–London

This afternoon it started to feel like a war of attrition. Arthur Cogan, acting for Col. Geoffrey Haswell, formerly the senior military officer in NDHQ's public affairs directorate, spent the whole day battering at General Boyle's defences.

Cogan, as I've noted before, tackles witnesses with all the ferocity of a defence lawyer trying to save his client from the noose. While the techniques may be effective in a criminal court, Cogan's usual milieu, they tend to be time-consuming and fractious in our inquiry. But every now and then, his scatter-gun approach hits home, and witnesses are rushed or prodded or goaded into making incriminating statements.

Cogan used to infuriate Peter Vita, the lawyer who was the original chief counsel for the government. Their confrontations were becoming nasty and personal before the July recess when Vita went back to Toronto and was replaced by Ottawa lawyer Brian Everden. Everden is sharp-witted but soft-spoken, much calmer than the pugnacious Vita. For this phase of our hearings, Everden is teamed with Norman Peel, an urbane, white-haired lawyer from London who has acted for the government in several of the Somalia-related courts martial. Peel has a slow, measured, rhetorical style of argument, like the beating of some great drum, that breaks up and neutralizes the rhythm of Cogan's machine-gun attacks.

Despite expectations of fireworks between Cogan and Boyle, the long cross-examination was more like trench warfare. Boyle refused to be lured into the open by Cogan's sallies.

By 4 P.M., I felt that everyone in the hearing room was on the ropes and just wanted to escape into the weekend.

On Monday, General Boyle will be in Colorado at an American military ceremony, enjoying the attention and respect that a chief of the defence staff commands. Then, next Tuesday, he'll face Cogan again and more allegations that his conduct has made him unfit to lead the Canadian Forces.

I heard today that Boyle's handlers believe that he has already won. This may be true in a technical sense – but it would appear that the public perception of evasion, sophistry, and blaming of subordinates has grown deeper and more damaging day by day, judging from everything I hear and read. All the newspaper editorials that I have seen have berated him for ducking responsibility and most have called for his resignation or firing. Three letters to the editor in the *Globe* this morning, two from retired senior military officers in British Columbia, expressed shock and dismay at his performance.

The *coup de grâce* this week came hurtling out of left field when former health minister Monique Bégin released a letter she had sent to the Krever inquiry accepting responsibility for the blood-supply problems under investigation. The sight of Bégin voluntarily taking her place alongside junior members of her old department, and insisting on being "named" by the inquiry if her former subordinates were, was immediately contrasted with Boyle's behaviour. As one of the *Globe* letter-writers stated, evasion is expected from politicians, and honourable acceptance of responsibility from military leaders, not the reverse. Bégin did more damage to Boyle than any of the lawyers this week.

Monday, August 26, 1996
En route London–Ottawa

Hazel and I went to the London "Y" at 7 A.M. At the desk outside the locker rooms, the teenaged attendant, the son of an old
friend, wanted to talk about the aggressive lawyer who had
questioned General Boyle last week. He meant Arthur Cogan.
"Yeah, that's him," he said. "Is he allowed to do that?"

We're not exactly the Watergate hearings on television, but
we're the closest Canadian equivalent.

Tuesday, August 27, 1996
Ottawa

Although the Somalia hearings tell me the opposite every day,
I do believe that life in Canada gets better and better. Late this
afternoon, after I had escaped from the hearing and was walking along Bank Street, greedily absorbing the last fragments of
afternoon sunlight, I noticed a tall black man in a flowing
white jacket, trousers, and black paratrooper-style boots trying to distribute pamphlets to pedestrians. Most pointedly
ignored him.

I fell into conversation with him. I think I must have been
desperate to talk about something other than Somalia, even
Islam, the subject of his pamphlets.

"I'm from Nova Scotia," volunteered this exotic figure.
"A real Bluenoser."

He looked more like something from *Lawrence of Arabia*.
Then he told me that I looked like a bureaucrat, which I
suppose I do, wearing my charcoal-grey suit and carrying my
black briefcase.

"You look like you've done all right," said this irreverent Muslim Maritimer. I reacted as if he'd accused me of something shameful.

He left me with a pamphlet. As I discovered later, it had no local address. If I wanted further information about the Five Pillars of Islam outlined in the pamphlet, I would have to write to a box number in Saudi Arabia. A religion that inefficient and hard-to-get can't be all bad, I thought to myself.

A few minutes after we parted, I found myself walking in the midst of an East Indian family group, the grandmother in a sari, her daughter and grandchildren in western dress, all talking in their own language. A swarthy Lebanese began to clear away the sidewalk displays outside his handbag shop.

When I grew up in the west end of Montreal, there was one French-speaking family on our street. At the end of the war, a black paraplegic veteran moved his family into special housing that had been built in a vacant lot across the street from our flat. It was the first black family that I had ever seen. Now a black Haligonian in flowing white linens hardly attracts a second glance in Ottawa. We have become immeasurably more diverse as Canadians while maintaining a level of social harmony that amazes visitors, even if we take it for granted.

The ordeal of General Boyle is approaching its end. The lawyers for other officers have almost exhausted their questions. Tomorrow will be his ninth and final day on the witness stand. The media have already given their verdict: resign or be fired. But the general apparently has no intention of complying. It looks as if he intends to weather the storm, and that the minister of defence will support him, if not enthusiastically, until our report is released.

Wednesday, August 28, 1996
Ottawa

It was a few minutes before 5 P.M. when General Boyle stepped down from the witness stand after nine days of testimony, damaged but defiant. He repeated at the very end that he will continue to serve as chief of the defence staff unless the government asks him to resign, and that isn't likely. Defence Minister David Collenette said yesterday that General Boyle "has been doing a very good job in difficult circumstances."

From the beginning, the general has insisted that he had no involvement in tampering with documents released by the military in response to an Access to Information request by Michael McAuliffe. This was the most serious accusation that faced him because it involved breaking the law. Although his explanations have been at times tortuous, and his defence forced him to accuse subordinates of lying and cheating, no one has produced a single piece of documentary evidence to show conclusively that he either knew or approved of the document tampering.

If there were such a memo, surely one of his accused subordinates would have produced it by now. The general seems confident that there isn't. But who knows? Previously unknown documents are still surfacing. Only a few days ago, while searching backup computer tapes from the Directorate of Public Affairs at NDHQ, one of our investigators discovered a 1994 memo prepared for Boyle's signature suggesting that the name of *Ottawa Citizen* journalist Greg Weston should be deleted from internal documents at NDHQ in anticipation of an Access to Information request. There is no evidence that Boyle ever signed the memo. This afternoon he denied that he had ever seen it. But it indicated the mentality that pervaded the NDHQ's public affairs branch when he was associate assistant deputy minister, policy and communications.

If it depended on the verdict of newspaper editorialists and columnists, Boyle would be in early retirement now. Typical was a piece published in Ottawa's *Le Droit* last Monday, reprinted from *Le Soleil* in Quebec, by the newspaper's editorial director J.-Jacques Samson.

"The Chief of the Defence Staff of the Canadian forces, Jean Boyle, is toast [*est cuit*]," he wrote. "He is no longer able to command."

But the public's attention span is short. A growing school of thought among followers of our inquiry predicts that Boyle will serve at least until the end of 1997, the termination of his two-year term. Our report may not be finished and made public much before that. Even if it is critical, he will be able by then to point to the reform measures that he has already started to institute, and retire honourably.

Friday, August 30, 1996
En route Ottawa–London

Col. Geoffrey Haswell, on the stand for the past two days, has been an unusual witness. He's the only one so far charged in connection with the fiasco in the public affairs directorate at NDHQ.*

Colonel Haswell didn't bring us closer to linking General Boyle with document tampering. Like many other witnesses, he's convinced Boyle knew what was going on in public affairs,

---

* He was eventually acquitted.

but he has no proof. During his testimony, however, he gave us an unprecedented glimpse into the way the military was handling its public relations during the Somalia crisis.

"Containment" was the word that he used to describe Boyle's whole approach to information, in concert with his assistant deputy minister, Dr. Ken Calder, and under the leadership of deputy minister Robert Fowler. The policy was to release as little information to the media and the public as possible.

Haswell was the first member of the directorate to admit that the controversial shift from RTQs (Response to Queries) to MRLs (Media Response Lines) had no other purpose but to hide RTQs from Access to Information. Other witnesses have tried to disguise it as part of a departmental reorganization. Haswell called it what it was – evasion of the law and a deliberate attempt to avoid public scrutiny and democratic control of the military.

This attitude was endemic in the highest levels of the public affairs directorate, where information policies were transformed into disinformation practices. Haswell described the practices of Ruth Cardinal, former director general of public affairs and currently a senior official in the Privy Council Office, whose comments on official memos were often written on yellow sticky papers that could later be removed if the documents were requested under Access to Information. He said that his staff sometimes tried to staple and tape the sticky papers to the memos to make it difficult for them to be detached because they regarded the information in them as vital.

He also made public a technique that journalists have become familiar with: insisting that documents requested under Access to Information are described exactly before their release is permitted. Unless the titles are exact, those seeking documents are told that they don't exist. Colonel Haswell said that he had recently been trying to use Access to Information himself to acquire documents related to his impending court appearance and had been foiled by this very tactic.

INTO SOMALIA
·
September to December 1996

In September 1996, the inquiry finally arrived in Somalia, so to speak. But even as we began to hear witnesses about events in Somalia, we had to deal with the aftermath of our documentation hearings the previous month.

In early October, we interrupted our schedule for an unexpected return appearance by Roberto Gonzalez, former director general of public affairs at National Defence Headquarters under Gen. Jean Boyle. Since his testimony the previous April, Gonzalez had remembered details of his dealings with General Boyle that contradicted parts of Boyle's testimony in August. In his new testimony, he linked Boyle more closely with the alteration of documents at NDHQ.

Two days later, on October 4, Defence Minister David Collenette resigned, explaining that he had written a letter improperly to immigration authorities on behalf of a constituent. (He was re-elected the following June and reappointed to the cabinet as transport minister.) This was followed four days later by Boyle's resignation as chief of the defence staff and his retirement from the military. (He subsequently went to work for a company manufacturing military aircraft.) Doug Young, a New Brunswick politician with a reputation for decisiveness, was shifted to Defence from the Transport portfolio.

Meanwhile, we were moving more deeply into the examination of events in Somalia. Conscious of time limitations and aware of the growing impatience of the government, we decided to focus at this stage on a critical event in Somalia – the fatal shooting of one Somali and the wounding of a second by Canadian soldiers on the night of March 4, 1993. We felt that a thorough examination of this event would reveal a great deal about command and control of Canadian soldiers by their senior officers. It would help us to understand the highly publicized murder of Shidane Arone several weeks later, as well as other documented examples of misconduct by Canadian soldiers. We believed that giving this kind of attention to the March 4 incident would save time in the end, but we also knew from experience that it would be a long process. Between October 1996 and the following March, we heard twenty-four witnesses on the March 4 incident at Belet Huen and its ramifications at National Defence Headquarters, from master corporals who took part in the incident up to the acting chief of the defence staff, Vice-Admiral Larry Murray. The eight days that Murray spent on the stand in January 1997 recalled the ordeal of his predecessor, Jean Boyle, but Murray survived the process.

Monday, September 9, 1996
Ottawa

The third and final phase of the hearings began today, a little more than a year since we held our first public session. We've slogged our way through the training of the Airborne regiment, its selection for the Somalia mission, and the videotaped horrors of its hazing ceremonies. We've completed a long but essential journey through the corridors of the public affairs directorate at NDHQ in Ottawa, where military and civilian personnel, through their approach to information management, tarnished the image of the Canadian Forces and almost brought down the chief of the defence staff.

Now we're finally into Somalia, examining what actually happened after Canadian soldiers started to arrive in December 1992. That will take us eventually to the aftermath of events in Somalia, the question of possible cover-ups, and the ultimate responsibility of senior military, bureaucratic, and political figures in Ottawa.

We're all feeling the pressure as time passes. There's an awareness that the inquiry already has exceeded its original time limit. Our lawyers are being told to exclude witnesses who aren't absolutely essential and to keep their examinations as brief and as pointed as possible. But the hearings process has its own dynamic. It often reveals unexpected areas that demand further exploration. Trying to accelerate is like trying to get a long freight train to act like a sports car. It has its own momentum and its own pace.

We may be drawn deeper into Somalia than we originally intended. Allan Thompson of the *Toronto Star*'s Ottawa bureau has been in Somalia in recent weeks interviewing people who worked for the Canadian soldiers and others who witnessed some of the more horrific events there. His most sensational story, on the front page last Saturday, claimed that a document accepted by Canadian military authorities who investigated the March 4, 1993, shooting of two Somalis at the Canadian camp at Belet Huen was forged. The document contained a statement by ten Somali civilians employed by the Canadians, supporting the shooting of one Somali and the wounding of another, saying they were known to be thieves. Now four of the Somalis are saying that their signatures on the document were forged. Following up editorially on its own exclusive story, the *Star* today urged an examination of these claims, if necessary in Somalia.

These revelations will renew discussions among ourselves, unresolved since the early stages of the inquiry, about the necessity of taking testimony from Somalis.

At the outset, I assumed that we would have to do this. I remember saying that hearing about crimes in Somalia only from their perpetrators was legally and politically indefensible. I recall asking whether an inquiry into the police killing of native people in Canada, for instance, could possibly avoid hearing from native Canadian witnesses as well as from the civil authorities. Since then, however, my position has shifted. The logistics of moving the inquiry to Somalia are overwhelmingly complicated, apart from the chaotic political conditions that still prevail there. And extending the inquiry into Somalia would considerably increase its duration and cost.

My position at this stage is that we can't decide on the question of hearing testimony from Somalis until we have heard more from the Canadian soldiers.

Meanwhile, there was a foretaste of further stories of misconduct by Canadian soldiers. Several communications from Canadian headquarters in Somalia, filed today, referred to drunken behaviour by Canadian troops on leave in neighbouring Kenya and in transit from Somalia to Canada. Complaints had been received that Canadian soldiers flying from Nairobi to Canada on a commercial flight had drunk the bar of a jumbo jet dry, threatened airline staff, and passed out in the aisles. The communications from Canadian headquarters drew attention to these incidents and threatened disciplinary action, including cancellation of leave for entire units, but there was no indication that anyone had actually been punished.

When I called home about ten o'clock this evening, Hazel told me that the inquiry was on the supper-hour television news again – something about a general attacking General Boyle.

"That's not what was going on today," I said, stretching from the phone to turn on the TV set. Sure enough, at the top of the news, there was a shot of a military-looking man in civilian dress standing below the peacekeepers' monument near the National Gallery in Ottawa, surrounded by reporters and cameramen.

"You're right," I said to Hazel. "It's on the news now."

I turned up the sound. Maj.-Gen. Clive Addy, who had retired just the day before, had invited journalists to his outdoor press conference to take a shot at his former leader, General Boyle, for not exerting leadership.

Commenting on Boyle's appearance before our inquiry, Addy said, "I was troubled by some of his responses in respect to accountability. His interpretation of accountability is somewhat different from what he imposes on others."

Then he went on to say that "leadership is in need of an urgent overhaul at all levels."

"Abuses of power at higher levels, both civilian and military, at the expense of the soldier and his well-being also need fixing."

This is the first time that a senior colleague of Boyle's had deliberately broken ranks. It may encourage others to become more critical of senior officers during our hearings. It certainly confirms that there are serious leadership problems at the very highest levels.

Tuesday, September 10, 1996
Ottawa

We're now starting half an hour earlier, at 9:30 A.M., and finishing our hearings at 4:30 P.M., half an hour later. This might not seem like an unusual day to the average nine-to-fiver, but it's unrelenting. Coffee breaks are often the occasion, as they were today, for quick conferences with our lawyers. Lunch today was eaten during a discussion of yesterday's *Toronto Star* reports of forged Somali documents. We barely had time to go to the bathroom before we were back in the hearing room at 2 P.M. After 4:30 P.M., I worked in the office until 7 P.M., rereading transcripts of General Boyle's testimony to prepare a summary for the others, as the chair has requested.

But just when the treadmill seems endless, something usually happens to grab your attention. Today it was word at noon from one of our lawyers that Roberto Gonzalez has decided to talk.

Gonzalez is the former director general of public affairs at NDHQ, the link between Boyle and the officers and civilian workers in the Media Liaison Office who altered documents provided to Michael McAuliffe. Boyle has steadfastly denied knowing about this. Gonzalez, in his testimony, had said that he must have told Boyle, but he could not recollect when and where this occurred. Today we apparently have received word from Gonzalez's lawyer that he now remembers the details of this exchange of information, not only with Boyle but with his superior, Dr. Ken Calder, and Deputy Minister Robert Fowler. Our lawyers are arranging to interview him as soon as possible. Even without new documentary evidence, Gonzalez's testimony may be enough to push the general from his shaky perch and to seriously damage the credibility of the others. Of course

Gonzalez's own credibility will be an issue if he testifies again. Why didn't he recall these details when he was on the stand under oath? And why is he coming forward now?

The reason might have something to do with Boyle's blaming of subordinates for not informing him. Perhaps that was the last straw for Gonzalez. Perhaps his decision also means that Boyle has been so weakened by his testimony before us that he can now be attacked with impunity. Perhaps Gonzalez's decision will encourage more people to break ranks and come forward. In any event, the news increased the pulse rate of our inquiry this afternoon.

An article in the current *New Yorker* about the British Darwinist Richard Dawkin, author of *The Selfish Gene*, describes his view that evolution is "a process of gene survival taking place in bodies that the gene occupies and then discards." It reminded me of the inquiry. Are myself and the other commissioners simply instruments of some gene that ensures the survival of democratic societies by subjecting them to these purging ordeals from time to time?

Wednesday, September 11, 1996
Ottawa

Frequently I notice him sitting in the small public gallery at the back of our hearing room, a slender, sharp-featured man who looks as if he might be an accountant. His appearance always gives me a lift. Particularly in recent weeks when General Boyle has been on the stand, the sight of Michael McAuliffe has reminded me that a single stubborn journalist is responsible for starting the train of events that led us to this point.

It was McAuliffe who invaded the world of National Defence Headquarters with nothing more than a notebook, a telephone, and persistence and exposed a mentality and practices that have almost destroyed the credibility of Canada's military hierarchy.

There never have been many journalists such as McAuliffe, and there will probably be fewer in the future as our newspaper industry shrinks and public broadcasters such as the CBC fall victim to their own bureaucracies and budget cutbacks. But McAuliffe remains for me at this time a relic of journalism's great past and a hopeful omen for the future.

Friday, September 13, 1996
En route Ottawa–London

The *Ottawa Sun* ran a column yesterday flatly predicting that General Boyle would resign within the next few weeks. It was the kind of article that isn't written without some sort of indirect approval from an authoritative source.

Last night CTV News broadcast an even more revealing item claiming that Defence Minister David Collenette hadn't intended last week to support Boyle as strongly as the media then assumed. It gave the impression that Collenette is now distancing himself from Boyle so that the general can resign and sink from prominence without catching Collenette in the undertow.

This morning there was a rumour that Boyle had been booed when introduced at a military mess dinner in Winnipeg last week. There's no confirmation of this, but the news reached one of our investigators from an apparently reliable source.

Boyle had said at the end of his appearance before us that he intended to assess the reaction among the troops. If the story is authentic, it indicates an incredibly high degree of disapproval. Even if it isn't, the fact that it is circulating is meaningful.

With Parliament heading back into session within a week or so, the defence minister can expect to face a barrage of questions from Opposition members and the media as a result of our hearings and Gen. Clive Addy's recent criticism. The news stories this week indicate that he perhaps has already decided to sacrifice Boyle in order to protect himself.

One of the many problems facing Collenette is that there is no obvious successor to Boyle, or at least none that the media regard as likely. The Somalia affair and its aftermath have involved so many senior officers that they have virtually destroyed the normal line of succession.

Wednesday, September 18, 1996
Ottawa

We've been caught in the eye of a political storm this week.

As Parliament reconvened after its summer recess, Prime Minister Jean Chrétien and Defence Minister David Collenette have been trying to defend themselves from Opposition parties demanding both Collenette's and Boyle's resignations. In the process, the beleaguered prime minister has struck us a glancing blow.

On Monday, in an apparent effort to show the openness of his administration, Chrétien took credit for creating our inquiry and drew attention to our thoroughness. At least that's what I think he intended to do. But before he had finished, he had accused us of treating prominent public servants "almost as if they were criminals." He compared our schedule to that of the Watergate inquiry under the Nixon administration, saying erroneously that the American investigation lasted only a few months. The *Globe and Mail* gave the correct figure yesterday – twenty months.

The problem here is that we are the government's own inquiry, created by it and entitled to its support unless we are demonstrably failing to do our job. The other principle at stake is judicial independence. Although we're not a court, we are a semi-judicial body that must remain independent of political influence. Even a hint from the prime minister that we are not behaving properly can be seen as an attempt to influence us.

It's frustrating not being able to respond to Chrétien's remarks, particularly for me. As I dodge the television reporters on the way into our hearings, apt phrases keep coming to mind. But I can't afford to say even something as innocuous as, "I think the inquiry can speak for itself and it's doing so every day, loud and clear." Nothing wrong with that, but as soon as you break through the wall of silence that we have erected about ourselves, the media sense an opening and will try to exploit it for days. It's not worth the trouble.

We may try to make our irritation known quietly to the prime minister through people in his office. Another response that someone suggested jokingly was to offer to provide the government with an interim report on General Boyle. That's the last thing they would want. Despite the public posture, I imagine that the government is quite happy to have us soldiering on up to, through, and beyond the next federal election.

Monday, September 23, 1996
En route London–Ottawa

My usual flight to Ottawa is cancelled, so I'm routed through Toronto's Pearson airport, adding an hour to the trip. I suggest to the clerk at the ticket counter in London that she should upgrade me to business class "because of the inconvenience" and she does! I must remember to try this again.

When people stop me these days to talk about the inquiry, they say, "How much longer?" But in the next breath, they want to talk about something that they have read or heard about the inquiry in the past week. They seem torn between resentment at having to pay attention to us for so long, a kind of horrified fascination with the never-ending revelations, and an insatiable appetite for more. The whole Somalia affair has become an agonizing addiction for Canadians. It has altered our image of ourselves as a non-violent people admired internationally as the peacekeepers of the world. It's now become one of those national events that will be remembered as watersheds, particularly in the worlds of defence and diplomacy. People will talk about before and after Somalia, perhaps for decades to come.

By the end of last week, it had become clear to us that the former director general of public affairs, Roberto Gonzalez, is getting ready to release a bombshell. Gonzalez has been holidaying in Montana for the past week but is scheduled to be interviewed on the phone by our lawyers sometime today. There were reports last Friday that Gonzalez is furious with General Boyle for allowing him to take the rap for altered documents and, equally, with government lawyers for advising him against pointing the finger at Boyle. Gonzalez now has his own lawyer, as do more and more of the senior military and Defence Department people appearing before our inquiry.

Friday, October 4, 1996
Toronto

My two fellow commissioners and the inquiry's secretary, Stan Cohen, were in Toronto today to attend my university retirement dinner at the Albany Club. We had lunch and an afternoon meeting of the commission at the Royal Military Institute on University Avenue.

The institute is an antique warren of oak-panelled chambers and military memorabilia dating back to the last century. Winding stairways and eccentric hallways contribute to an internal geography whose confusion was explained to us by Judge Rutherford, a former president of the institute. It was created by merging two Victorian mansions into a single structure.

More effectively than the University Club a few doors south, the institute conveys the feeling of a British gentlemen's club. From the porter at the front door to the waiters in the sunny, cream-coloured dining room upstairs, its servants seem to carry that old-fashioned title with a dignity that is as pleasing as it is anachronistic. Equally rare these days is the fug of tobacco smoke in the bar. As we entered, Nick Stethem, an executive of the club and frequent television commentator on military affairs, put aside his cigar for a moment and welcomed us.

The first of the messages arrives during the soup course. Judge Rutherford is called to the phone. He returns to tell us

that rumours are sweeping Ottawa about an impending resignation by Defence Minister David Collenette. By the main
course, Nick Stethem has come upstairs from the bar to tell us
that CTV has asked him to stand by to comment on a cabinet
shuffle. We are just being served coffee when word arrives that
Newsworld is carrying Collenette's press conference live from
Ottawa. We pick up our cups and troop downstairs to the institute's television set in one of the main lounges.

Collenette is resigning, all right, but not because of anything
to do with Somalia. He tells the press conference that a member of his staff has discovered a letter written by himself to the
Immigration and Refugee Board on behalf of a constituent.
This is a violation of ethical guidelines established by the prime
minister, says Collenette to a strongly sceptical audience of
journalists . . . sceptical because the discovery of the letter allows
Collenette to resign over a relatively minor matter, leaving the
door open for an early return to the cabinet, perhaps even
before the election expected next spring. The prime minister
hints at as much later in the afternoon.

Members of the institute clustered about the television set
are as doubtful as the press. The resignation is too convenient,
too obvious a way for Collenette to sidestep the whole Somalia
issue.

It also leaves Gen. Jean Boyle exposed to enemy fire. As soon
as Collenette stops speaking, journalists at his press conference
start to ask questions about Boyle. Collenette has made a point
of stating that his staff had written the offending letter but that
he had signed it; therefore, he is responsible. A politician as
astute as Collenette knows perfectly well that this admission of
responsibility will be compared immediately with the chief of

the defence staff's earlier attempt, before our inquiry, to divert part of the blame for much more serious mistakes toward his subordinates, and to hold them responsible for not serving him more effectively. By couching his resignation in these terms, Collenette significantly and deliberately increases the pressure on Boyle.

We adjourn to a small conference room adjacent to the library of the institute to deliberate. On Monday, we will start to hear testimony on the first of the serious incidents in Somalia – the March 4, 1993, shooting of two Somalis who were apparently attempting to steal from the Canadian military compound in Belet Huen. One died and the other was wounded. We expect to hear allegations of set-up and cover-up – that the Somalis were lured into a trap, shot in contravention of the military's own rules of engagement, and that delays and mistakes in reporting this event through official channels were deliberate. If the testimony clearly indicates this, we hope that it will help to shorten our investigation of similar allegations arising from other incidents.

We're all conscious of the growing pressure; all of us are anxious to complete the inquiry as soon as possible and move on to other things. Within the next few weeks we will have to ask the government for another extension – this time the final one – to the end of next year. This would mean completing our public hearings by the end of June at the latest.

Our lawyers already have a list of more than ninety potential witnesses. They've been told to eliminate all but the most essential. They've also been told to stop posing a long list of routine questions on racism and the use of alcohol among the Canadian troops in Somalia to virtually every witness. The evidence on both these issues is already clear. Racist terms, from the relatively mild "Smufti" through "nig-nog" to "nigger," were commonly used by some soldiers and officers in Somalia. There was nothing done to discourage it, at least on an official level. The two-beers-per-man-per-day policy, it's already clear, was enforced so erratically as to be ineffective.

My academic early-retirement dinner tonight was attended by about 130 old friends, colleagues, former students, and media personalities. Lloyd Robertson took a night off from CTV News to narrate a biographical video. I wrote my first television script for Lloyd almost forty years ago when both of us were working in Winnipeg.

Sunday, October 6, 1996
Ottawa

Collenette's successor as defence minister is Doug Young, formerly minister of transport. The media today are quoting Collenette as saying that Young "comes from the stiletto school of politics."

"We both play hardball," Collenette told the media. "The difference is that I am a bit more clinical in the way I disembowel people."

This type of comment is fuelling speculation that General Boyle will have to step down soon after his first meeting with the new minister tomorrow. Nothing like this is said inadvertently in Ottawa. Collenette is consciously pushing Boyle closer to the edge of the precipice.

Tuesday, October 8, 1996
Ottawa

There was a conference over salad and fruit today, during our lunch-hour recess, with one of our military advisers. I asked him informally what he thought of Jean Boyle's future. The news media this morning had focused on the meeting yesterday between the new defence minister, Doug Young, and the chief of the defence staff. Some analysts were surprised that Boyle had made it through the day, and had started to wonder whether he might even last longer than expected. Others remarked on Young's minimal endorsement of Boyle. The new minister had said only that Boyle would remain CDS as long as he had the confidence of the government. Our consultant said that Boyle would try to stick it out – "He's stubborn and he's a fighter."

About thirty minutes later, just as we prepared to resume our hearings, word came through that Boyle had resigned.

In his letter to the minister, the general indicated that he felt blameless, but that events had conspired to make his continuing leadership impossible. He was sacrificing himself as the most effective contribution he could make, under the circumstances, to the members of the Armed Forces.

Already the published and broadcast judgements on Boyle are much harsher than this interpretation. He is being blamed not so much for his involvement in document tampering as for his performance before our inquiry. His tortuous explanations of accountability, and his attempts to deflect blame toward his subordinates, did far more damage to his credibility than any of his actions at NDHQ.

If Boyle had simply accepted responsibility for his subordinates' violation of Access to Information legislation, if he had coupled a frank admission of responsibility with an offer of resignation, public opinion might well have supported his continuation as the head of the Armed Forces. At worst, he would have resigned with honour, perhaps to await reappointment at some future date. Now it looks as if he is being forced out, after having almost torpedoed the career of the minister who appointed him.

David Collenette's resignation on another and minor matter, with the assistance of the prime minister, has allowed Collenette to escape relatively unscathed, but the government probably could not forgive Boyle for endangering the minister. In the end, he must have clearly understood, by the politicians' public pronouncements and their private advice, that he had no choice but to fall on his own sword.

Historians will remark in future on the almost ridiculously insignificant nature of the action that felled him. It was a too-clever attempt to evade a persistent journalist by providing him with altered documents. The documents themselves were relatively innocuous. As Boyle and the others constantly reminded us, these Responses to Queries were prepared as guides for officers answering questions from the media. What could be less secret than a document prepared for public consumption?

This was true for the main part of the RTQs; the problem lay in the "background" section sometimes tacked on to the end, where confidential information was often provided for the benefit of the officers briefing the media.

As long as Michael McAuliffe's request for RTQs was informal, tampering with the documents provided to him, by removing the "background" sections as well as the covering sheets showing which officers had approved the RTQ, was devious but hardly reprehensible. Even so, General Boyle's first inclination was not to do it, as he told us. He preferred the more straight-forward route of asking McAuliffe to go through the formal Access to Information procedure to acquire the RTQs. If Boyle had stuck to his guns, he would still be chief of the defence staff. Instead, he let himself be talked into the tricky response to McAuliffe's informal request, and to become personally involved by approving it.

When McAuliffe predictably asked for the same material under Access to Information – and if he hadn't, some other journalist would have eventually – Boyle's Directorate of Public Affairs could still have avoided trouble by providing the full RTQs as required by law and confessing to the relatively minor alterations made in responding to the earlier request. The embarrassment to the Defence Department and Boyle would have been minimal, almost not worth mentioning. Instead, the decision was made, at some level in Boyle's own Directorate of Public Affairs, to send the same altered versions in response to the Access to Information request. At this point, they crossed the line into illegality.

Boyle's knowledge of this remains unclear, but his detailed awareness of the first informal request created doubts about his professed ignorance of the second application under Access to Information.

Finally, his failure to convincingly accept responsibility for the illegal response to Access to Information cost him his job. In the annals of Canadian political history, it is hard to recall such an important appointment being lost over an incident that was, at least in origin, so inconsequential.

Boyle's resignation does help to clear the way for a renewal of the Armed Forces. Our inquiry has a role to play here over the long term, provided that we can harmonize our work schedule with that of the new minister.

Thursday, October 10, 1996
En route Ottawa–London

There has been speculation this week that we might do some sort of deal with Defence Minister Doug Young, who has been talking publicly about wanting to see a report from us by next spring. It is being suggested that we might undertake to write a brief report recommending the awarding of a Somalia campaign medal, a move that would give Young instant popularity in the Armed Forces.*

One of the arguments in favour of this is that such campaign medals are not really medals at all but merely ribbons and have nothing to do with the merit of individual soldiers. They simply indicate that the Armed Forces member has served in a particular theatre. By recommending that the campaign medal be awarded, we would be indicating that the Canadian Forces in Somalia had accomplished their mission, which is true. They were sent there to ensure more peaceful conditions for the distribution of humanitarian aid, thereby saving the lives of thousands of Somalis threatened by starvation. No one has pretended that the Canadians and other members of the coalition forces in Somalia failed to do this.

However, the medal has become a symbolic issue in Canada. No subject was mentioned more frequently or more emotionally during our visits to Canadian military bases in Quebec,

---

* He later did it anyway without consulting us.

Ontario, and Alberta last year. To award the medal at this point would be seen as a gesture toward exoneration for the many problems that occurred in Somalia and in relation to it. I'm certain that the medal will be approved some day, and may even be supported by us in the context of a final report that sorts out the achievements and the problems our soldiers encountered, fostered, and even created in Somalia. But this is not the time.

In any event, this speculation now seems to have vanished as quickly as it appeared, and we'll return to business as usual the week after next.

Monday, October 21, 1996
Ottawa

Sitting in the Barrymore Theatre in New York last week, watching a performance of Peter Hall's production of Oscar Wilde's *An Ideal Husband*, I couldn't escape from General Boyle. One of the play's principal characters is a British cabinet minister who, at the start of his career, sold secret government information to an Austrian investor. Years later, at the height of his success, the minister is confronted by the Austrian's rapacious widow, still in possession of a compromising secret letter.

In Wilde's play, the minister is saved by a friend who produces equally embarrassing information about the widow.

If only life were so tidy! In Boyle's case, the equivalent of the "letter" was his concurrence in a petty little scheme of bureaucratic skulduggery aimed at getting the better of a journalist. When the damning information threatened to become public, there was no friend to save him. Instead, he decided to tough it out, but only succeeded in digging himself in deeper.

It's amazing how quickly and completely he has disappeared. When Hazel and I returned on the weekend from our five-day holiday in New York, media attention in Canada, which had been obsessed with Boyle, had shifted elsewhere.

Wednesday, October 23, 1996
Ottawa

Momentum is slowly building up once more. Now we're moving into the interior of what is known as the "March 4 incident," dragging our lengthening train of lawyers behind us. Almost reluctantly, the media, despite its short attention span, is also being dragged into the story, unable to resist the horrors that are beginning to emerge.

In Kingston last week, Prime Minister Jean Chrétien went further than he should have done in criticizing our inquiry for taking so long. Liberals had hoped originally that we would be finished long before the 1997 general election. Despite the new minister's calls for an early end to the inquiry, everyone knows that it will continue through the election campaign expected next spring, with incalculable consequences for both Liberals and Conservatives. Politicians don't like unpredictability.

We can definitely sense the cold wind of disapproval wafting down on us from above. But all the government can do is make noises in public, try to embarrass us by claiming that we are dragging our heels, and increase its reluctance to provide us with additional time and money. In the end, the government has no real alternative but to let us proceed. In the complex network of loyalties, patronage, and influence that makes this city work, the independent public inquiry is truly an anomaly.

None of the three of us asked for this job, and none of us expected it to go on for up to three years. Both Judge Létourneau and Judge Rutherford would like nothing better than to return to the bench tomorrow. I'm the only one of us who benefits financially from the inquiry – at about 25 per cent of what the lawyers are paid – but I'd happily give it up tomorrow. We're as much prisoners of the process as the government itself.

Wednesday, October 30, 1996
Ottawa

The photographs that I looked at the other day were in an album, the same kind that usually contains pictures of birthday parties, children, special occasions. These photographs showed what a high-velocity bullet can do to a human body. They were copies of Polaroid photographs taken on the night of March 4, three years ago, by a medical technician inside a Bison personnel carrier less than an hour after Canadian soldiers had killed their first Somali intruder.

No one knows why the photos were taken. One of today's witnesses, a sergeant in the medical platoon that night, thought that they were another example of the "hero" or "trophy" photos that have landed Canadian soldiers in so much trouble in Somalia, Bosnia, and the Gulf when they appeared in the media. For whatever reason, a medical technician that night opened the body bag that enclosed the remains of a Somali named Ahmed Arush and took some snaps.

The picture shows an adult male, in his twenties, with gaping wounds in his neck and the side of his face, his head skewed out of normal shape by the force of the blast. His right eye is missing, knocked into or out of his head. His guts, like some sort of obscene sausage, protrude from a wound in his abdomen.

Although they were taken three years ago and thousands of miles away, the pictures still have the ability to sicken. It's no wonder that the memories of that night have continued to trouble individual soldiers, to threaten the careers of officers, and to disturb the national conscience.

In month after month of testimony, this was the first day when you could smell death in the hearing room. You could almost see the body bag being taken from the Bison into the medical station, being opened, and the body covered in blood emerging into the light.

The sergeant in charge that night – stocky, brusque, apparently proud of his professional sang-froid – drew a crude picture of the body for us on a flip chart, like a child's drawing except that it was scarred with dots and shaded areas marking the entry and exit points of the bullets. He drew two eyes to show which one was missing, then a nose and then – as we all wondered if this was what we really were about to see – a mouth with a slight smile. He stepped back, said something inaudible, then swiped the marker back and forth on the face to turn the smile into a grim slash.

Maj. Barry Armstrong, the doctor who would soon become a centre of controversy, examined the body and said immediately that the wounds looked suspicious. He told everyone in the room that it looked as if the Somali might have been killed while lying on the ground. Later that night, he was to use the term "dispatched" in his initial report.

The body was used almost immediately to demonstrate a tracheotomy for the younger medical corpsmen, to teach them how to punch a breathing hole into the neck of a gravely wounded soldier. Then it was used to teach them how to prepare a corpse for transportation – the anal opening plugged, the eyes closed, the skin washed with antiseptic, the hands crossed over the chest and bound with bandages. Only after that, having served his final purpose for the Canadian army, as an aid to medical instruction, was Arush put back into his body bag and sent into town.

Arush was caught apparently trying to break into the Canadian compound at night, according to testimony so far. But he knew that many others before him had been caught, arrested, turned over to local authorities, and soon released. He had no way of knowing that armed soldiers were waiting that night in ambush.

As soon as he was detected, he tried to run away. Given the previous Canadian response to dozens of similar situations, the first shots that hit him must have taken him completely by surprise. He was unarmed, he wasn't threatening anyone – and these were Canadian soldiers. They weren't like the French, who had drawn a line in the sand around their camp and announced that they would shoot anyone who crossed it.

We don't yet know where Arush fell after the first shot, and where he was when subsequent shots killed him. Still running, with a gaping wound in his stomach? Lying on the ground? Dispatched?

At the end of the afternoon, the childish portrait of Arush was still on the easel as we filed out of the room, the slash of the mouth grim in the one-eyed skull.

Sunday, November 11, 1996, Remembrance Day
En route London–Ottawa

Canadians seemed this year to pay more attention than usual to commemorating the dead of two world wars. News media reported larger than usual crowds at the customary cenotaph ceremonies. Schoolchildren were more in evidence. Newspapers published more than the perfunctory notices of recent years. Radio and television schedules were dominated by wartime histories and the recollections of those who survived, military and civilian.

I'm not sure why this is happening right now. The military has certainly been in the news since Somalia but often in a negative light. Is it nostalgia for an earlier time when military service was synonymous with patriotism and self-sacrifice?

Monday, November 12, 1996
Ottawa

The new minister of defence, Doug Young, said on the CBC this morning that he "certainly wouldn't want to be in an election campaign with the inquiry still going on, having people telling me that I'm trying to cover something up." When Michael McAuliffe asked him: "Is it more important for you to have a speedy inquiry or more important to have a full inquiry?" Young responded: "It's very important for me to end the inquiry."

This followed Young's comments last week that he is hoping "to get a signal" from us that "the hearings will end by March and work can begin on their report." And Young seems to be taking his cue from earlier comments by the prime minister.

These comments aren't accidental, and it isn't difficult to see the game that Young is now playing on behalf of the government. With an election expected in the spring, the Liberals are starting to repair fences with the military. Young's announcement of new spending on equipment last week was part of this strategy. His impatience with the inquiry is also calculated to win favour with some Canadian soldiers who now want to put Somalia behind them and forget about it. But it's a dangerous game treading a thin line between urging efficiency on us and appearing to want to close us down to prevent political embarrassment. Young's linking of the effects of our work on the coming election campaign brings political considerations across the barrier that separates and insulates us from government interference.

At the start of our hearings this morning, Raphael Schacter, counsel for Lt.-Col. Carol Mathieu, took Young to task for his comments to the media, reminding him that it was the government that had set our terms of reference and that officers such as Colonel Mathieu had a right to fully answer accusations brought before the inquiry. Judge Létourneau, in response, remarked on the long delays that we had encountered in getting documentation from the government and that newly discovered documents were continuing to reach us almost a year and a half after our original order for their production.

Wednesday, November 13, 1996
Ottawa

Months ago, our researchers began to suspect that communications between Somalia and NDHQ in 1993 were being logged and perhaps even recorded by the Communications Securities Establishment (CSE). CSE is the super-secret electronic "spy" agency that eavesdrops on many different types of international communications, seeking intelligence of use to Canada. For many years, its very existence was unknown to Canadians and, even today, its activities are mysterious, although occasionally mentioned in the media.

Our initial inquiries about CSE-monitored communications relating to Somalia were met by the bureaucratic equivalent of the blank stare. Finally, we asked the Defence Department, which manages CSE for the government, if it believed that CSE fell under our initial order last year for disclosure of documents. Last week, we learned that it does*.

This afternoon, as a result of this, the security official who gave me my initial top-secret clearance at the beginning of the inquiry reappeared to clear me up to another level. I had been under the impression that my previous top-secret clearance meant exactly that. I wasn't aware that there was another, invisible layer above, so secret that even "top-secrets" such as myself were unaware of it.

Among other things, I now have to notify the government whenever I travel outside of North America and, if I do, whether I encounter any strange characters who seem to be interested in my top-secret activities.

I was told that I would go through this process in reverse at the end of the inquiry and would be instructed at that point how to handle the mental cargo of top-secret information I would have absorbed by then. With my memory, I don't think anyone has to worry.

---

* Nothing of significance ever came from this source.

Thursday, November 14, 1996
En route Ottawa–London

We've spent three full days this week examining a young master corporal, Ben Klick, of the Princess Patricia's Canadian Light Infantry. He was seventeen when he enlisted in Vancouver, the son of parents who both served in the air force. Now in his twenties, he's a poster image of the ideal soldier with his straight posture, crew-cut blond hair, and clean features. On the sleeves of his military uniform, below the corporal's stripes, he wears the crossed rifles of the qualified marksman, his special military trade. He has ranked among the top-ten Ontario marksmen and has competed nationally.

It was because of this skill that Capt. Michel Rainville selected him for special duty on the night of March 4, 1993, at the Canadian camp at Belet Huen. Captain Rainville had been ordered to beef up security at the engineers' compound, which had been plagued by petty thievery as well as a more serious theft of a fuel pump used to service two U.S. helicopters standing by for medical evacuations.

Rainville decided, apparently on his own and with no reference to senior officers as far as we know, that the fuel pump had been stolen by saboteurs and that the mission of his reconnaissance platoon was to capture these saboteurs.

Up to that time, no one had mentioned sabotage in connection with the persistent thievery. The fuel pump, for example, had been left unguarded in an open field on the night it was stolen. If sabotage had been intended, it would have been a relatively simple matter to ignite the thousands of gallons of fuel stored nearby.

By deciding that his mission was to stop sabotage, Rainville set the stage for an escalation of violence. The Rules of Engagement didn't allow Canadians to employ deadly force against thieves. Sabotage, however, was classified as a hostile act that permitted a graduated response leading to shooting to kill. Corporal Klick's assignment that night, as he lay in ambush beside Captain Rainville in a truck in the engineers' compound, was to use his marksman's skill if necessary to protect his comrades who were lying in wait outside the compound for the "saboteurs."

The predictable result of this set-up, on March 4, was the wounding of one Somali and the death of another. Despite immediate allegations of murder by one of the Airborne's doctors, there was only a perfunctory inquiry and no autopsy. Only after the killing of sixteen-year-old Shidane Arone several weeks later did the military police start to investigate.

Corporal Klick produced a handwritten statement of what he had heard and seen that night. This was done two days after the event. It raised some troubling questions about the sequence of events. When the MPs finally started an inquiry, Klick was interviewed at length in Belet Huen, where he provided a version of events that was closer to Captain Rainville's description. At the end of that session, he warned the MPs that he and his comrades had decided that the police inquiry was politically motivated to accommodate then defence minister Kim Campbell. Shortly after, he and other members of the reconnaissance platoon were flown from Somalia to Nairobi, Kenya, for further questions by the MPs. They refused to co-operate.

Corporal Klick had no choice but to appear before us. If he had refused, we could have ordered him to attend. And now, he produces in response to our questions a third version of events, even more protective of Captain Rainville. He insists that there are no conflicts or contradictions in this. When pressed, he will concede that his first statement is probably the most accurate; but he also is happy to offer new details that are now clear to him and which, in many instances, materially alter his original narrative. And he does this skilfully. Corporal Klick is no dumb soldier. He's a match for commissioners and lawyers. He has an ability to talk himself out of tough spots by trying to lose the original question in a flood of irrelevant detail. When brought up short, he looks hurt that his attempt to be helpful has been misinterpreted.

He produces new information to bolster his theme. For instance, he claims that an American non-commissioned officer had questioned the wounded Somali and confirmed that he was a saboteur operating under the orders of one of the factions in Somalia. In the 170,000-plus documents that we have collected so far, including a written report by this American soldier on the March 4 incident, there is no mention of this interrogation leading to this confession.

Former captain Michel Rainville, acquitted of charges related to Somalia but released from the army, is in our hearing room every day at this stage, seated in the public benches directly across from the witness stand where his former soldiers are testifying. He's a thin, intense young man in his thirties, in a grey business suit, ash-blond hair now longer than it was when he was a soldier. Most of the time he just sits and stares at the witnesses.

Yesterday, over the objections of Rainville's lawyer, Judge Létourneau ordered the former captain to sit on the other side of the room, out of the witnesses' line of sight.

Re | Red Cross

P. 204

Reference to Krever inquiry. Gov't refuses to supply information to Krever — Gov't to Blame

17, 1996

Ottawa

At the e... vernment refused to hand over requested documents to the Krever inquiry into our national blood supply. Canadians are dying from AIDS-infected blood transfusions received many years ago. The inquiry was created by Ottawa to find out if safeguards were put into effect soon enough and, if not, who was to blame. But when it became evident that government itself might be to blame, Ottawa started to obstruct its own inquiry. Now it's refusing to give the Krever inquiry 1984 draft legislation on the blood supply that was never enacted, citing cabinet secrecy. So with one hand, the federal government creates an independent inquiry and, with the other, refuses to co-operate with it. At the same time, it takes steps purportedly to resolve the problem, making the inquiry seem redundant.

Along the same lines, Ottawa announced a few days ago that it will send 1,500 Canadian soldiers to Zaire to ensure the distribution of food to hundreds of thousands of starving refugees. In Zaire and neighbouring Rwanda, the delivery of aid is complicated by warring factions that use the refugees for their own political purposes. This is exactly the situation that developed in Somalia in 1992, with the same kind of feverish television coverage. Then, it was the Americans who took the lead. Prime Minister Brian Mulroney made a personal commitment to President George Bush, and subsequently the Canadian Airborne Regiment was dispatched to ignominy and eventual disbandment.

Now, as if we've learned nothing, it is Canada that has taken the lead and talked the Americans into following. Perhaps remembering Somalia, and the futility of its involvement there, Washington has been cautious. Why then is Canada leading the way? If any country has reason to draw lessons of caution from the Somalia experience three years ago, it is us.

Apparently we have drawn lessons, but not of caution. With an election expected next year, the government has been trying to shove Somalia into the background. Defence Minister Doug Young's decision to award the Somalia campaign medal was part of that effort, as was his insistence that we wind up our hearings before next spring's expected election. But what better way to make everyone forget Somalia than to achieve a successful intervention in Zaire? That would quickly make the inquiry look like yesterday's news. While the nation celebrates a rediscovery of the international role and national honour that we lost sight of in Somalia, we commissioners would be the spoilsports, poking around in the Somalia mess.

I'm not saying that these political considerations are the only motives behind the dispatching of Canadian troops to Africa this weekend. Things are never that simple. But I'm also not the only one to suspect that there are ulterior reasons. If the Zaire intervention goes well, "Canada and Jean Chrétien reap a cornucopia of benefits," wrote the *Globe and Mail*'s editor, William Thorsell, yesterday. "The Canadian military makes a lightning-strike public-relations comeback from its darkest days."

If this is the plan, it's already starting to unravel. Even as Canadians soldiers started to fly from Trenton, Ontario, yesterday in their ancient Hercules transports, the starving refugees in Zaire began to trek back into Rwanda by the hundreds of thousands. Today the government of Rwanda told the world that it didn't want foreign troops intervening. Food and money, yes, but no soldiers. Canada's response, so far,

has been to say that our soldiers land there anyway, whether
they are wanted or not. This is a far cry from Pearsonian
peacekeeping.

If there is one thing that Somalia should have taught us, it's
that we understand almost nothing about the political and
tribal complexities of African countries, that it's futile to try to
resolve them through short-term military intervention, and that
in doing so we run the risk of aggravating local situations. This
would be obvious to anyone who has paid any attention at all
to our hearings over the past year. Now the government seems
intent on making the same mistakes on an even larger, more
visible scale.

Tuesday, November 19, 1996
Ottawa

Prime Minister Jean Chrétien's attempt to put himself into the
running for a Nobel Peace Prize is beginning to look like the
miscalculation of the decade. Instead of being welcomed into
Africa as the saviours of starving thousands, Canadian soldiers
have been refused entry by the Rwandan government. Hundreds of our soldiers are now holed up in Uganda and Kenya
waiting for the word to go somewhere. It could well be straight
home, along the airlift route through Europe and Africa that
has already cost Canada hundreds of thousands of dollars to
organize.

Washington said yesterday that it is reconsidering its earlier
commitment, made in response to a personal appeal from Chrétien. It now looks unlikely that American soldiers will go to
Africa, although U.S. planes might still be used to transport

relief supplies. In Ottawa, Defence Minister Doug Young has been backpedalling as adroitly as possible, preparing the Canadian public for cancellation of the mission after a tremendous public relations campaign in favour of it.

Somehow Chrétien has managed to make Canada look politically naïve and politically devious at the same time – naïve to believe that we could walk into a complex political situation in Africa without political repercussions, and devious because our real agenda remains hidden, or at least unacknowledged by the government.

The official line in Ottawa has been that the prime minister was emotionally moved by television images of starving Africans in the refugee camps in Zaire. This has been a hard sell, considering Chrétien's previous lukewarm approach to humanitarian crises in developing countries. It's been difficult to suddenly portray this pragmatic, calculating politician as Saint Francis of Assisi. The second line of the official apologia has emphasized the influential role played by UN special envoy Raymond Chrétien, the prime minister's nephew and a former Canadian ambassador to Africa. But now, instead of looking like an experienced diplomat and problem-solver, Raymond Chrétien has been ignominiously told by the Rwandans to mind his own business. The great African rescue operation is now turning into a desperate effort to rescue ourselves from a public relations disaster that will simply confirm the damage to our reputation done in Somalia.

"The payoff could well be world recognition for a job well done," wrote David Pugliese in the *Ottawa Citizen* at the end of last week. "Or the mission could blow up in the face of Canada's beleaguered Armed Forces.... Some suggest the mission is a way to redeem the Forces and take the political heat, created by the Somalia Inquiry, off both the government and the military."

While I'm concerned about the refugees in Africa, and the tribal warfare that has created poverty in the midst of agricultural plenty in Rwanda, my feelings about the ill-fated Canadian intervention are certainly affected by our own experiences with the same government.

The pressure is on, no doubt about it. Yesterday, after our hearings, we had a private meeting with a representative from the Privy Council Office, the inquiry's paymaster. The whole exercise is conducted in veiled terms. References are made to work schedules, research budgets, the need for economy in government. Nothing is stated directly, but the message is clear: Get this over with.

We too want to finish as quickly as possible, but we have terms of reference to fulfil and a complex legal procedure to follow. The only way that we can accelerate is by restricting our investigation. We've now started to do precisely this. Done carefully, up to a point it probably results in more efficiency. After that, you're starting to consider skipping over areas of importance – areas, no doubt, that the government and military would love to see overlooked, or treated superficially.

Under this pressure, we're proposing a more condensed schedule of public hearings ending by next July. Even this concerns me. If we commit ourselves to a deadline such as this, I'm worried that we will become vulnerable to stalling tactics by the government or other parties who want to curtail our investigation. If this happens, we could find ourselves rushing toward a deadline hobbled by legalistic delays of one kind or another and distracted from our main purpose.

I hope, after all these years, that I'm not naïve about the way things operate in Ottawa. Political considerations are a part of everything that happens in this city. But subtly undermining the freedom and effectiveness of an independent public inquiry is something even President Richard Nixon wasn't able to do in the United States. That's what we're starting to see in outline in our own case.

Perhaps I'm jumping to conclusions too quickly, but the longer this exercise goes on, the more sceptical I'm becoming about the good faith of our political masters, our military officers, and the Defence Department bureaucrats who work with them.

CLOSURE

———•———

January to February 1997

Before we had a chance to resume our hearings in January after the Christmas break, Defence Minister Doug Young announced, on January 10, that we would have to complete our hearings by the end of March and hand in our report at the end of June. This was the first time that a Canadian government had terminated an independent public inquiry. We objected publicly to the decision; internally, we had to decide what we could do in the limited time available.

We could see that completing testimony on the March 4 incident would take us another two months. That would barely leave time for final statements by officers who had been notified that they might be censured by the inquiry. There would be no hearings into the March 16 murder of Shidane Arone or allegations of subsequent cover-up in Ottawa.

Why didn't we decide to go straight into March 16 and the cover-up question? It didn't take long to realize the impossibility of doing this. Rushing senior officers and officials to the stand in the dying weeks of our hearings, without time to prepare properly, would only have discredited the careful work that we had already done. We decided to continue with the March 4 incident so that we could at least report on that with some confidence.

We also had to accelerate the writing of the report. It would have to start immediately, with the early chapters of the report being drafted while we completed our hearings. Then we would have about a month to complete it in April, in order to leave time for translation and printing by the end of June. No inquiry had ever faced this kind of deadline.

Thursday, January 2, 1997
London

We haven't been sitting over the holidays, but the military has continued to make news, all of it bad. First there was the dismissal of Canada's third-highest officer, Lt.-Gen. Armand Roy, for claiming unauthorized expenses. Newspapers reported that the total amount was in the range of $70,000 to $80,000 and had to do with the general's posting to Land Force Command in the Montreal suburb of St. Hubert while his home was in the city proper. The general allegedly collected special allowances for a distant posting while commuting across the St. Lawrence River from Montreal. He was allowed to step down with pension, leaving the Canadian Forces with an acting chief of the defence staff and two of the next three top positions vacant.

Despite the leadership vacuum at the top, Defence Minister Doug Young announced earlier this week that he is freezing promotions of all officers for three months. The news media explained this unprecedented move by saying that Young felt uncomfortable with recent recommendations for promotion, a signal that the high command is still unable or unwilling to clean its own house. Young intends to submit his own recommendations for reform to the prime minister before the end of March.

Another media barrage started yesterday when Quebec newspapers reported that Canada's first female infantry officer, Sandra Perron, was tied to a tree, left barefoot in the snow for two hours, and punched in the stomach by a superior officer during a training exercise in 1992. She resigned from the Forces last January. Although Perron refused to criticize the training exercise, and insisted that she was proud of having survived it, the story and newspaper pictures of her tied to a tree in the snow, head bowed, caused another furore.

Today it turned out that the officer in charge of Perron's training exercise was former captain Michel Rainville, who is still waiting to appear before us as the instigator of the March 4 incident in Somalia. Rainville is quoted in the media admitting that he had hit the woman officer in the stomach but with the flat of his hand. If he had not, he said, "she would have lost credibility" with the other officer candidates.

Friday, January 10, 1997
London

The week concluded with Defence Minister Doug Young announcing that our inquiry would have until the end of March to complete its public hearings. His new deadline for our final report is June 30, six months earlier than our requested extension.

The announcement stunned all of us. I had expected that Young might clip a month or two from our request, but his decision to invoke closure is unprecedented. Even four decades of watching politicians at close range didn't prepare me for this.

We're asked to meet at 2 P.M. on Sunday in Ottawa to consider our response. I call my secretary, Kim, in Ottawa to re-book my flights. Then I start thinking about my own reaction to Young's outrageous decision. The answering machine at home starts to record calls from news media. I return all the calls, many from friends, old colleagues, and former students, explaining that I can't yet say anything. From the outset, I've been determined not to be regarded as the predictable source of leaks from the inquiry and, so far, I've succeeded.

Saturday, January 12, 1997
London

The news media have been slow to react to Young's announcement. The journalists don't seem to understand the unprecedented nature of what he has done or the effect that it will have on the scope of our investigation. So far they've taken at face value his assertion that we have been moving too slowly and that the military deserves to have quick answers.

Sunday, January 21, 1997
En route London–Toronto–Ottawa

On the first and second leg of my flight to Ottawa, I haul my antique laptop computer onto my knees and start to work on a

draft statement for tomorrow. The chair will provide most of
the facts on our side of the case. Judge Rutherford will address
his remarks to former and current members of the Armed
Forces. This leaves me free to speak in a more personal vein. I
start out by talking about the possibility of resigning from the
inquiry. By the time we touch down in Ottawa, with a stop at
Pearson airport in Toronto, I have completed a draft statement
that satisfies me. This is what I wrote:

> Frankly my first reaction was to resign.
>
> When I was asked to serve on this inquiry in the spring
> of 1995, I accepted the government's assurances that
> what was wanted was a full and fair investigation. I had
> no reason to doubt the public statements of a minister of
> the Crown. The scope of the inquiry was confirmed by
> our terms of reference, which ordered us to look beyond
> the events in Somalia to broader questions of leadership
> and accountability and to determine whether events in
> Somalia were the work of "a few rotten apples" or
> whether flaws in our system made something like Soma-
> lia inevitable.
>
> Now the government has unilaterally broken the con-
> tract that it had made with myself and my fellow com-
> missioners. It has curtailed our inquiry in a way that will
> prevent us from fulfilling our terms of reference and
> answering some of the most crucial questions that the
> government itself had presented to us. This is not just a
> matter of shaving a few months from our schedule, let's
> be clear about that. This is a drastic curtailment of our
> work. As far as I can determine, it is unprecedented in the
> history of national public inquiries in Canada.

The fact that this decision was linked publicly to political considerations made it even more outrageous.

So when the government broke the terms of its contract with me, I had every right to resign. Some might say it would have been the correct and honourable response.

By staying, I have agreed to participate under protest in an incomplete and flawed process. I've done this because of the support and encouragement that we have had all along from many sectors of our military and civilian population. Just because the government has broken faith with me doesn't mean that I can break faith with those who have supported and encouraged us, often at significant risk to their own careers and reputations in the case of some of our soldiers. I decided that the best way to keep faith with them would be to continue with our crippled inquiry to demonstrate, as we proceed, exactly how serious this order of closure is, exactly how much we will not be able to look at. This will be even more apparent in a few months than it is now.

I also appreciate the amount of good work that has already been done, in our hearings and in the research and staff work that will eventually be made public. It is vital to complete as much of this as possible, partly because it will be useful and partly to demonstrate how much we won't be able to finish.

I'd like to close these remarks by stating that I've been impressed since the beginning of this process by the fact that a public inquiry like ours really is a unique part of our system. I've been a close observer and student of Canadian politics for the past forty years, in Quebec and Manitoba before spending a decade in the Press Gallery here in Ottawa, and I know that genuine independence is a very rare commodity. In this town almost everything is connected to something else by invisible networks of power and indebtedness. But a public inquiry like ours really does stand outside the system. Watching my two fellow commissioners, I have come to appreciate that the phrase "independence of the judiciary" is a living reality. For a government to act in a way that infringes on the independence of a public inquiry is alien to our political tradition and endangers principles of accountability.

In future I'm sure there will be many people who will think twice about serving on public inquiries because of this example.

We met at 2 P.M. to discuss our response to the minister. It was obvious that the others were as upset as I was and that our press conference at 9:30 A.M. tomorrow will be a declaration of defiance. Yes, we will continue to serve on the inquiry under protest, but there will be no attempt to soft-pedal our sense of outrage or the crippling effect that Defence Minister Doug Young's decision will have on our work.

Although there is speculation that we're being curtailed because we're doing our job too well, and getting too close for comfort to the centres of power, another current explanation is that the government doesn't want us producing bad news that would disturb the coming election campaign. Young has made this connection himself in his comments to the media.

Tomorrow, our press conference will be an unprecedented response to Young's unprecedented order. This should trigger a chain reaction of comment in the media. Then, as we continue our hearings, the brutal curtailment of our inquiry will become clearer. Canadians have not yet understood that Young's order will prevent us from fulfilling our most important mandate – to investigate failures of leadership at the most senior levels. It will call into question the government's ability to effect the kind of sweeping reforms that are now required.

It's hard to forecast public reaction, but it's at least possible that the shutting down of the Somalia inquiry will eventually assume symbolic importance as a token of this government's arrogance. As someone said today during our discussions, the government wouldn't have dared to do this if there had been a strong opposition in Parliament, a credible alternative to the government in the coming election. Young's decision on the inquiry seems to be based on an assumption that the Liberals are invincible, that they can get away with almost anything.

Tonight the CBC broadcast the first of a two-part dramatic television treatment of the cancellation of the Avro Arrow following the defeat of the Liberals in 1958 by the Diefenbaker Conservatives. The issue in that election was arrogance. Ontario Liberals suffered a stunning defeat in the 1990 provincial election because they appeared to believe that they, too, were invulnerable. There is nothing that Canadian voters dislike more strongly than this kind of political hubris that takes electoral victory for granted.

Right now it's impossible to believe that the Tories, with only one MP in the House, could overthrow the Liberals in the coming election. So far, none of the polls forecast that even as a remote possibility, although the Tories have been gaining slowly. But many things can happen between now and an election in the spring or fall. If Prime Minister Chrétien's reputation for sincerity and decency starts to crumble, the process of disintegration could accelerate swiftly.

Monday, January 13, 1997
Ottawa

Today at 9:30 A.M., the three of us walked in front of a solid
wall of television cameras, photographers, and journalists as we
made our way to the table at the head of our hearing room on
the ninth floor of the Vanguard Building, in downtown Ottawa.
Then Judge Létourneau began the process of responding to the
government's order. Our statements, the press conference that
followed, statements by lawyers representing various parties
before the inquiry, and our own lawyers occupied the whole
morning and part of the afternoon. It was almost 3 P.M. before
we continued, in an atmosphere of anti-climax, the testimony
of Master Cpl. Brent Countway, a member of the reconnaissance platoon that had killed a Somali intruder on the night of
March 4, 1993. Tonight these events were the lead items on all
national television newscasts. The process of creating a national
consensus on the government's action has begun.

Before the news, I watched the second and final part of the
CBC's dramatized version of the Arrow story. Here was another
government portrayed as destroying an important Canadian
industry, a national institution, for partisan reasons that seem
irrational, almost unbelievable more than four decades later.
Ever since, the Arrow has symbolized both the potential for
excellence and the self-destructiveness of this country. In the
final scenes, the physical destruction of the Arrow ordered by
the Diefenbaker government was heart-wrenching.

Today a Liberal government attempted to dismantle something far more important than the Arrow – the institution of
the independent public inquiry. Lawyers for the various parties
before us, even those representing officers under suspicion by

our inquiry, castigated the government for terminating the process. The inquiry is a quasi-judicial institution, they said. The government's action is close to political interference with the courts and a serious threat to democracy.

During the press conference and on open-line radio shows later, I was asked repeatedly to provide a reason for the government's decision. This was for the government to answer, I responded. But I did say that the reason must have been a powerful one for the government to take such a step.

Until now, the inquiry's focus has been the Tory government in power during the Somalia expedition. Now the Liberals have left themselves open to charges of participating in the cover-up, of attempting to cover up the cover-up. Defence Minister Doug Young has said, in effect, that the government didn't want the inquiry to overlap with a federal election campaign. But there must be more to it than that. One explanation, and the one that seems most likely to me at this point, is that the government anticipated an even more negative public reaction if the inquiry continued, that it feared revelations about its own involvement in the cover-up that outweighed the risks of closing us down.

The media suspect that I and the others know what it is that the Liberals fear, but I haven't the foggiest idea. Our investigations into the final stages of the alleged Somalia cover-up, and subsequent developments in Ottawa when the Liberals were in power, haven't reached the stage where we have a clear picture of what was happening. "Perhaps we don't appreciate the importance of some of the things we've been looking at," I remarked to one of our lawyers this afternoon.

Whatever it is, it will now remain concealed throughout the campaign and perhaps for years. Hidden but not forgotten. The government has created a strong suspicion that it has something to hide. The questions will not just go away. Like the Arrow, the wreckage of our dismantled inquiry will exist for years as a symbol of political arrogance.

Many people are interpreting this as the ultimate victory of the civilian and military bureaucrats at the head of our defence establishment. They are saying that these generals and deputy ministers have shown themselves to be more powerful than our political institutions. If this is true, the end of our inquiry will also mark the end of an opportunity for Canada to introduce real changes in our top-heavy defence establishment. The senior brass and bureaucrats will have protected their own, with the exception of General Boyle. The lower ranks will have borne the brunt of punishment. Soldiers who believed in our ability to expose wrongdoing at the very highest levels and to clean house at National Defence Headquarters have been betrayed and, in the cases of some who have voluntarily testified before us, left vulnerable to retribution.

Tuesday, January 14, 1997
Ottawa

The phone in my room rang at 6:30 this morning – a local radio station wanting an interview about yesterday's events. I agreed sleepily, and was on the air about thirty minutes later.

I tried to talk about the central issue of government interference with a quasi-judicial inquiry, but the talk-show host wanted to be more specific. "Are you going to get to Kim Campbell?" he asked. When I assured him that we weren't likely to see Campbell, Robert Fowler, or former chief of the defence staff John de Chastelain on the stand, he seemed flabbergasted. "What about the murder of Shidane Arone?" Nor that, I said. "But that's outrageous!" he cried.

Slowly the enormity of the government's decision seems to be penetrating the public mind. Apart from the Liberal-oriented *Toronto Star*, most newspaper editorials today were critical of the government. On the CBC's "The National" tonight, the lead story was about the family of Master Cpl. Clayton Matchee. They complained about being deprived of their only hope of learning more about his attempted suicide following the death of Shidane Arone. Both Conservative and Bloc Québécois parties are urging the government to recall Parliament to debate the closing of the inquiry.

Meanwhile, Doug Young was up at 4 A.M. in Vancouver to appear on CTV's "Canada A.M." shortly after 7 A.M. in Ontario. He talked about not being able to wait for our report "for ten or fifteen years," a wild exaggeration that seemed to indicate a certain recklessness under pressure. *Le Devoir* published an interview with Young this morning in which he said that he already knew all the secrets at National Defence Headquarters, and therefore didn't need the inquiry to inform him.

Tonight I took my twenty-seven-year-old son, Nicholas, out for a birthday dinner at a restaurant near the Byward Market. Jeffrey Simpson, the *Globe* columnist, was at a nearby table. He predicted that Young will launch a whole series of reforms of the military within the next few months to show that he's now in charge and that the inquiry isn't necessary. This will eventually overshadow concern about our inquiry. Young presumably has assured the prime minister that the firestorm over the inquiry will die down within a few weeks. If an election is held in the spring, Young's reforms will push the fate of the inquiry into the background.

Jeffrey is probably right. And yet, this might be one of those times when there is synergy between the public mood and a specific situation, as there was in 1957 when the Pipeline Debate and the use of parliamentary closure came to represent the arrogance of a Liberal government apparently secure in office. In that case, the unravelling came quickly and unexpectedly. The termination of our inquiry might be the kind of issue that symbolizes the complacency of this government. If it is, the controversy could have a longer life than Doug Young imagines.

At the inquiry, former captain Michel Rainville, in charge of the reconnaissance platoon that killed a Somali intruder on March 4, is now on the stand. Behind the scenes, at lunch-hour meetings, and after the day's hearing had ended, we discussed our schedule for the next few months. Adapting our hearings in future to the new requirements is like trying to reverse the course of the *Queen Mary* in mid-ocean. Some of our lawyers are having difficulty aborting lines of investigation that have taken months to prepare in order to accelerate our hearings toward an examination of cover-up of events in Somalia. This isn't the way lawyers like to work; they don't like to take a step unless they know exactly where it will lead. The new schedule requires improvisation and a willingness to take a few risks, which make our careful lawyers nervous, and not without reason. There are dangers in moving ahead too quickly. If we bring senior officers to the stand to discuss cover-up and we can't prove anything, it will tend to confirm the government's wisdom in closing us. It's a difficult call, but by the end of the day, we had decided to leave routine matters behind us as quickly as possible and move at least part way into the final stage of the inquiry dealing with the alleged cover-up of events in Somalia.

Wednesday, January 15, 1997
Ottawa

Everyone is discouraged today. The excitement of responding
to the government's decision over the weekend, Monday's press
conference, and the flurry of sympathetic media attention since
then is wearing off. In its place is the growing realization that
we have been overpowered by the government and that the
weapons at our disposal are laughably inadequate.

The phone didn't ring this morning until 7:30 when an old
friend from London asked me to provide a few comments for
his morning radio show. I did it as a personal favour; we had
decided yesterday to disappear from the media again so that we
won't look as if we're waging a political campaign against the
government. The two judges are instinctively wary of this; I'm
much happier in an atmosphere of public controversy, but I
agree now that the media and others have to take up the fight.

My friend in London asks about a possible reference to the
Supreme Court. I explain once again that public inquiries are
protected from government interference only by tradition and
the force of public opinion. I surprise myself by using the word
"humiliated" for the first time. I say that I am frustrated and
humiliated. Later I wondered why I had said that, although I
realized that it was true. Even when right is on your side, being
beaten is always, inevitably disgraceful. It's like being fired from
a job without cause. You can tell yourself that it's not your fault,
but you still feel blameworthy, somehow tainted by failure.

Our psychological slump is aggravated by the increasing
workload as we continue our struggle to adjust to the new
deadline. Meetings fill every minute not occupied by our continuing public hearings. The schedule changes almost hourly.

Until this afternoon I was expecting to return home to London as usual on Thursday night, coming back here on Sunday. Now we've had to schedule another meeting on Friday, and I will have to phone Hazel later tonight to tell her that I won't make it on Thursday. Both of us are finding the long separations difficult.

Some of the work we have done is being rendered useless by the curtailment of the inquiry. After all our care to serve Section 13 notices on potential wrongdoers so that we can name them in the report, and so that they have plenty of time to defend themselves before our hearings end, most are now being withdrawn. The curtailed schedule of hearings will make it difficult to allow everyone to respond to the Section 13 notices. As a result, the notices might be challenged. But withdrawing the notices means that we can't blame some individual officers or civil servants for specific failures related to events in Somalia. We will be able to provide only narrative descriptions of situations of failure without laying blame specifically. People may draw their own conclusions, but the report will be much less pointed than we want it to be. Of course that will suit senior government officials and military officers.

This afternoon, for example, we had to withdraw the Section 13 notice that we had served months ago on a senior officer because he was threatening to refuse to testify unless we did so, and we no longer have the time to go to court to compel him to testify. The lawyers for some officers fully understand the constraints that the new schedule has placed on us.

The minister of defence is still saying publicly that we have plenty of time to call witnesses and deal with important questions. The fact is, his new deadline already has eroded much of our power. You can feel the inquiry's structure coming apart like the Avro Arrow in the CBC television drama; even if the government relented next week, and restored our end-of-the-year deadline, it would take several months just to make up for the disruption of the past week.

One of our younger lawyers notified us today that he had received a job offer from a large Ottawa legal firm and requested permission to leave the inquiry within a few months. Others have asked our senior lawyers if it is permissible to start sending out letters of application to law firms, including those representing clients before the inquiry. This isn't the way that we had envisaged the final stage at all.

The pressure on Gilles Létourneau, as chair, and Stan Cohen, as secretary, is unbelievable. They both look exhausted.

Stan today prepared a document to be tabled at our hearing tomorrow: a listing of our outside research papers with the commitment that these will be published along with our final report. We're doing this because we're actually afraid that the government might try to stop us from publishing these papers. Only a week ago, that attitude would have seemed paranoid; today it's regarded as taking reasonable precautions. There's also some discussion of publishing the report and other documentation in CD format so that as much material as possible is widely available.*

It's like being in a besieged city. We're frantically preserving the archives and preparing messages for posterity before the barbarians come over the walls to pillage and exterminate.

One of the lawyers used the term "banana republic" the other day, and, in fact, it doesn't feel much like Canada right now. The two judges seem to be stunned by this display of

---

* This was done.

naked, ruthless political power. These days, as a country, we do seem to be deliberately shedding many of the values and traditions that were among our proudest possessions. What is happening to the inquiry is only a small example.

I hope this is the lowest point, or close to it. Within a few more days, we should have a clearer idea of where we are heading in our final two months of hearings, and how much progress we can make. Morale in the organization will respond to the challenge of gaining momentum again, refocusing our hearings, bringing questions of cover-up to the fore as quickly as possible, and moving as far up the chain of command as we can before the minister's order brings us to a halt.

If we can go out under a full head of steam, shot down like the Arrow just as we are about to break the sound barrier at NDHQ, the effect should be electrifying. It would certainly make all of us feel better.

Friday, January 17, 1997
En route Ottawa–London

I'm glad to get away from Ottawa even for a few days. I was up at 5:30 A.M. and headed out to the airport in arctic darkness. The thermometer showed -32°C. When I lived here I felt that no other Canadian city could seem as cold and alien in the winter. The green belt surrounding the airport, a verdant gateway to the city in the summer, looks as desolate and hostile as the Canadian Shield in winter.

At the end of our first week under the government's order, one of our problems is a growing sense of paranoia. Because none of us could believe that the government would actually shut us down, now we're ready to believe almost anything. We're starting to anticipate all manner of devices that it could use to delay publication of even our abbreviated report. So suspicious have I become that I've started to wonder if we've been the target of a campaign of manipulation from the very beginning. A columnist this week was recalling the cancelled appointment of Anne-Marie Doyle as one of the three commissioners in the spring of 1995. At the time, as I wrote in this journal, I attributed this to the confusion and mismanagement that often hamper senior levels of government. Now my opinion seems naïve. Was the columnist right to suspect that this appointment was designed to sabotage the inquiry from the start, to place a government "mole" among us? A week ago, that interpretation would have seemed incredible. Now I'm appalled to discover that I'm ready to consider such ideas.

And what about the stonewalling involved in the slow response to our repeated requests for documents in 1995 and 1996, all the while professing a sincere desire to assist us? More than ever, the creation of the Somalia Inquiry Liaison Team (SILT) at National Defence Headquarters, which we originally accepted at face value as a necessary interface between the inquiry and the military, seems part of a deliberate campaign to make our progress as slow and as difficult as possible. The SILT group was always part of the national defence structure and it now seems naïve of us not to have fully appreciated this. But what else could we have done? Declare war against the department at the outset? I think we had to assume a certain amount of good faith on their part until we were forced to take a more realistic view. But, in the process, we lost many valuable months.

Maybe I am getting paranoid. It is certainly time to get away from Ottawa. I hope things will look a little better on Monday.

Sunday, January 19, 1997
En route London–Ottawa

"Cross-Country Check-Up" on CBC Radio this afternoon asks listeners to express opinions on the termination of our inquiry and proposals for reform of the military. Only one caller during the two-hour program supported Doug Young. Rarely has Ottawa made a decision that has encountered such universal condemnation. Most of the callers, apparently under the impression that the government can still be pressured to reverse its decision, said that the inquiry should be allowed to continue. I'm not at all sure that it can. None of the media commentators who have been critical of the government have speculated about such a reversal, and frankly I don't see it happening.

———

Saturday and Sunday afternoon were spent as usual at the nursing home in London where both of "The Mothers," as we now refer to them, are living.

Hazel's mother is becoming more and more confused. Although she still looks forward to playing cribbage with me, I now have to lead her through every step of the game. It's heart-rending to see this woman who was a keen bridge player only a few years ago losing count of the cards as she deals and paying almost no attention to the running score – although there is still a glimmer of triumph when she wins.

On my mother's bedside table there is an old black notebook – a journal kept by my father during a European tour in 1919. It is less a diary of events than a long love letter to my mother, whom he had met about a year before. The European trip was a project of his mother's, who was determined to stall and eventually destroy their courtship. My father was miserable most of the time, longed to see my future mother again and mortally afraid that she might change her mind during his absence. His mother was already planning to send him to stay with her family in Philadelphia when he returned from Europe. But by the end of the trip, his journal indicated that he had decided, for the first time in his life, to oppose his mother, stay in Montreal, and become engaged.

In 1981, about fifteen years after his death, my mother filled several pages at the end of my father's journal, still mourning his absence. She noted that this was volume two of the journal and that the first volume had been destroyed. "And that's another story," she wrote. I guessed that my father's mother had discovered and destroyed it.

In her wheelchair, with no short-term memory at all and even the distant years fading day by day from her recollection, my mother expresses her love for my father over and over. She says that he was a very good man, so patient, that she was so lucky to have been his wife. And she still grimaces at the memory of her mother-in-law.

I sit on the edge of her bed and read to her the words that my father wrote in a village in Normandy, for her eyes only, almost eighty years ago. She listens and sometimes calls me by my father's name, "Hullett."

Monday, January 20, 1997
Ottawa

"I don't know," said Capt. Paul Hope at the end of the afternoon. He had just been asked by one of our lawyers, John

McManus, whether he now felt that he had been part of a cover-up of the March 4 incident. Not at the time, he said, but now he's not certain.

Captain Hope, the Airborne's intelligence officer in Somalia, had just come to the end of a long day on the stand.

He began by explaining that he should never have been selected by his commanding officer, Lt.-Col. Carol Mathieu, to investigate the shooting. Mathieu gave him the assignment on his return from seventy-two hours of rest and relaxation in Nairobi in neighbouring Kenya. But Hope didn't have enough experience; he didn't have enough time; and he shouldn't have been asked to investigate his own unit, not to mention his own commanding officer. From the outset, these factors hampered his investigation. Were they meant to? Hope isn't sure now.

As a result, he didn't interview all the witnesses to the events on March 4. When there were conflicting versions, he gave the most weight to the account of Capt. Michel Rainville, whose leadership of the operation would eventually come into question.

The decisive moment of the investigation arrived when Hope received the report of Maj. Barry Armstrong, which suggested that the shooting of Arush might well be murder. This was far beyond anything that Hope had expected. He immediately handed the hot potato to Mathieu, in effect saying, "What am I supposed to do about this?" Mathieu never answered that question. Armstrong's statement was attached to the end of Hope's report as "a big unanswered question mark," to quote my own words at this afternoon's hearing.

This was the genesis of the eventual cover-up, right there in the first forty-eight hours after the killing of Ahmed Arush and the wounding of his companion.

It now looks as if we have a situation similar to the one that unseated Gen. Jean Boyle, where a low-level and apparently minor fabrication eventually led to larger and more complex efforts at concealment.

Captain Hope now wonders if he was set up to spin the first strands of an elaborate web. He, and we, may never know.

Wednesday, January 22, 1997
Ottawa

That's where it all began, retired colonel Allan Wells indicated today, echoing the words I wrote here yesterday. It all started with the report that Maj. Barry Armstrong addressed to Col. Carol Mathieu in Belet Huen within hours of the fatal shooting of Ahmed Arush on March 4. Instead of acting on it, Colonel Mathieu simply attached it without comment to the report of the initial investigation carried out by Captain Hope. From then on, a chain reaction of events led from Belet Huen to Canadian headquarters in the Somalia capital of Mogadishu to National Defence Headquarters in Ottawa, where Colonel Wells was director general of security.

Wells is retired now and living in the Ottawa suburb of Nepean, except during hunting season when he goes home to Newfoundland. One of our lawyers, trying to reach him during the fall, found herself talking to the owner of the general store and the only phone in town. She said she would pass on the message to the colonel when she next saw him walking past the store.

Even in civilian clothes, the burly Wells looks and sounds a bit like a sergeant-major. More than thirty years in the army, almost all of them in the military police, have left him with a gruff, deliberate manner. Nothing rattles him. He looks at everything slowly and deliberately.

On March 5, 1993, the day after the shooting, one of his officers came to him with information that there was some suspicion that the incident had involved the use of "excessive force." Three times over the next few weeks, Wells asked his immediate superior, Vice-Admiral Larry Murray, deputy chief of the defence staff, whether he could send miliary police to Somalia to investigate the shooting. According to Wells, all his queries were ignored.

At one point, Murray told him that the investigation would be done by American military police. When the dumbfounded Wells objected, nothing more was heard about this or any other investigation until the March 16 murder of Shidane Arone hit the media. In the wake of that horrifying event, serious investigations of the March 4 case began.

Later that year, Wells found himself ordering an investigation of allegations of cover-up by his own boss, Murray. Because of his dealings with Murray, this created a situation where he was investigating an event in which he had been a participant. The potential for conflict of interest was clear to him, as were other risks involved in the investigation. The way Wells put it, it wasn't exactly a "career-enhancing assignment."

Media interest is picking up again because Vice-Admiral Murray is now the acting chief of the defence staff, having succeeded General Boyle. Journalists have been speculating that he would already have been named chief of the defence staff were it not for the fact that he was questioned in 1993 about his possible involvement in the cover-up of the March 4 incident. Although this internal investigation cleared him, it consisted of nothing more than an interview. No one else was questioned.

Now, racing against the clock, we're interviewing other potential witnesses, doing the job that should have been done in 1993.

Next Monday, Murray himself will take the stand in a showdown that will be reminiscent of Boyle's testimony, except that the allegations are much more serious than tampering with a few documents. As in Boyle's case, how he defends himself on the stand and on camera will be as important as what he says.

———————

The quickened pace of our hearings is taking its toll on our lawyers. There have been some serious disagreements about the scheduling of witnesses. Some of our counsel have tried to maintain an orderly, logical sequence of witnesses in order to methodically build the strongest possible case. But there simply isn't always time for this, and compromises have to be made. Witnesses are being rushed into the hearing room in an effort to get as much testimony on the record as possible before the curtain falls. For some of our lawyers, this goes against all their training and instincts. Tempers have been frayed; the possibility of resignations has been mentioned.

Today we announced officially that we would be sitting five days a week until the end of February, five and a half hours a day. This barely leaves time for the organizational meetings that must be held to keep everything on track. It also takes little account of the strain on a witness who testifies from 9:30 A.M. to 4:30 P.M. Colonel Wells, for instance, was visibly tiring during the final hour this afternoon. His answers were becoming longer and less precise, so that the last half-hour was not as productive as it might have been.

And we now hear that at least one of Doug Young's experts, contracted to produce "quick and dirty" studies of the military to support his planned announcement of reforms at the end of March, has asked us to supply him with research studies that have taken us over a year to commission and assemble from outside consultants. Why should we supply material that Young will then use to justify his experts' work and to take another swipe at our own alleged slowness and lack of productivity?

We've responded by telling the expert to ask the government to allow us to release the study. We would then make it public in order to show everyone a little of what we have been doing.

A new Environics poll this morning showed that Prime Minister Chrétien is running behind his party for the first time since the last election. The Liberals have also slipped in the poll but not nearly enough to create any expectations about a close contest in the election expected this spring. A piece of good news for the Tories was the announcement that former major-general Lewis MacKenzie, the "hero of Sarajevo," will run for the Conservatives in Ontario.

What role the Somalia inquiry will play in the campaign is unclear, except that the issue so far has produced remarkably few letters to the editor. *Globe* columnist Jeffrey Simpson was right when he said the firestorm would last about two weeks. It's already dying down.

Friday, January 24, 1997
En route Ottawa–London

Last night I took a taxi across the Ottawa River to the Museum of Civilization for a book launch. One of my former television co-hosts in Montreal in the 1960s, Mairuth Sarsfield, née

Hodge, has written the novel that has been germinating within her for most of her life. It is a story about growing up in the black community in Montreal in the 1940s and 1950s. When I introduced her to the audience at the launch, before she read to us, I talked about the different and separate worlds of Montreal at that time – Mairuth in Little Burgundy, my own middle-class neighbourhood of Notre Dame de Grâce in the west end, Mordecai Richler's Jewish immigrant community on St. Urbain Street, and all the future writers and poets in the French-speaking east and north ends.

In the 1960s, when Mairuth and I worked together, there was a sense that the barriers were slowly disappearing between these different worlds. We all lived an adventure of discovery, and dreamed of a more unified city and country.

I said last night that this was typical of our generation at that time, in many places. In the 1970s, on assignment in Northern Ireland, I met Catholics and Protestants of my own age who also talked about the 1960s as a time of hope. They were already disillusioned, as we are now, particularly those of us who still inhabit Quebec physically or in spirit.

Sunday, January 26, 1997
En route London–Toronto–Ottawa

I find it more and more difficult to maintain my political equilibrium, not to get thrown off-balance by unfortunate developments, to remember that life is a complex mixture of good and evil. I've always had an optimistic temperament. I dislike people who see the negative side of things, who see Armageddon in every current event.

But it's never been so difficult to maintain a detached view. Last week, for instance, information commissioner John Grace released his report on the destruction of documents that were central to the tainted-blood inquiry. These minutes of meetings were destroyed with the approval of a committee of senior civil servants only a few weeks after they were requested by a *Globe and Mail* journalist under Access to Information. One of the civil servants worked for the federal Health Department; in fact, he was in charge of the department's compliance with Access to Information. And he's still there.

Grace, who is also a former journalist, noted in his report that thousands of Canadians were infected with AIDS or hepatitis C between 1982 and 1989, the period that the Canadian Blood Committee in Ottawa selected when it destroyed transcripts and tapes of its meetings.

How could a civil servant get away with blatantly flouting the law? Because, as Grace said, Access to Information legislation contains no penalties. When the law was passed, Grace and most Canadians believed that public exposure would be enough to ensure adherence. That is true no longer.

Is this another indication of moral corruption in the civil service? Is it the same phenomenon that our inquiry has exposed in senior ranks of the military? Does it show that the concept of service in the public service has been replaced by selfish careerism, and that personal benefit and the survival of the institution have replaced the ideal of service that once inspired and animated the best people in Ottawa?

At a Robert Burns dinner in London last night, an annual event at the home of our friends Helen and Brian Luckman, I found myself seated beside a law professor from Western who was making the same observations about universities. Once, they were guided by professors who saw the university as a temple of learning. Teaching was considered a vocation, a superior calling. Now administrators have taken over. Presidents of universities are rated by their success in reducing faculty, increasing class sizes and raising funds from wealthy individuals and businesses, regardless of the crippling effect this can have on academic independence. Recent experience had left this law professor demoralized and cynical.

On a recent visit to a London hospital, I had trouble distinguishing among nurses, secretaries, and maintenance staff, among doctors, male nurses, and technicians. Most of the nurses wore baggy sweatpants, sloppy cotton pullovers, and running shoes. There was an air of casual, even lackadaisical, informality in the medical quarters while the waiting room was filled with people who had been there, in some cases, for hours.

I can remember a time when nurses in their starched uniforms were almost like nuns. The uniforms spoke of dedication to professional ideals, cleanliness, a concept of service that made great demands on its practitioners. The uniform commanded respect.

These standards of dedication, sacrifice, and honour are the ones that have lost their hold on most professions in the brief space of my own lifetime. This is not to say that every teacher, nurse, doctor, or military officer used to be a paragon of virtue. Performance always falls short of professed ideals. But today the principles that used to inspire public service have faded into the background. Selfish interests have moved to the forefront, slowly but insidiously. Only after weeks like this do I understand how far we have travelled from the ideals of service that used to merit our respect.

In the civil service, this loss of idealism produces inefficiency, and an absence of accountability. In universities, it risks contaminating a new generation of students with the cynical bitterness of their teachers. Hospitals can't help people if their own personnel and systems are infected by cynicism. In the *Globe and Mail* last Saturday, a Canadian doctor was quoted urging Canadians to provide constant care of sick family members when they are in hospital because our hospitals can no longer ensure fully adequate nursing care. This doctor actually held up to Canadians the example of entire families camping in African hospital enclosures to assist in feeding, cleaning, and nursing their sick relatives.

The same doctors who complain about the deteriorating system, however, recently bludgeoned the Ontario government into giving them a pay raise while more nurses were cut from hospitals that are trying desperately to adjust to funding restrictions set by the provincial government.

But it is in the military, because of its training in the art of war, that this type of demoralization becomes dangerous. Soldiers without proper leadership can develop quickly into gangs of bullies and thugs. We've now seen this in Bosnia, Somalia, and perhaps in Haiti.

Our inquiry has revealed some of the frightening effects of this demoralization and corruption within the Canadian officer corps. I can't help thinking that Canadians will wake up some morning and realize with a shock how effectively they have destroyed the very institutions that helped to create the national characteristics we value most highly. If this process goes on long enough, it will seriously weaken a new generation's ability to continue our progress. This in itself is a form of "debt" that we are handing down to our children.

Monday, January 27, 1997
Ottawa

Vice-Admiral Larry Murray, acting chief of the defence staff and Jean Boyle's successor, stood on the same spot this morning that General Boyle had occupied last year at the start of his exit from the military's top job. Many concluded at the time that Boyle's style on the witness stand was more damning than what he actually said. He often appeared nervous and evasive. When he blamed subordinates for mistakes, he looked like a man trying to duck responsibility.

He also had an unfortunate knack of saying exactly the wrong thing at times, in a way that made headlines the next day. Hours of careful testimony would go out the window when he would produce one of these maladroit responses.

Murray seemed determined not to make the same mistake. If anything, he was overprepared. In the first few hours, he tried to cram vast amounts of detail into answers to relatively simple questions. Gradually it became evident that this was his usual style. Direct questions would produce a barrage of complex information that would eventually obscure the point of the original question.

This was so distracting that I began to deliberately ignore it. When I asked Murray a question, I could tell within a few seconds whether he was going to provide an answer. If he wasn't, I would try to ignore the verbiage, try to remember what I wanted to know, and frame the follow-up question that I would have to ask. Sometimes, pretending to take notes, I would write down the key words of my next question so that I wouldn't forget them. Otherwise the flow of Murray's words had an hypnotic effect.

This was accentuated by his appearance. Compared to the tall, strapping Boyle who still radiated some of the glamour of the fighter pilot that he had once been, Murray is ascetically thin, almost frail. There is little to remind you of the destroyer skipper that he once was. Everything about him is sparse and muted. His short greying hair is receding, like a skullcap slowly being pushed to the back of his head. His chin retreats slightly. His voice is low and unremarkable. Only after a period of time, as he talks, does the force of his intelligence start to impress. It's as if you begin to perceive him darting about behind the huge apparatus of words that he is producing, nimble and adroit, like a puppet master.

I noticed his eyes. The lids are heavy, hooding the pupils that stare out at you with a kind of bird-like intensity. When he finishes a response, the head swivels and the eyes turn away decisively, discouraging any further questions.

Murray's problem this week is, unlike his answers, quite simple. After the March 4 killing in Somalia, it took more than five weeks for him to authorize the sending of military police from Canada to investigate. By then, the trail was stone-cold. In the meantime, at least some Canadian soldiers presumably had understood the message that Ottawa appeared to be sending, that no one in authority was very worried about the killing and wounding of a few Somali thieves. This attitude contributed to the events of March 16 when Shidane Arone was captured and beaten to death.

Murray provides many explanations for the delay. He was not given vital information from Somalia right after the event. Reports were slow to arrive. Some subordinates urged caution. When we confronted him with damaging evidence, he either didn't remember crucial meetings or he denied the testimony of others. In particular today, he contradicted the testimony of retired colonel Allan Wells, who had said last week that he had urged Murray several times, soon after March 4, to send military investigators to Somalia. Murray insisted there was only a single discussion about this, and that its tenor and content were not exactly as Wells had remembered them.

At this stage I have no idea how Murray's performance is being assessed by the media and the public. If previous testimony by Boyle and others is any guide, I would guess that people are finding little comfort in the picture of a military leader trying to hide behind complex explanations of what appear to be simple sequences of events.

After all, I keep reminding myself, a man died on the night of March 4. He was shot in the back while running away. Surely it was imperative to find out quickly what had happened. The longer the delay, the greater the suspicion that individuals are trying to protect themselves by altering or hiding critical information. And, indeed, this seems to be the pattern. Protection of individual reputations and the "image" of the military become primary concerns. This is now a familiar sequence, and it seems to be reoccurring in relation to the March 4 incident.

Wednesday, January 29, 1997
Ottawa

Vice-Admiral Larry Murray took the stand this morning. The question again was: Why did it take more than five weeks to begin a thorough investigation of the March 4 incident? For every delay along the way, Murray had an explanation. Sometimes it was the necessity to trust his commanders in the field; sometimes it was the workload that almost overwhelmed him and his subordinates; once, it was an essential trip to Cambodia on official business.

For the final two weeks of delay, when all the information at last was in Ottawa in the hands of legal advisers at National Defence Headquarters, there was no clear explanation. Murray admitted to us that things had been "creeping along" at this point.

At the end of the day, there remained the strong suspicion that the delay in investigating March 4 contributed directly to the March 16 incident when Shidane Arone was killed. A quick response after March 4 by commanders in the field and Ottawa might have tightened discipline at a critical moment. The soldiers would have sensed that their actions were being closely monitored and that deviation from the rules would be dealt with decisively.

It's ironic that Gen. Jean Boyle's worst offence was in relation to Access to Information legislation, a "paper" crime, while the March 4 incident cost one Somali his life and probably contributed to the death of a second. Boyle resigned, but Murray appears to be on his way to gaining the military's top job permanently.

We still have to hear from the two commanders in the field, Col. Serge Labbé and Lt.-Col. Carol Mathieu. In their cases, there are documents that are hard to explain. But it looks as if Ottawa will be effectively insulated.

It's a story that now is all too familiar: cautious leaders at National Defence Headquarters were intent on not doing anything wrong at the cost of failing to do something correctly. It's often difficult to point to one place in this flawed process and say, "This is where it went wrong, and this is the person responsible." It's usually a case of people failing to act quickly and decisively when a problem arises. The whole process is one of evading responsibility, keeping things quiet, and acting only at the last minute when further delay becomes impossible.

This process shields individuals at the most senior levels, but it has corrupted the entire military from the top down.

Thursday, January 30, 1997
Ottawa

Kim Campbell was prime minister for only a few months in 1993, but her political impact is still being felt.

Last year I was puzzled when the Chrétien government appointed her consul general in Los Angeles, and even more intrigued by earlier rumours that she would go to Moscow as Canada's ambassador provided that she could get a clean report from our inquiry. This was never requested formally, but there were a few discreet inquiries.

I couldn't quite understand why the Liberals were willing, even anxious, to find a comfortable niche for her. Now she seems to be providing an answer but raising more questions in the process.

On television tonight, Campbell is repeating more strongly her claims that her own department kept vital information from her during the Somalia crisis. Her former aides are also all over the media today with allegations that lawyers for the Defence

Department in 1993 first tried to frighten off Campbell from taking an interest in Somalia by warning her against interfering politically in the department and then, when that didn't work, tried to destroy the document containing this advice. An affidavit released yesterday by one of the aides referred to this as an attempt at "intimidation and blackmail."

The current furore provides a retrospective rationale for Campbell's diplomatic appointment. Perhaps the Liberals hoped to earn her gratitude and reticence. If so, they badly miscalculated. Her insistent demands for a public airing of her complaints, and a chance to clear her name, are keeping the controversy over the closing of the inquiry on the front pages. Her former aides are also clamouring for a chance to get at the Defence Department in front of our inquiry.

We've already said that our curtailed schedule won't give us time to deal with the Campbell controversy, which centres on the March 16 death of Shidane Arone. It now looks as if we won't be able to hear more than half a dozen witnesses by the end of February when the axe falls on our hearings, at least as far as new testimony is concerned. It will take all of March to provide those already criticized at previous hearings with an opportunity to make statements and call witnesses in their defence. This final phase of the hearings is required in the interests of fairness. So Campbell must realize that her demands to appear before us are both futile and highly embarrassing for the government.

Personally I'm delighted by what she is doing, in view of the government's unprecedented and indefensible decision to terminate the inquiry. When we come to the end of our hearings, Campbell's questions and accusations of cover-up and document destruction will be left hanging in the air to echo throughout the next election campaign.

Sunday, February 2, 1997
En route London–Ottawa

The plane was an hour late leaving Toronto. And right now I'm sitting in the back row, in the middle seat, the noisiest and most uncomfortable. It will be after 10 P.M. before I leave the airport in Ottawa, almost 11 P.M. by the time I'm in my hotel room.

Living like this seems more and more insane. Despite a fear of flying so severe that in the early years I could never manage to eat on a plane, I spent half my life in the stratosphere as a young journalist. I loved to travel, and eventually the fear became a kind of terrified numbness. During election campaigns in the 1960s, I learned to write on a portable typewriter balanced on my knees and discovered that it distracted me. This laptop serves the same purpose.

Arriving home late on Fridays, leaving at the end of the afternoon on Sundays, the weekends seem little more than a quick catch in the breath, a hiccup, before work starts again. Both Hazel and I are growing more and more impatient with this routine.

Boarding the crowded shuttle, struggling down the narrow central aisle, I catch sight of a Liberal member of Parliament heading back to Ottawa.

"I watched the whole press conference that Monday," she says, referring to our reaction to the inquiry's closure. "I've been asking my constituents about it. You know, there's hardly any reaction at all."

Monday, February 3, 1997
Ottawa

That it has made so little impression on Canadians is the hardest thing to accept.

I try to recognize the realities of politics and to understand other points of view. I can't expect others to feel as strongly as I do about the fate of "our" inquiry. But it's ours only in a very limited sense. It really belongs to the people of Canada, whose government brought it into being and who support it with their tax dollars. Instead of giving Canadians a sense of ownership in government, what has happened has created alienation and resentment.

People have been prepared to believe the government's deliberately exaggerated statements about our budget and the length of time we are taking because they have come to expect profligacy from the government itself. So the government that has created this cynicism among Canadians now uses it to undermine an inquiry that it created to restore its own credibility.

Canadians are also tired of bad news. In this respect, Defence Minister Doug Young has read the public mood correctly. His criticism of our slow progress and his promise of quick action have gained the support of a majority of Canadians. Since he announced the termination of our inquiry, the Liberals' popularity has dropped by only 1 per cent. This hardly represents massive public disapproval.

Today the special inquiry into military justice created by Young opened a cross-country series of hearings in Halifax. It has eight weeks to do its job. No wonder it has been trying desperately to acquire our research. Young hasn't given any indication of the amount of money that this unnecessary duplication of inquiries is costing.

Also today, Parliament reconvened after a seven-week break. The "gagging" of the inquiry was among the first subjects raised during Question Period, but the government also chose today to announce that its budget will be brought down on February 18. Predictably, that bumped the Opposition's performance in Question Period to second place in the newscasts, a further demonstration of the government's ability to control the media's agenda as well as its own.

Canadians' apathy in the face of abuses of authority is another factor in our smoothly engineered demise. I shouldn't be surprised. It was during the October Crisis of 1970 that I began to appreciate the depth of toleration that Canadians have for the untrammelled exercise of power. The Trudeau government then used a never-defined and never-substantiated threat of civil disorder to suspend civil liberties, arrest hundreds of people in Montreal, and hold them without charge or without access to lawyers for weeks. There was little political reaction against this, even when it became evident that no threat existed. On the contrary, Canadians applauded the government action and ridiculed its critics.

There is some alarm in Canada today because "60 Minutes" on the ABC network in the United States last night broadcast a report critical of this country's toleration of suspected Nazi war criminals. This is an old story for Canadian news media; it is embarrassing now only because Americans are hearing about it. Otherwise, Canadians would continue to defer to authority in this case as they did when Jewish refugees from Europe were refused entry into Canada during the Second World War.

Despite all this, I'm still shocked by the generally passive reaction to the shutdown of the inquiry, the acceptance of a blatant government manoeuvre to protect itself from criticism, a flagrant disregard of a long and unbroken tradition of respect for the independence of public inquiries. Nothing seems to be stirring in the conscience of the body politic. There is no alarm. There is every sign that Canadians are not just apathetic in the face of this abuse; most of them support it.

Sometimes it seems that democracy isn't even skin-deep in this country. It vanishes at the first challenge. By sheer good luck, the challenges have never been severe enough to create major changes in our democratic institutions or damage our smugness about our political institutions. That sense of political confidence is poorly deserved and, like all illusions, more dangerous to our survival as a free country than any of the external challenges that we might face.

Wednesday, February 5, 1997
Ottawa

We've resolved a nasty little tussle behind the scenes.

When the government last month set our new deadline, Defence Minister Doug Young also appointed several blue-ribbon panels to provide him with quick input for the military reforms that he has promised to announce by the end of next month. One of these was composed of historians, including Jack Granatstein, who continued to take pot shots at us even as he pocketed his contract from the minister. He referred to Judge Létourneau as the "Grand Inquisitor." Earlier he had defended General Boyle when he appeared before our "kangaroo court," as Granatstein called it.

Young appointed a second panel to review the military justice system. It is headed by former chief justice Brian Dickson and includes retired lieutenant-general Charles Belzile and former Tory MP J. W. "Bud" Bird. On Monday, this panel held the first of a series of public hearings in Halifax, but its real focus so far has been a concerted attempt to gain access to our research on military justice. It's widely known among the legal and academic community that Prof. Martin Friedland of the University of Toronto had completed a wide-ranging study for us by the end of last year.

Access to this study would provide the panel with an up-to-date theoretical base for its findings, but why should we assist the "competition" in this way? Wouldn't that just confirm Young's implied assertion that his experts could do, in a few months, what it had taken us more than two years to achieve? This was the unfortunate rivalry that the minister had created.

Our response was to offer to provide the study only if we were given control over the publication of all our studies. Some of us have become so suspicious of the government that we believe the Liberals might not only delay publication of our report after the end of June, on some pretext or other, but prevent us from publishing our research.

Today we received a government order giving us control over our own publishing schedule, and the Friedland study is on its way to the advisory group. We intend to publish it about two weeks before the minister announces his reforms.

———

On Monday, we worked until 9 P.M., with a short break for supper, to complete the plan of our final report. Two writer/editors who specialize in this type of work have been contracted to compile and arrange our massive store of research material, expert studies, testimony from hearings, more than 150,000 archived documents, and eventually our own recommendations into a well-organized report that will be as readable as possible.

Royal commission reports aren't expected to be works of literature, but they have enduring value as sources of information and assessment about a particular field, and they should be as accessible as possible. Writing and editing this mass of material is an awesome task.

The challenge here is to marry the chronological narrative, starting with the selection and preparation of the Airborne for Somalia and concluding with its disembarkation from that chaotic land, to a structure that will also highlight such basic themes of our inquiry as leadership, accountability, military discipline, and so forth. After several days of wrestling with this, a format emerged that seemed not only workable but also exciting. Like marathon runners approaching the finish line, we began to see the end, and to feel a sense of achievement through the exhaustion and depression that has afflicted everyone since Young took the axe to us last month.

––––––––––

On Monday, Vice-Admiral Larry Murray ended more than a week of testimony. Unlike his predecessor, Jean Boyle, Murray not only survived the ordeal but also enhanced his reputation. Against his soft-spoken determination, our struggle to extract information from him seemed to some to come close to badgering. Today I received an anonymous letter from "Canadians against rudeness regardless of sick sources," addressed to "Monsieur Desbarats – Kangaroo #3, Somalia Trial." It accused us of bringing about the "downfall of the inquiry method" through our "inane discussions" and "tortuous proceedings."

For anyone who listened closely, there was much material to arouse concern in Murray's testimony. But when he was backed into a corner, he threw up a mind-numbing, eye-glazing barrier of complex military vocabulary that was almost impossible to follow, like some sort of monotone Gilbert and Sullivan recitation at warp speed. It was useless for television purposes; not a single damaging clip could be extracted from this flood. Viewers who didn't switch channels to escape must have been confused and bored by his performance. That was fine with the vice-admiral, I imagine. Like a flotilla escaping its enemies by disappearing into a fog bank, he sailed away from us after sustaining only minor damage.

When we were discussing the outline of our report last Monday, someone wondered how we were going to handle the subject of "unanswered questions." These are already starting to surface at our hearings, and in the news media.

Vice-Admiral Murray was followed on the stand today by Maj. Marc Philippe, a French-speaking military lawyer who was attached to Canadian headquarters in Mogadishu as Colonel Labbé's legal adviser. Although Murray had been successful in claiming ignorance of certain key events in Somalia, there was an avenue of communication between Somalia and NDHQ that we hadn't yet explored. While most information was passed through the chain of command, from senior officers in Somalia to their superiors in Ottawa, Major Philippe communicated directly with his colleagues and bosses in the Judge Advocat General's office.

What Major Philippe knew, how much he communicated to Ottawa and when, have become vital questions. Even if commanding officers were delaying or blocking information, Philippe had access to much of it. If it can be shown that he forwarded it to Ottawa, the lack of vital information at Murray's level becomes harder to explain. If there was a barrier, it might be in the JAG office, which has direct and constant access to the chief of the defence staff.

The most meaningful part of Philippe's testimony centred on Major Armstrong's statement about the "dispatch" of one of the Somalis on the night of March 4. We know that this statement didn't reach Ottawa until weeks after the event. Philippe saw it in Somalia. Did he tell his superiors in the JAG about it? Without being as specific as we would have liked, Philippe did say that he must have. He couldn't remember exactly when he informed someone, but he was almost certain that he had.

Placing this information in Ottawa at this point brings suspicion closer to the inner circle at NDHQ. But we're not going to have enough time in the coming weeks to close the loop decisively.

All these unanswered questions are starting to accumulate underfoot like dirty snow on the streets of Ottawa.

What the legal advisers at NDHQ knew is closely linked to complaints by former prime minister Kim Campbell that she was deliberately kept in ignorance. Her former aides were on television again this morning, accusing officers at NDHQ of keeping information from them and the minister. Among their chief targets are military lawyers working for the Judge Advocate General. Campbell's former aides are furious that the interruption of the inquiry will prevent them from responding to the JAG's version of events, which has already appeared in the news media. Because of the enforced cut-off by Young, this part of the cover-up picture will remain hidden, a source of speculation for years to come.

Thursday, February 6, 1997
Ottawa

Doug Young was at it again in the House of Commons yesterday, repeating his claim that we still have plenty of time to call whatever witnesses we choose – Kim Campbell, Robert Fowler, John Anderson, anyone. As a lawyer, Young must realize how ridiculous this is; as a politician, I'm sure he's aware of the damage that he's causing to the inquiry.

No one I've met in recent days understands why we can't do what the minister says. We've tried several times to explain that we are required by law to devote almost the entire month of March to listening to submissions from those who are defending themselves in front of the inquiry, and hearing their witnesses. We don't have any choice. If we evade this obligation, lawyers will claim that the whole process is unfair and take us to court immediately, delaying our work and the report for months.

This leaves us three more weeks to hear two central players: Col. Serge Labbé, the commander of Canadian Forces in Somalia, and Lt.-Col. Carol Mathieu, the officer commanding the Canadian Airborne Regiment at that time. Each one is expected to take at least a week. Whatever days remain in February might be used to complete the interrupted testimony of Col. Michael O'Brien, one of the key figures at National Defence Headquarters in Ottawa when the soldiers were in Africa.

As a journalist, I think that I can understand why the media have been unable to explain all this properly. To begin with, journalists in Ottawa tend not to believe anyone. When two versions of events conflict, both are presumed to be self-serving. It also takes time to explain why the minister, in this case, is technically wrong, and journalists don't have time for technical explanations, particularly on television. The Big Lie is even more effective these days than it was in the era of print.

This cynicism leads journalists to give equal weight to the government's reasons for terminating us, and to our protests. This supposedly is objective reporting. But is it realistic to place both parties, in this case, on the same footing? The government has an obvious self-interest in ending the inquiry before an election. We have no such partisan interest in completing the job that we were given by the same government.

My sharpest disappointment has been the inability or unwillingness of journalists to perceive the real issue at stake here – the independence of public inquiries. Even editorial writers have paid insufficient attention to this principle. If the government attempted to close down a court in the middle of a trial, there would be an uproar – or, at least, I hope there would. Dictating an end to our hearings is very close to tampering with the courts, but on this issue, very little has been said.

I have to be careful here that I'm not exaggerating the importance of all this simply because I'm involved. The inquiry is our creation, even if the government gave birth to it. We've transformed its printed terms of reference into a living organism. Now its natural development has been halted, its power stunted. We all feel a kind of parental dismay.

But no, it's not just that. The freedom of an independent inquiry is not something that the government should be able to curtail without penalty. Up to now, custom had protected inquiries from political interference. Now that a government has defied tradition, and apparently with impunity, the example is there. It won't be long before it's tried again.

For a government with a strong majority to carelessly ignore the independence of a public inquiry, and for blatantly political purposes, is almost inconceivable. The media's slow and muted response is even more surprising. Have decades of growing corporate dominance of the media, an increasing focus on the bottom line, and years of traumatic downsizing of editorial staffs reduced the moral sensitivity of journalists and their capacity for indignation? Are they afraid to give offence even when confronted with an obvious challenge to freedom? Do they no longer understand that the erosion of freedom in one part of the system is a threat to the free expression that is the lifeblood of journalism?

A sense of morality, a passion for freedom, and a large and fearless capacity for righteous anger are at the heart of journalism. Otherwise, it's nothing but selling ads.

Sunday, February 9, 1997
Toronto's Pearson Airport

The Toronto–Ottawa flight is thirty minutes late for the second week in a row. I sit in the waiting room, unzip the laptop, and turn it on. The blue screen smiles up at me, an old friend, my confidant.

I'm thinking about Col. Serge Labbé, who began his testimony last Friday and will continue tomorrow. Until Somalia, he was said to be regarded as a likely candidate for chief of the defence staff. Subsequently his promotion from colonel was delayed, and he was sent into the limbo of NATO headquarters in Belgium to work on long-range planning. When Labbé is on the witness stand, he's at the crossroads of his career. . . .

(At this point, my four-year-old 286 laptop emitted a pro-longed beep and went into total paralysis. Nothing I did could budge it or stop the noise. I imagined everyone in the airport was looking at this man who couldn't control his own computer. Finally, I shut it off. When I rebooted it, the computer allowed me to store the two paragraphs that I had written but to do nothing else. When I boarded the plane a short time later, I took out my fountain pen and continued the old-fashioned way. . . .)

I feel bereft, writing with a fountain pen on the flight to Ottawa. Scrunched into the middle seat in the noisy second row from the back doesn't make me feel any better.

I had been about to say that Col. Serge Labbé, at his first appearance before us last Friday, was impressive, at least at the start. He must be in his forties but looks younger. Apart from his boyish, almost-too-handsome features, everything about him is straight from the military catalogue: dark hair cut medium-short, erect posture, and immaculate uniform. His deep voice is authoritative but pleasantly modulated. He is flawlessly bilingual, speaking English without a trace of accent, if anything a little too precisely. He is almost too articulate.

For the first few hours, his performance was impressive. It was easy to understand his dominance over subordinates, the legendary ability to command that sets one leader apart from others. Facts flowed from him smoothly. He showed himself to be a master of our massive and often confusing documentation. And he argued his interpretation of events passionately, refus-ing to give an inch when challenged. Eventually it was this uncompromising posture that began to reveal another side of Labbé, an overweening self-confidence.

When pressed by Judge Létourneau, Labbé insisted that the death of sixteen-year-old Shidane Arone had been the only serious flaw in the entire mission. In every other respect, it had been an outstanding success. Testimony that we've heard and the military's own after-action analyses have demonstrated that this position is so indefensible as to be almost ridiculous.

I wondered why he hadn't decided to adopt a more moderate position. Why wasn't he content to admit a few faults, and to say that he had done the best possible job under difficult circumstances?

Tuesday, February 11, 1997
Ottawa

At 9:30 A.M. tomorrow, instead of continuing with Colonel Labbé's testimony, we will hold a thirty-minute press conference to combat what I've found myself referring to, in my private mutterings, as the Big Lie. Judge Létourneau has prepared a statement to correct "the apparent confusion that exists in Parliament and elsewhere concerning how much time remains for Commissioners to hear new evidence."

This has been bothering me since last Friday, when Defence Minister Doug Young repeated his assertion, during a debate in the House, that our inquiry had plenty of time before his end-of-March deadline to hear testimony from whomever we wished. He has said this repeatedly in response to charges that he is terminating our inquiry to prevent us from investigating the role of senior people in the department, including Robert Fowler and other friends of the current government.

Young has repeated this so often that many people now believe it. He is shifting responsibility for the cover-up from himself to us. This is serious. I felt that we had to make a concerted effort to set the record straight, and I started to press this point within the inquiry group at the end of last week. During the weekend, the more I thought about it, the more convinced I became that we had to act. The longer the Big Lie remained unopposed, the harder it would be to erase it.

In our own discussions, it became evident that others were more cautious than I. Understandably, the two judges are reluctant to become involved in political controversy. I was close to deciding to go public on my own when agreement was reached to hold the press conference. Any hesitation among the others disappeared later today when it was learned that during Question Period Prime Minister Chrétien had repeated the allegation. That clinched it.

Now we'll have to see whether the media respond to the press conference. I suspect that they will, sensing that we are attacking the government's credibility. It's war – a simple scenario that fits headlines and the format of television news. It may not succeed in stopping the Big Lie, but at least we will have tried. At least we will not have condoned it by our silence.

Tomorrow I will have to decide whether I want to give the issue a little extra push by opening the door for twenty-four hours to interviews with the media. This is almost impossible to do in a limited way. If you agree to one newspaper or television interview, you almost have to agree to all requests. I've carefully avoided such exposure since the inquiry began, but this issue is critical. Canadians have got to understand the enormity of what's at stake with the interference in the work of an independent inquiry now compounded by the government's attempt to shift responsibility for the result. The tactic is so bizarre that it's hard to believe it's succeeding.

Wednesday, February 12, 1997
Ottawa

If there is one thing that the media understand, it's a fight. Although we said the same things in the press conference that we have been repeating for weeks without effect, today it got the media's attention and, through the journalists, the attention of Parliament and the country, at least for twenty-four hours.

The journalists at the press conference focused on the issue of political interference. To be more exact, they tried hard to get us to charge the government with political interference. But everyone knows the motive is political. Doug Young himself had said months ago that he didn't want the inquiry continuing during an election campaign.

I took a few swipes at my old colleagues in the Press Gallery by saying that the media appeared to have lost its sense of "moral outrage." Journalists had been so preoccupied with the politics of the situation, whether the government had public support for shutting down the inquiry, whether it was going to ultimately "win" on this issue, that they had lost sight of the real issue. It was the unprecedented closure of an independent inquiry that should have been engaging its attention.

Susan Harada of CBC-TV news asked me why I wasn't demonstrating more outrage. I reminded her that I didn't specialize in soapbox appeals during my days in the media, but obliged her by saying that I certainly was horrified by what the government had done.

Tonight we are the top story on all newscasts, followed by a report on the expulsion of a Reform MP from the House during Question Period for going beyond the bounds of parliamentary propriety in his attacks on the government for closing us down. At lunchtime, I did a telephone interview with Michael Enright for "As It Happens"; after our afternoon session, I went to the National Press Building on Wellington Street for a television interview with Don Newman; then to the World Exchange Building to tape a "Canada A.M." interview for use tomorrow; then back to the National Press Building this evening for a live CBC interview with Allison Smith of Newsworld. Several more radio and television interviews before breakfast tomorrow morning will complete the follow-up to the press conference.

Events today won't change the government's mind, of course, or perhaps substantially alter the course of media comment and public opinion, but we've done what we can do to protect ourselves from the government's campaign to deflect responsibility for the cover-up toward us. We've placed the facts as we see them forcefully before the public. That's all we can do without appearing to be engaged in a political campaign.

Now there are rumours everywhere that some of the lawyers for senior military officers will attempt to use the issue of political interference to prevent us from continuing. They would argue that the curtailment of the inquiry will prevent their clients from having their full day in court.

Friday, February 14, 1997
En route Ottawa–London

The *Globe* reported this morning that Kim Campbell is being told by the government that she can either push her Somalia case publicly or continue as consul general in Los Angeles, but not both. Campbell has been making almost as much news as Doug Young recently as she tours Eastern Canada to promote the paperback edition of her autobiography.

The *Globe* story is unattributed but has that authoritative ring to it. It's a deliberate plant by someone in Ottawa who wants to send a warning to Campbell. I suspect this because the story includes the fact that Campbell used official notepaper to communicate at least one of her recent statements on Somalia. That embarrassing detail presumably would not have been provided by her.

This turn of events strengthens suspicion about the motive for Campbell's appointment last year. It wasn't that the Liberals felt they owed something to the former Conservative prime minister. Now it can be surmised that they expected something. They were trying to buy her silence.

After the Los Angeles appointment, the government apparently assumed that she wouldn't bite the hand that was feeding her. This has turned out to be a risky assumption for the government to make.

All this is just speculation, of course, but seems more and more plausible as the pieces fall into place.

I've been hearing stories about an off-the-record session between journalists and senior members of the cabinet, months ago, in the course of which the early demise of the inquiry was forecast. Someone recalled the other day that it was after the resignation of General Boyle that the prime minister criticized us in the House for treating senior bureaucrats and military officers harshly. From the vantage point of the end of this week, it looks as if our problems with the government at that time were more severe than we ever imagined.

Boyle's resignation must have been the turning point. Our investigation of claims that documents in NDHQ had been altered or destroyed must have taken the government by surprise. It wasn't expressly mentioned in our terms of reference. The only reason we followed this trail was to assure ourselves that we had all the documents we needed. The government must have watched in helpless anxiety as we toiled along the paper trail that led eventually to Boyle. This was a development that no one had foreseen.

If the military had made a concerted effort to produce all its documents for us to begin with, as the government had ordered and as the military had agreed, the pursuit of Boyle would never have happened. We started it only because of doubts that our own order for production of documents, in April 1995, was effective. Because of our growing suspicion that the document flow was being managed, we became more persistent. Perhaps this was an instance where the strategy of the government, if there was one, proved to be counter-productive.

Perhaps this also explains the questions put to me months ago over dinner by my friend's wife, from the perspective of her experience in the upper realms of the Ottawa bureaucracy. She kept trying to find out why I had been appointed. Whom did I know in the party? She seemed genuinely astonished that, as she laughingly said, the system actually seemed to have worked as it was supposed to. It had selected, perhaps by mistake, three commissioners for its inquiry who were truly independent. In this sense, the closing of our inquiry is a token of our independence and effectiveness. It was the only way that they could stop us.

Hazel heard a commentator on television speculating yesterday about Judge Létourneau's history as a civil servant in Quebec under the Lévesque government. The suggestion was that this closet separatist was now deliberately wreaking havoc among the federalists in the Chrétien government. If someone in the government is spreading this stuff, it shows their desperation.

In a media scrum outside the House today, Defence Minister Doug Young is supposed to have said that the March 4 incident was "murder" and that everyone knew it. We were told this by our staff over lunch. Then, shortly before the afternoon session, we heard that Young had tried to undo the damage in the House. It sounds incredible, as if Young is losing control.

Sunday, February 23, 1997
En route London–Ottawa

I abandoned these notes for a week. Hazel was with me in Ottawa and I didn't want to spend more time than I had to away from her. It helped to have her there in the evenings, to forget the inquiry for a few hours, particularly last week.

On Friday morning, during our coffee break, we were told that a judge of the Federal Court had ruled against Gilles in the Beno case. Judge Douglas Campbell, a new member of the

Federal Court, Trial Division, from British Columbia, had decided that Gilles's warning to General Beno during his testimony to stop "fiddling around" and his subsequent alleged comments about the general during a breakfast in Calgary showed bias. The ruling would prevent Gilles from taking part in any deliberations or decisions relating to General Beno. This would have to be done by Judge Rutherford and myself.

The decision, despite its limited scope, couldn't have come at a worse time. Driving from Ottawa to London on Friday night in heavy rain, Hazel and I listened to initial reports and reactions on CBC Radio. The finding of bias against Gilles was reported along with comments about the unfairness of our current process from lawyers representing senior military officers. This combination of personal "bias" and systemic "unfairness" will confuse the public and will probably help the government to defuse criticism of what it has done.

Judge Campbell's decision seemed to surprise everyone. I thought it was significant that he focused on one and a half sentences among the thousands of pages of transcript that our hearings have produced – Gilles's remark to General Beno: "I might as well tell you that you won't gain much by fiddling around. It was a clear question and you won't gain much. . . ." It seemed to me that this comment had to be considered in the light of General Beno's entire testimony and not just the response that he was giving at the time. A commissioner, after all, is not sitting as a judge. His or her principal duty is to inquire and that may demand tough and persistent questions during public hearings. There is a risk here that future commissioners will be hamstrung if their attempts to get at the truth from a reluctant or cagey witness can be construed as indicating personal bias.

Of course the ruling is going to be appealed, but that will probably take months. Long before that happens, the hearings will be over; possibly the report will be finished, too, or what's left of it.

There were suggestions on Friday, in the press on Saturday, and in phone calls to my home over the weekend that we should withdraw all the Section 13 notices. This would mean that our report would focus exclusively on systemic problems within the military. No blame would be attached to any individual. This would certainly simplify our job. If we withdrew the Section 13 notices, we could again try to place responsibility for emasculating the inquiry where it belongs, on the government. Unfortunately, the court ruling against the chair would be used by the government to confuse the issue, perhaps even to make it look as if we have been forced by the ruling to abandon criticism not only of General Beno but of all the brass.

If we move ahead with the Section 13 notices, it's clear that lawyers for many of the recipients will go to court. They will try to block the hearings and our report on the grounds that our compressed schedule makes it impossible for their clients to get a fair hearing. Again, this could either prevent us from reporting at all or force us to report only systemic problems. Any attempt to place responsibility on individuals would be delayed until the courts had settled the issue of fairness. This delay could amount to several years, by which time questions of individual responsibility will be of academic interest only.

My instinct on Friday was not to withdraw the Section 13 notices but to force the lawyers to go to court to close us down. Canadians won't grasp our reasoning if we withdraw them ourselves. Fighting will be messy, and may damage us even more in the long run, but I think it's the only honourable course, and the one that people will understand. I said on Friday that we shouldn't scuttle the ship; we should go down with guns blazing. But it looks as if we are going down.

I still can't quite believe it. The government is going to get away with it. In the United States, even a president couldn't stop the Watergate investigation. Here, a single cabinet minister can call a halt to a federal inquiry for admittedly political reasons and no one gets excited. It's enough to make you cry.

ENDGAME
•————————
February 1997

T he unexpected closure of the inquiry triggered a bewildering series of legal actions by those who wanted us to continue and those who didn't. John Dixon, one of former prime minister Kim Campbell's aides, went to court in British Columbia to oppose the closure, with some initial success. Senior officers who faced censure by the inquiry used its interruption to claim that they wouldn't have time to defend themselves properly. Some of them asked the courts to delay the publication of our report so that sections dealing with them could be deleted or changed.

The bias case against Judge Létourneau was rejected on appeal, but that ruling itself was appealed by lawyers for General Beno.

Despite the various political and legal distractions, we continued to follow the consequences of the March 4 incident up the chain of command in Somalia and Ottawa. Col. Serge Labbé, the commander of the Canadian Airborne Regiment Battle Group in Somalia, spent eight days on the stand in February, followed by seven days of testimony from Lt.-Col. Carol Mathieu, the commander of the Airborne regiment.

Originally we had not intended to hear testimony from Maj. Barry Armstrong, the doctor who had first raised questions about events on March 4. The reasons for our hesitation in calling him are explained below in the journal. In the end, Major Armstrong spent three days on the stand in mid-March and turned out to be one of our most compelling witnesses.

He was followed by five witnesses testifying on behalf of senior officers. On March 16, we heard our 116th and final witness after 183 days of hearings since October 2, 1995, and almost 38,000 pages of testimony.

Tuesday, February 23, 1997
Ottawa

Well, we're going to go down fighting. We had a meeting at noon today, between hearings, to see how everyone felt after a weekend to think things over. There was consensus. We're not going to throw in the towel. The Section 13s will stay in force, and we'll brace ourselves for the legal onslaught. It won't be long in arriving. Lawyers for many of the senior officers were meeting this afternoon, presumably to discuss some sort of common strategy. We assume that legal action will be taken to try to prevent us from continuing with our work.

At another meeting that started after the end of our afternoon hearing and continued until 6:30 P.M. we started winnowing the list of more than eighty witnesses for the defence submitted by many of our Section 13 recipients. With only three weeks set aside in March to hear these witnesses, and the possibility of a further week in April, we estimate an average of one witness per day, perhaps twenty all told. We selected about ten today. The process will continue tomorrow as the lawyers continue to propose witnesses.

We realize that these decisions will provide ammunition for the lawyers who are claiming unfairness, but we have no other options. The government has dictated the timetable.

Incidentally, Defence Minister Doug Young and his supporters have been claiming that our inquiry isn't the first to be curtailed. They've cited two others. I've done some research, and it turns out to be true. In May 1984, Ottawa appointed Judge Francis G. Carter to head up a one-person Commission of Inquiry into Marketing Practices for the Potato Industry in Eastern Canada. It was terminated the following November, before any hearings were held. The *Globe and Mail* reported at the time that it was "the victim of Ottawa's cost-cutting mood."

And earlier, in 1979, the Trudeau government created a National Commission on Inflation, seen as a successor to its Anti-Inflation Board. The Conservatives under Joe Clark made an electoral promise to get rid of it and did just that following their victory. The commission was disbanded in July 1979.

These closures aren't remotely comparable to what the government has now done. Its decision to shut down a major inquiry of national interest remains unprecedented in its brazen defiance of tradition, fair play, and respect for our judicial institutions.

Wednesday, February 16, 1997
Ottawa

The inquiry team met again today after the close of hearings at 4:30 P.M. We're still trying to cope with a flood of requests from senior officers who want to call witnesses in their defence next

month. Some individuals have asked for more than twenty witnesses, exceeding the total number that we can hear in the four
weeks we've allotted, and even that involves running over the
government's end-of-March deadline by a week.

We'll never be able to satisfy them. In any case, there's an air
of futility about the whole exercise. It seems to be a foregone
conclusion that lawyers for these senior officers will go to
court, singly or in a group, to try to stop us.

We're also working against the clock to promulgate rules for
the March hearings, which begin the week after next.

This is the shambles that Defence Minister Doug Young has
created. It's like trying to manoeuvre a battleship that has been
crippled by a direct hit. The jury-rigged rudder is almost useless. Emergency power somehow keeps us underway but at
reduced speed. Almost every hour brings a new crisis.

The story out of Vancouver this morning was that Kim
Campbell's former aide, John Dixon, has asked the Federal
Court to order us to complete our investigation. Dixon says he
wants to clear his name by having an opportunity to deny claims
that Campbell, as defence minister, was told of the March 16,
1993, killing of Shidane Arone at the same time as senior officers at National Defence Headquarters. Before Young's curtailment of our schedule last month, Dixon was scheduled to testify
later this spring. Now he won't be heard at all, unless the Federal Court in Vancouver orders the government to extend our
mandate. If the government won't do that, according to Dixon,
it should be ordered to revise our terms of reference, eliminating
the points that we will not now have time to cover.

Dixon was on Newsworld this morning. I watched him
over a bowl of bananas and granola. Now a lecturer in crimi-
nology at a Vancouver college, he expresses our position more

forcefully than we can at the moment. He accused Young of uttering "nickel-plated nonsense" when the minister said that Canadians already had all the answers about Somalia. Dixon said he probably knew as much as anyone in Canada, after having served in Campbell's office in 1993, but he still had many questions that deserved to be answered.

Dixon's court action and others will keep the inquiry in the news for weeks to come, prolonging the pressure on Young and the government as they try to clear the decks for the spring election campaign. None of us feel that there's any chance of the government changing its mind at this stage, but it's fascinating to watch the pressure build from both sides – those who want the inquiry to continue and those who want not only to stop us but to prevent us from reporting at all.

––––––––

At night, I often have what I call inquiry dreams. They never have a plot. They're neither frightening nor pleasant. I can only describe them as legal or judicial. I wake up with a feeling of having read, argued, and listened to incredibly complex legal arguments for hours, as if I had been inside an evolving legal opinion, the subject of which is unknown to me. Is this what lawyers dream?

Sunday, March 9, 1997
Ottawa

Back in Ottawa after a week's break from our public hearings. I haven't touched this journal for ten days. At the end of the week before last, I was simply too tired and dispirited. After six consecutive weeks of hearings, and mounting legal obstacles, all of us were finding it difficult to continue. I took research reports back to London with me to read during the break and didn't open a page. I wanted to spend as much time as I could with Hazel on household routines – shopping, fixing a broken latch on the garden gate, hanging curtains, moving furniture, cleaning out the humidifier and putting it away for the summer, all the things I haven't had time to do. It's difficult to explain to Hazel (or myself) why I should force myself to work toward a report that the government no longer wants, the public doesn't seem to care about, and that may never see the light of day.

Journalists have continued to uncover new and damning evidence of cover-up. Last Friday, David Pugliese of the *Ottawa Citizen* published documents obtained through Access to Information. The undated documents showed that the Defence Department had recommended to Defence Minister Doug Young that the government should shut down the inquiry because it was taking too long and "the national interest will not permit further delay." It also suggested that our terms of reference were too broad.

This is just another indication of the hermetically sealed world that politicians, bureaucrats, and the military seem to inhabit – a world where it is seen as normal and legitimate to ask a department under investigation whether the investigation should continue, and whether the list of "charges" that the government asked the inquiry to investigate is acceptable. This was like asking the accused whether the indictment was drawn up properly and then, when the person in the dock complains about the charges, shutting down the trial.

Today, in the Sunday *Star*, Allan Thompson of the newspaper's Ottawa bureau reported an undercover attempt in 1994 to discredit Maj. Barry Armstrong, the army surgeon who blew the whistle on the March 4 event and other incidents in Somalia.

In November 1994, Thompson received a telephone call from one of Defence Minister David Collenette's aides. "The source said," according to Thompson's story, "that if I were to call and ask the Defence Department for a copy of the autopsy report, it would be made available."

The autopsy was the one performed by forensic pathologist James Ferris on the body of Ahmed Arush two months after the Somali was killed by Canadian soldiers. Although decomposition made the examination difficult, the Ferris report failed to substantiate Armstrong's allegation that Arush had been "dispatched" after being wounded by Canadian soldiers.

After receiving this tip, Thompson called a public affairs officer at National Defence Headquarters, navy Lieut. Al Wong, and asked for the report. It was faxed to him before the end of the day.

Thompson then relied on other documents that we had tabled at the inquiry to show that the three-year-old leak was carefully orchestrated. Senior officials wrote memos to indicate that the report was handed over only after being requested by the *Star*. There was no mention, of course, of the initial tip-off from the minister's office.

Thompson also cited other documents that we had tabled that indicated that former deputy minister Robert Fowler and other senior officials may have been involved in the decision to release the pathologist's report.

"Defence officials didn't want the release to be seen as an overt attempt to discredit Armstrong," Thompson explained. "So they evidently decided to orchestrate a leak of the document that wouldn't look like a leak. And they used me to do it."

This is one of the few times, perhaps the only time in my recollection, where a journalist has admitted being used during a campaign of misinformation and has pointed the finger at the source of his "scoop." Although Thompson didn't mention the name of his "trusted government source" in the minister's office, his confession in print may make it more difficult for him to gain the confidence of other sources in future. He deserves a great deal of credit for exposing this blatant attempt at misinformation and his own willing participation at the time.

I'm no longer surprised by these revelations, although eighteen months ago I would have regarded them as fantastic. I can't understand why Canadians aren't simply outraged by what has happened. It makes the Watergate burglary look like a schoolboy's prank, yet no one in this country seems to be very excited.

Tomorrow morning we resume hearings with Major Armstrong on the stand. Lawyers for some of the senior officers will do their best to destroy him, but Thompson's story will make it more difficult.

Tonight is another one of those times when, thanks to Allan Thompson, I'm proud to call myself a journalist. When it comes to honesty and contributing to the public good, we certainly don't have to take second place to politicians, bureaucrats, and senior military officers. Watching the media at work and seeing the results of good journalism in the coverage of Somalia and its aftermath have been among the few positive aspects of this whole experience.

Monday, March 10, 1997
Ottawa

Almost the last straw last night was reading, before going to bed, an article in the current issue of *Maclean's*, which was, at least in part, a veiled attack on Gilles Létourneau. Commenting

on the "flood" of legal challenges "about to swamp the beleaguered commission," the article quotes an anonymous retired
judge "who is a personal friend of Létourneau's" as being concerned "that his reputation will be irrevocably damaged."

This article is a worrisome example of how far astray contemporary journalism can wander in its search for objectivity.
I'm sure that the writer thought that he was being "fair" by
balancing his account of the defence minister's difficulties –
"Hardly a day goes by without Young having to fend off charges
in and out of the House of Commons that the government is
trying to bury the Somalia scandal before the approaching federal election" – with a few negative comments about Létourneau. But balance in information is more than a matter of
dividing up the available space between opposing versions of
the same story. This is a poor substitute for trying to assess an
event as objectively as possible. In this case, the *Maclean's* journalist created the impression of a stand-off between Young and
Létourneau, as if each were equally to blame for an inquiry that
"now seems all but doomed to failure."

The comparison is as misleading as it is ludicrous, a subtle
kind of disinformation that does little to inform the public. On
one side of the ledger it places the defence minister, a man who
made history by terminating a public inquiry for admittedly
political reasons, and who remains defiantly unapologetic
about his assault on democracy. On the other side, it compares
Young with a judge whose only "fault" has been, in the eyes of
some, an excess of zeal in the pursuit of truth. That Gilles
Létourneau might not always be the most diplomatic of judges,
that he might have expressed impatience at the lengthy and
often evasive answers of senior officers testifying before the
inquiry, is hardly a reason for equating him with Young.

The *Maclean's* article concluded by asking whether Létourneau's reputation, which it stated had grown brighter "throughout his career," will survive the Somalia inquiry, without
presenting any evidence that our problems are the result of anything but the inherent complexity of our task and the efforts of
senior bureaucrats and officers in the Defence Department to
avoid responsibility for the Somalia affair at any cost.

This supposedly even-handed treatment of the issues facing
the inquiry is no help to Canadians trying to understand what
the Somalia controversy is all about.

So this morning, after a brief radio interview with Peter
Gzowski on "Morningside" to discuss the promising changes
that Neil Reynolds is making as the new editor of the *Ottawa
Citizen*, I pushed myself through the remnants of an overnight
snowfall toward Slater and O'Connor streets, making my reluctant progress toward another day of hearings.

I've often noticed that days that begin badly sometimes end
up well, and vice versa. Even if it isn't true, believing it is helps
me to survive the first depressing hours of a bad day. In this
case, the clouds began to lift as soon as Gilles walked into our
conference room just before the hearings reconvened. A few
days spent Ski-Dooing along the trails of northern Quebec last
week had helped him to regain perspective.

My own cure for depression began in earnest as Maj. Vincent
Buonamici began to testify. He is the next-to-last witness whom
we will hear before our investigative hearings come to a close.

Major Buonamici, along with the Airborne's former surgeon, Maj. Barry Armstrong, has been a thorn in the side of the
ruling establishment at NDHQ since Somalia. It was Buonamici
who was involved in investigating Armstrong's allegations and
who became persuaded, in the process, that the high command

in both Somalia and Ottawa was probably involved in a cover-up. He had the temerity to submit a report to Vice-Admiral Larry Murray, the current acting chief of the defence staff, that appeared to implicate Murray himself in the "inexplicable delays" that hampered investigation of the March 4 shooting. It was more than five weeks after that incident before Canadian military police were permitted to commence their investigation.

Buonamici today repeated his claim that only the March 16 murder of Shidane Arone, and the realization at NDHQ that the impending media storm would bring the March 4 incident into sharp focus, persuaded senior officers to finally authorize a police investigation. By then, the trail in Somalia had grown cold. Although the delay in sending police to investigate remains inexplicable, testified Buonamici, he is convinced that it was the result of a deliberate conspiracy at National Defence Headquarters. He also believes that no one will be able to prove this unless someone on the inside eventually comes forward.

No wonder they have made life difficult for Buonamici at NDHQ in recent years. His conspiracy hypothesis blows the "few bad apples" explanation for the murder of Arone right out of the water. It relates that tragedy directly to the slow, business-as-usual approach to the March 4 killing. According to Buonamici, this progressive cover-up sent a signal to the more unruly elements in the Airborne regiment and set the stage for the murder of Arone almost two weeks later.

On the stand today, Buonamici earned himself a place among that small band of witnesses who have freely testified before our inquiry without any apparent motive of self-interest. He obviously speaks from conviction, and his hypotheses provide a credible rationale for some of the more puzzling decisions in Ottawa after the March 4 killing.

Buonamici has a large Italianate head with a generous nose and full lips, in profile reminiscent of the young Mussolini. His uniform doesn't look as if it has been glued and pressed to his stocky frame. You can still see the human being inside the military dress.

Why is it that other officers who most closely approach the conventional military ideal, the ones in spotless uniforms with the shortest haircuts, the cleanest profiles, and the most perfect military vocabularies, are the ones who in the end appear to be the least trustworthy?

Tuesday, March 11, 1997
Ottawa

This morning I awoke not with that familiar sense of having spent the night wandering in a legal labyrinth but with a feeling of indignation. It had taken about forty-eight hours for a news report last weekend to work its way through my subconscious. This morning it had crystallized into a hardened feeling of resentment that the military should have wanted to terminate our inquiry "in the national interest." This was one of the reasons, according to last Saturday's report in Southam newspapers, that the Defence Department urged Doug Young to close us down: that "the national interest will not permit further delay."

The arrogance of this suggestion shows that the Defence Department has learned absolutely nothing from Somalia, the mistakes in Bosnia, events in Haiti, its own board of inquiry after Somalia or our inquiry. It still has the presumption to equate the national interest with the survival of the command structure at NDHQ.

The Armed Forces and the defence minister have conspired to shut down the inquiry under the pretence that changes are urgently required. The minister will announce his own list of reforms before the end of this month, changes that will have to await the outcome of the next election before they are fully implemented and when, likely as not, a new minister will be appointed with his or her own list of priorities. Another review of Young's review will then take place. Meanwhile, the department and the Armed Forces will continue much as they have in the past, having learned nothing.

The department's ostensible rationale for shutting us down, although it cloaks the hard politics of its real reason, reveals the unchanging nature of the military mind. To say that the national interest will permit no further delay in winding up the inquiry is to reveal a longing in the Armed Forces for a return to what it regards as normality. Normal times, for the military, are when Canadians either ignore or mildly support the Armed Forces; normal times definitely do not involve being subjected to constant critical examination. Our generals and admirals have enjoyed a kind of benign neglect for most of their careers. They can't understand why it has changed or why they can't now return to the good old days.

They have failed totally to comprehend that a new era has begun in which the military will be expected to function as do other institutions in our democratic society. It will be expected to open itself to scrutiny, to communicate honestly with the public, and to be accountable for its actions. The mystique of military service, the close bonding of the warrior class and its resistance to civilian interference, lasted much longer than it should have after the end of the Cold War. Somalia and the inquiry, I like to think, have ended it forever.

If the military had understood this, it would have welcomed our inquiry as an ally in the work of essential reform. Instead, it has fought us every inch of the way, rejected our legitimacy, resented our questioning, and finally defeated us with the help of a compliant minister and federal cabinet.

It is not the inquiry that has been defeated but the military's opportunity for constructive internal reform. When we leave the field of battle, the generals will not return to "peacetime," as they fondly remember it. Canadians have seen too much to continue to accept the generals at their own estimation. When a fossilized leadership incurs further disasters in future, and shows again and again that it simply cannot learn from experience, Somalia and the inquiry will be remembered as a lost opportunity, hope stifled, reform deliberately aborted.

Canadians have been watching and drawing their own conclusions. As my daughter Michelle, her husband, Dave, and their two children and I sat down this evening in a Swiss Chalet restaurant at the south end of Bank Street, a woman approached the table to say that she admires what the inquiry has been trying to do. Yesterday a taxi driver said almost the same thing to me. The other commissioners constantly repeat this type of story – chance encounters where people seem to want to express their gratitude for our attempt to bring light into the dark corners of our military culture. This is a new experience for all of us, this outpouring of gratitude. It seems un-Canadian in its fervour. It has persuaded us that the effort has not been wasted, that even if our report is stifled or mutilated the inquiry has affected Canadians deeply.

The longer the generals and senior bureaucrats in the Defence Department take to understand this, the more tragic the results will be. Something much worse than Somalia could be waiting for us in the future.

Wednesday, March 12, 1997
Ottawa

The man who started it all, Maj. Barry Armstrong, took the stand today. It was the first time that I had seen him, apart from a few television clips that showed him in his surgery in Belet Huen. I was more curious about him than any of our previous 115 witnesses, including the most senior military leaders. This was the man who, almost exactly four years ago, first alerted his own leaders and subsequently all Canadians to the possibility that Canadian soldiers had committed murder in Somalia.

The inquiry itself is largely Major Armstrong's creation. It was his persistent revelations, along with the death of Shidane Arone and the television broadcasts of the hazing rituals, that created the public outrage that forced the government to react by disbanding the Airborne regiment and appointing me and my fellow commissioners.

I didn't know what to expect. Only a few weeks ago, Lt.-Col. Carol Mathieu, Major Armstrong's commander in Somalia, had described him as almost "certifiable." Other officers have cast doubt on his military qualifications and questioned his right to express an opinion on any aspect of military behaviour. We now know, from recent newspaper stories, that the Defence Department made him the target of a campaign of misinformation designed to discredit him in the eyes of the public.

The only concrete evidence of eccentricity that Mathieu had been able to produce for us was the claim that Armstrong liked to climb to the roof of his hospital in Belet Huen and look at the stars. While I couldn't imagine either Mathieu or his superior, Colonel Labbé, ever doing something like this, it didn't strike me as particularly reprehensible. On the contrary, I rather

liked the image of the doctor beneath the night skies of the
Somalia desert, perhaps imagining himself to be Lawrence of
Arabia while his colleagues watched old videos and drank beer
in their tents.

After some of the derogatory comments about Armstrong's
military background, I was surprised to learn that it was quite
extensive. It dated back to his university days. His postgradu-
ate medical training was taken while he was in the military. He
served as the base doctor for Canadian Forces in Germany for
several years. In effect, his whole career has been spent as an
army surgeon, a highly qualified one. After Somalia, he served
in Bosnia before returning to duties in Canada. So while he
might never have served in the trenches, he was steeped in military culture. The army was his world.

The style of his evidence also surprised me. He was methodical, soft-spoken, and conservative in his presentation, not the
wild-eyed zealot that I had been led to expect. He sounded
credible when he said that it was only with great hesitation and
reluctance that he came to the conclusion, on the night of
March 4, that something had gone terribly wrong. He could see
that the dead Somali had been shot in the back and was probably alive when he had been shot again and killed. This was the
story that his wounds told to Armstrong as the body lay on a
table in the military hospital in the Canadian camp at Belet
Huen. Later, when he treated the wounded Somali, he noted
that gunshot wounds were visible not only on his backside and
legs but on the soles of his feet, indicating that he had been shot
while running away.

Later that same night, when his surgery was finished and he
had just tumbled into bed, Armstrong was woken up and summoned to the phone. Canadian headquarters in Mogadishu

was calling. National Defence Headquarters in Ottawa was already concerned about the shooting. The news media in Canada had learned that the dead Somali apparently had been shot in the back.

According to Armstrong, he was told that night that officials in Somalia and Ottawa were already involved in "damage control." He claimed that in his communication with the duty officer at Canadian headquarters in Mogadishu, he used the word "murder" in describing his fears about what had happened and that he repeated this suspicion the next day to his commanding officer in Belet Huen, Lt.-Col. Carol Mathieu.

If Armstrong really did communicate this concern to his superior officers within twenty-four hours of the event, there should have been an immediate police investigation. Instead, there was a series of internal inquiries, and it wasn't until some time after Arone had been killed, almost two weeks later, that NDHQ ordered a police investigation.

Many explanations have been given to us for this slow response, but Armstrong's testimony throws suspicion on all of them. Who to believe? The testimony of many senior officers that provides collectively a rationale of sorts for their slow response to the March 4 shooting? Or the words of a military doctor who risked isolation from his comrades and ridicule from his superiors in order to expose what he believed to be the truth?

The first impression, of a thoughtful and conscientious soldier coming to grips with an appalling reality and single-handedly trying to send a warning signal up the chain of command, with no encouragement from anyone, is convincing up to this point. Major Armstrong had waited a long time for this opportunity and it was his finest hour.

This evening, I went to the CBC studio in the National Press Building to do a remote taped interview with Brian Stewart for the magazine section of "The National" tonight. I watched the program before writing these notes. It consisted of a review of events in Somalia, the disbanding of the Airborne, and the appointment and work of our inquiry. The session with me closed the program. The general tone was highly critical of the defence minister, who had refused to be interviewed for the program. Stewart asked me at one point if this was going to be Canada's Dreyfus Affair. Would it now drag on and on? I said that the analogy I had heard recently was Dieppe, the tragic and bungled Canadian raid on the French coast. For many years the real facts about Dieppe and the responsibility for the operation were concealed. This only served to deepen the mystery and confusion and to ensure that Dieppe would live for many years in newspaper and magazine articles, books, and television specials. Because of the government's termination of the inquiry for political reasons, I told Stewart, Somalia will never die.

Friday, March 14, 1997
En route Toronto–London

Another late winter storm blankets central Ontario. I start watching the Weather Channel on Wednesdays to see what Friday travel disasters are in store. This one was a lethal mix of snow, sleet, and freezing rain, which the Air Canada Airbus has just climbed through in a hurry, rushing to rise above the murky clouds, leaving a dimly glowing oval to mark the location of the city below.

Scheduled to fly out at 4 P.M., I had to rebook for 8 P.M. as the afternoon hearing dragged on. I made it to the airport at

6 P.M. The clerk at the counter found me a seat on a delayed
6 P.M. flight and I boarded at 6:30 P.M. Loading the luggage and
de-icing took another hour before we took off about twenty
minutes ago. This is one routine I won't miss at all.

When Maj. Barry Armstrong stepped down from the stand about
5 P.M. this afternoon, he was our 116th and final witness after
more than a year and a half of public hearings. Next week we'll
hear from witnesses selected by some of the senior officers to
speak in their defence, but the real hearings, in a sense, are over.

Under pressure of time today, some lawyers became testy
and, at one point, started to yell at one another until Gilles
intervened. "Order!" he shouted. It was the first time since the
hearings started that he has had to do this, a tribute to his management of the process.

Major Armstrong turned out to be a fitting final witness. During the past four years he has had to endure a campaign of concerted vilification. It continued throughout his appearance before
us. Even on his last day, lawyers for other members of the military tried unsuccessfully to introduce affidavits alleging everything from professional incompetence to selling Canadian drugs
to Somalis, supposedly a threat made by Armstrong in an effort
to persuade authorities to provide him with essential equipment.

Occasionally the crude tactics backfired. When one lawyer
asked the doctor about reports that he had said prisoners during the Gulf War were treated far worse than those in Somalia,
it gave Armstrong a chance to delineate the differences between
the Gulf War, fought against an armed enemy, and the occupation of Somalia, a ruined country controlled by an assortment
of feuding warlords. But even in the Gulf, said Armstrong, punishment had been swift and severe for a Canadian soldier who

had struck an Iraqi prisoner with the butt of his rifle. There was no such punishment for Canadian soldiers who tied up Somali thieves, attached signs to them, and put them on public display.

Throughout his two and a half days on the stand, the tall, scholarly doctor with the pockmarked complexion and the rimless glasses maintained his composure against all the lawyers. He remained serious and methodical, and never overstated his case. Yes, he could be wrong, he admitted. But his concerns about the killing of the Somali on March 4 were real, they were based on his observations of the corpse and soldiers' stories circulating in the camp. He couldn't understand how Canadian soldiers could shoot a thief who was running away. All he asked for was an adequate explanation.

Sunday, March 16, 1997
En route London–Ottawa

Weekend newspapers, even the Liberal-leaning *Toronto Star*, which so far has tended to side with the government, continued to focus on the unanswered questions. In its editorial today, the *Star* listed the questions that we are being forced to leave hanging in the air, including: whether the Arone murder was deliberately covered up; how much former defence minister Kim Campbell, her former deputy Robert Fowler, and former chief of the defence staff John Anderson knew; and whether the current Liberal government had any part in a cover-up. "Has the kind of thinking that allowed the now-disbanded Airborne Regiment to run amok in Somalia been eradicated?" the editorial asked. The *Star* presented this as the minimum that now needs to be answered.

Unfortunately, the *Star* then went on to suggest that our investigation should be continued by a committee of the Senate, a proposal that Tory Senator Lowell Murray hopes to bring to a vote in the Upper House this coming week.

I'm surprised that the *Star* doesn't understand how idiotic this proposal is. If the inquiry should be continued, why not let us proceed? Why abolish an independent inquiry that is equipped to probe these questions and then turn over the job to an unprepared Senate committee that will be handicapped by partisan concerns? If the government has decided to cancel us, surely it isn't going to allow a Liberal-dominated Senate committee to examine these questions fully? The *Star*'s proposal makes no sense, unless its authors assume cynically that it has no hope of being adopted and can therefore be safely endorsed.

More pointed and accurate was Andrew Coyne's column on the page facing the same editorial. Coyne wrote that Major Armstrong had "revealed himself to be a man of decency, integrity, intelligence – and courage...."

Coyne ended his column tellingly: "It is simply staggering that with so many loose ends, so many unanswered allegations, the inquiry should be rushed to a premature close. Somebody killed Ahmed Arush, whether by fair means or foul. A number of people seem to have gone to great lengths to prevent us from knowing why. And the worst of it is, they're getting away with it."

Even if Prime Minister Chrétien wins the election, Somalia probably will not go away. I don't believe that the facts can be hidden indefinitely. Answering some of the outstanding questions will remain a challenge to enterprising journalists for years to come. There's nothing the media like better than an unresolved mystery. Somewhere, sometime, a journalist will unearth a document or a new source that throws light on another piece of the puzzle. This truth will provide leverage for more discoveries and revelations. Sources will come forward, driven by guilt, or a belated sense of honour.

Bureaucrats and military officers may be more inclined to talk when they reach the end of their careers than they are today. Politicians will write their memoirs. My hunch is that most of the Somalia story will be known within the next five to ten years. It's even possible that future revelations could result in the appointment of another inquiry to complete our work.

Monday, March 17, 1997
Ottawa

Sgt. John Collins retired from the Airborne several years ago after more than thirty years in the army. He arrived this morning to testify on behalf of Lt.-Col. Paul Morneault, the commanding officer who was removed from the regiment by the high command weeks before Sergeant Collins and his mates left for Somalia in December 1993. Collins was a soldier of the old school. When he joined up, as he said, a Grade Three education was enough. Now soldiers are better educated, according to the lean, silver-haired sergeant with the deep gravelly voice, but not better behaved.

"In the old days, you gave an order and it was obeyed," he said. "Now they question everything."

Even in the sterile surroundings of our hearing room, Collins carried with him something of the barracks. You could easily imagine him with a beer in hand and his boots on the table in the sergeants' mess at the end of the day. Except that, as he said, "It's an eight-to-four job now."

———

According to the *Ottawa Citizen* this morning, Defence Minister Young's reform blueprint, to be announced next week, will be a very flimsy attempt to upstage our own report. He wants to continue to do the impossible – maintain a traditional multipurpose defence force (which we really no longer have) without increasing the military budget.

Many of his reforms will have the effect of tinkering with the system; his quick-and-dirty studies will join dozens of earlier reports gathering dust at National Defence Headquarters. And after the election, Young will probably move on to another portfolio, having tabled his studies for further consideration, damaged our inquiry, and neutralized defence as an election issue. Or at least that's obviously his plan.

Tuesday, March 18, 1997
Ottawa

We all seem to feel as if we've reached the top of the mountain and are now starting the descent. The substantive hearings have ended. The three of us still troop downstairs from our offices on the eleventh floor to the hearing room on the ninth every morning, but the witnesses are no longer ours. They are called to defend the actions and reputations of officers liable to be criticized in our report. They are now few in number because most of the officers and their lawyers have withdrawn from this

stage of the hearing in protest while they try to stop us in court.
With only a half-dozen lawyers present, the room looks empty.
The testimony and cross-examination is brief and perfunctory.
Within a day or two, this final stage will end.

Soon the hearing room where we have spent the better part
of eighteen months – with its lawyers, cameras, stenographers,
and translators, the set where Canadians have witnessed the
rare spectacle of Canada's high command defending itself in
public – will go dark, as empty as an abandoned theatre. The
echoes of this unusual performance will be heard for many
years, but at this moment, as the minister of defence brings
down the curtain before the final act, I am conscious only of the
deepening, ominous silence.

Upstairs, the words of our report are filling computer
screens. Draft versions of text are beginning to take shape.
Daily meetings are scheduled for the next two weeks to discuss
our recommendations and multiple revisions of the report,
which will eventually run to several thousand pages.

Although the recommendations are still being elaborated,
none of us are anticipating any serious difficulty in reaching a
consensus. Almost since the beginning, there has been a sense
of common purpose running through our deliberations, of
unavoidable conclusions seeming to emerge from testimony in
an almost organic way. The research papers by outside consultants and our own staff have contributed to this process.

The ease with which we are achieving agreement says something about the need for reform in the military. Much of what
we will recommend, I'm sure, will reflect proposals that have
been appearing and reappearing for many years, often in
reports issuing from the military itself. But this time, the recommendations arise not from theory but from the traumatic

events in Somalia in 1993. This is what will give them authority and power, we can hope, despite the attempt by Defence Minister Doug Young next week to neutralize reform and allow the military to continue in its old, familiar paths.

In the introduction to his research report on misconduct in the military, released by us this week, Martin Friedland, professor of law and former law dean at the University of Toronto, reminded us that the murder of Shidane Arone on the night of March 16, 1993, occurred exactly twenty-five years to the day after the My Lai massacre in Vietnam.

"That event and its cover-up and investigation was a crucial defining moment for the American public and military," wrote Friedland. "This event and its aftermath will also turn out to be a crucial defining moment for the Canadian public and the Canadian military."

Friedland quoted one of our internal documents, the report of a visit of our researchers to senior U.S. army officials in Washington in the summer of 1995. Our people were told by the Americans that "the U.S. Army has reached the stage where they are sure that a situation such as the conduct of 2 Commando at Belet Huen could not occur in the U.S. Army."

"The task of the Somalia Inquiry, in my view, is to set the stage so that the Canadian military will be able to say the same," wrote Friedland.

Friday, March 21, 1997
En route Ottawa–London

I sit in the departure lounge at Pearson airport waiting for my connection to London and wonder at the absurdity of it all.

Yesterday afternoon, Stan Cohen, the inquiry's secretary, came into my office with a look of amazement on his face. The Senate had just passed a Liberal motion creating a special committee to look into the murder of Shidane Arone in Somalia and a possible cover-up. We were both stunned. This story is rapidly passing the point of rational development. Stan politely suggested that I should refrain from commenting publicly about this. I wouldn't know what to say anyway.

The Liberals undoubtedly think that they've been clever about this. By proposing an inquiry that will be stillborn when this Parliament is terminated by the expected spring election, they hope to appear willing to continue the investigation, secure in the knowledge that nothing will happen in the time available. Because the special committee will die when Parliament does, a new Parliament would have to re-create it when it convenes. Even if this occurs, and I wouldn't bet on it, the committee probably couldn't begin to do anything until next fall. As a report on Global TV yesterday pointed out, the committee might be able to report about the time that our final and complete report would have been ready.

The ability of the Senate to deal with this effectively is certainly open to question. It will have neither the legal expertise nor the research resources that have been available to us. Lawyers for the various parties will not be able to cross-examine. Partisan battles within the committee will undermine its ability to look for the truth.

The government has been too clever by half. Defence Minister Doug Young again stalked away from reporters yesterday when they asked him to reconcile government support for a Senate inquiry with his recent statements that our inquiry was no longer needed because Canadians already know all the answers about Somalia.

The government's contradictory stance puts Young in an impossible position because it undercuts his rationale for closing us down. If his position was based on anything but political expediency at this point, he would resign.

Last night there was an informal gathering in Ottawa to thank our three military advisers, all of them retired senior officers, Lt.-Gen. Jack Vance, Col. Ted Nurse, and Lt.-Col. Doug Bland. With more than forty years of military service behind him, and once considered to be a leading candidate for chief of the defence staff, Jack Vance has come to symbolize for me some of the military ideals that seem at times to have all but disappeared. He and Doug and Ted have been able to look critically at their own profession, alienating in the process some of their friends who are still in the military. But they have reassured us that there are many others in the Forces, particularly among younger officers, who understand and support what we are doing.

The three occupy offices along the short corridor leading from our hearing room to the conference room where we take coffee breaks, eat lunch, and hold most of our in-house meetings. On some days, when senior officers have been evasive on the witness stand, contradicting one another, and putting their own interests ahead of the welfare of the Forces, the three of us leave the hearing room overcome by a sense of hopelessness. If these time-servers are the best that our military can produce, if they represent the values that the system selects for promotion, our task seems futile. Just walking past the offices of Jack, Doug, and Ted reminds us, on these bleak days, that integrity, intelligence, and idealism have motivated officers in the past and that there are still others like this in the Forces.

On many days, one or the other has wandered into our conference room to share a coffee with us, to listen to our cries of exasperation, and to prevent us from slipping into total despair. If our report is inspired by a belief in the possibility of change in the military, by an act of faith in the officer class of the future and the men whom they will lead by example, it will be due in large part to the presence as well as the work of these three advisers. All three of us, as commissioners, tried to say this at the dinner last night in one way or another.

WRITING THE REPORT

March to April 1997

A s soon as our hearings ended in March, we started to work full time on the final report. As the journal indicates, the amount of material that we were trying to organize and assess was almost overwhelming, despite the preparatory work that had been done. Although my whole life has been spent reading and writing for a living, never had I read so intensively over such a prolonged time.

Not unexpectedly, translating the report proved to be a nightmare. Although we had an army of expert translators working on sections of the report as soon as they were finalized, there were problems of consistency in vocabulary and style. Being the only fully bilingual commissioner with French as a native language, Judge Létourneau had to read and approve every line of the French translation. This added immensely to his work in the final weeks.

Legal objections to releasing the report continued right up to the week before our deadline at the end of June and weren't resolved until the last minute.

Monday, March 24, 1997
Ottawa

This morning we started to immerse ourselves in the writing of the report. Research studies and drafts of various sections have been circulating for months, but now, for the first time, we are considering the material as a whole and making final decisions.

Because of my background in journalism, people on the outside expect me to have a major role in writing our report. A few even seemed to assume that I had been selected specifically with this task in mind. Frankly, it's the last thing in the world I would want. Assembling, writing, and editing a royal commission report is perhaps the most unrewarding task in the world. This is a job for technicians who have the skills needed to absorb mountains of data, sort it into neat piles, and process it into something recognizable and meaningful.

I'm not saying that I don't admire people who can do this. It's a special ability that is in high demand in Ottawa, where the production of speeches, manuals, press releases, studies, and reports of every size and description provides employment for a small army of anonymous writers. But better them than me.

We're fortunate to have two skilful practitioners currently taking thousands of pages of testimony, internal research reports, and preliminary drafts, as well as suggestions from the three of us, and making a structured document out of them. We're also lucky that Stan Cohen, the inquiry's secretary, is a quick, fluent writer with a nice turn of phrase.

Of course that doesn't mean that I can keep my hands off the copy. When I receive drafts from the writers, I read them as an editor as well as a commissioner, covering them with corrections and suggestions.

We had a brief discussion on split infinitives this morning. The writers wanted to know my position on them. Not preferable but sometimes unavoidable, I said. That's the way they felt. We banded together against rigid grammatical orthodoxy. Later a phrase in one of the drafts to the effect that "the commander decides his priorities" triggered a discussion about the use of gender neutral terms. Stan Cohen absolutely refused to use the he/she form. We compromised by deciding to use plural forms whenever possible. Gilles said that trying to translate the he/she format would produce a stylistic abomination because of the gender-related forms of nouns, verbs, and adjectives in French.

Because we are dealing in this phase with factual texts describing such things as the military justice system, the political history and social customs of Somalia, and the structure of the military chain of command, we are moving quickly through the material. In the next few days, we will encounter sections with more interpretation leading toward our conclusions.

So far the three of us have avoided discussing our recommendations in specific detail. After two years of working together, I think that we all sense agreement on the major reforms that are needed. If I think back, we've probably touched on most of these informally during hundreds of coffee breaks, casual chats in our offices, and more formal sessions. In this sense, it's almost like living inside a single large brain. I'll be very surprised if we have any serious disagreements as we approach our deadline.

Even for someone like myself who spent years meeting daily deadlines, this writing process seems fast – taking the results of two years of work and, in a few weeks, reaching agreement on a final draft. But it's the best way. Our energy level is high. We all realize that we haven't time to waste on lengthy discussions of minor points or advocacy of personal positions. Like soldiers at the end of a long march, we sense that, at the barracks, our opportunity to put our feet up, look back on the mission, and swap stories over a drink or two is just around the corner.

Thursday, March 27, 1997
En route Ottawa–London

The *Globe and Mail* buried the story deep inside the paper, but the *Ottawa Citizen* gave it greater prominence. This morning, one of Southam's Vancouver correspondents indicated in the *Citizen* that a judge of the Federal Court, sitting in British Columbia, was expected to rule against the government's decision to terminate the inquiry.

It was 8:30 A.M. in Vancouver when Judge Sandra J. Simpson released her decision – 11:30 A.M. in Ottawa as we frantically pressed on with editing our report for the June deadline. We were in the ninth-floor boardroom when Stan Cohen was called to the phone. He returned a few minutes later with the gist of the judgement scribbled on a piece of foolscap.

It certainly looks as if Judge Simpson has given Defence Minister Doug Young and the government its comeuppance. Unprecedented as was Young's decision to close us down, Judge Simpson's ruling also breaks new ground. Rarely has a Canadian court interfered with a political decision of government in such a direct fashion.

Doug Young and the cabinet are now in the hotseat. It looks as if his take-charge style has turned a small but worrisome election problem for the government into a high-profile issue, and perhaps ended his career.

At first sight, it looks as if the government will have no option but to let us continue. Even if it appeals today's decision, it will have to provide us with some guidance in the meantime. We can't simply be left in limbo for the next few months.

Of course the cabinet could follow one of the courses suggested by the judge – cutting back our terms of reference to correspond to our shortened deadline. But that would make explicit the government's intention to prevent us from investigating the cover-up and probably also result in Young's resignation.

By lunch time, phone messages from the media were piling up on my desk, but we're not saying anything for the time being. The court's decision has driven the ball into the government's court. We can only react to whatever the government decides to do next week. I can imagine the consternation in the Langevin Block this afternoon as they try to figure out a strategy, and how they will spin it for the media.

One of the underlying issues, as law professors are already pointing out today, is the principle of separation of government and the courts. The government doesn't have the right to interfere with the courts. How far can the courts go in interfering with what is essentially a political decision made by the government? My own instinct is to say – not very far. In a democracy, the government has the right to make a bone-headed decision and live with the consequences. Some of our lawyers tell me this is a more complex subject than the way I've just expressed it, particularly since the Charter of Rights was adopted. If the government's decision can be seen as infringing on the rights of citizens, then the courts might have a role in this case.

In her ruling, Judge Simpson decided that the government's order-in-council shutting us down was beyond the government's powers and suffered from "lack of clarity and impossibility of performance." She ordered the government to impose a new deadline giving the inquiry "the time it reasonably requires to complete its mandate," or to reduce our terms of reference and set new deadlines to give the inquiry "the time it reasonably requires to complete its reduced assignment," or to take whatever other steps necessary to fulfil her order.

Whatever the outcome, it looks as if we'll make legal as well as military and political history before we're finished.

———

On a personal level, the Simpson decision left me in a state of shock. Since Young's announcement in mid-January, Hazel and I have been adjusting happily to the early closure, anticipating that I would finish work on the inquiry in about a month. We've been looking forward to finally spending more time together. I can't describe how sick and tired both of us are of the long separations. Now I'm facing the prospect of the inquiry continuing well into next year, if we start up again.

I'm typing this in the departure lounge at Pearson airport, waiting for the connecting flight to London and imagining how upset Hazel is going to be when I arrive home.

March 31, 1997, Easter Monday
London

On Saturday, the *Globe* carried a written statement released by Doug Young late Friday, repeating his June deadline for our final report. He stated this again yesterday on CTV's "Question

Period." The only way he can do this, I assume, is by amending our terms of reference. I expect he'll do this.

I don't know why I didn't anticipate this more clearly on Friday. It seems to make sense from Young's point of view, even if it is reprehensible. After all, Young and the government have already absorbed most of their punishment from the media for shutting us down. Revising the terms of reference, although another unprecedented act, only makes it official and clarifies the government's intentions. If this is what happens, there will be another short, fierce outcry from the media, but there's still no sign that the issue is commanding public attention.

So the brief moment of public euphoria and private despair that seized us on Friday has passed. Young won't budge. The cover-up will simply become explicit, and Canadians will swallow even that.

Wednesday, April 2, 1997
Ottawa

This morning we continued our process of editing and approving sections of our final report while Stan Cohen maintained the contact with the Privy Council Office that started yesterday. I am sure that the PCO will not want to physically remove sections of our terms of reference, presumably because that would make it clear to everyone that the government doesn't want us to investigate a cover-up. I suspect that they intend to propose an addition to the terms of reference that would instruct us to report on whatever we have been able to investigate and conclude by the end of June.

Our lawyers can't seem to agree on whether this responds to Judge Simpson's order. If it doesn't, John Dixon in British Columbia, or someone else, may well go to court to try to over-throw the new order-in-council. But at least our dilemma is resolved for the time being. Whether we agree with it or not, the new order-in-council will supersede the Simpson ruling. We work out a terse two-sentence statement expressing our unhap-piness with the closure but also our understanding of the force of the new order-in-council, which we have no choice but to obey.

We reached this decision in instalments, breaking away periodically from our work on the final report as updates on the government's intentions were brought to us. In mid-afternoon, we interrupted our discussions again to read the text of Judge Simpson's judgment, which praised the work of our inquiry, defended the integrity of our process, and casti-gated the government for closing us down without specifically amending our terms of reference to disclose what it did not want us to do.

For political reasons, the government's new order will try to evade this requirement, but it's all a smokescreen to conceal what the minister actually has done. I don't believe that anyone is fooled by it.

————

Just before five this afternoon, I left our meeting a few minutes early to rush by taxi to Government House for the second annual presentation of journalism awards by Governor Gen-eral Roméo LeBlanc. The awards are a project of the Canadian Journalism Foundation initiated by Toronto philanthropist

Eric Jackman. Several weeks ago, in London, I chaired the committee that selected CBC Newfoundland's television news and current affairs unit as this year's outstanding journalistic organization. Another committee headed by Peter Herrndorf, president of TVOntario, selected Peter Gzowski for this year's Lifetime Achievement Award.

I was late arriving at Government House and was ushered quickly into a salon where the official party had assembled. The governor general came forward to welcome me, introducing me to his wife and some of the other guests, most of whom I knew. Then he said that I'd become a familiar face on television again and began to ask me about the inquiry as did others in the group.

The governor general's wife, at my left elbow, is the sister of former deputy defence minister Robert Fowler. I had to be a bit careful in my responses.

Before I left the reception following the awards ceremony, I talked with Peter Gzowski for a few moments about retirement. In his speech accepting the award, he had said that he intends to do his last "Morningside" show next month from Moose Jaw, where he was a very young city editor of the local newspaper near the start of his career. It was only a few years after that, in the early 1960s, that I first met Peter in Montreal. I was on the *Montreal Star* in my home city, having spent five years in Winnipeg, and Peter had also returned east to be the Quebec correspondent for *Maclean's*. I vaguely remember a dinner party at his duplex in Montreal ... other wives, other times. Then Peter went back to Ontario and I stayed in Quebec until the end of the 1960s, when I went to Ottawa to work for the *Toronto Star*. Peter and I never worked together, never became close friends, but we've always recognized one another as members of the same generation of journalists and also, I think, as misfits, Peter with his Polish name, me with my French-Canadian, both proud of our ancestors in this country and viewing Canada from a slightly oblique angle, not quite in the mainstream of our respective home provinces, Ontario and Quebec.

Friday, April 4, 1997
En route Ottawa–London

I guess that's it.

After a hamburger and chips at Harvey's with my daughter Jane, helping to ease her through the final stressful weeks of her graduate program at Carleton University, I returned to my hotel last night to hear the phone ringing as I unlocked the door. It was Roger Smith of CTV to tell me that the Privy Council Office had issued its new order. As we expected, it simply told us to report on whatever we had investigated up to that point, without specifying what we should omit.

It enables the minister to avoid telling us specifically not to report on the allegations of cover-up. The government has shut us down to protect itself. That must be clear to everyone.

I suppose it's possible that someone may try to challenge this in court, but, by then, our report will be finished and on its way to the government.

After talking with Smith on the phone, I started to read a 210-page draft of the chapter in our final report that deals with the March 4 killing at Belet Huen. I had until noon today to finish reading it, assemble my comments, and bring them to an afternoon meeting with the writers, researchers, and other commissioners.

Parts of our report are highly technical and, frankly, boring to anyone but a specialist in military affairs, but this chapter tells a story. All the contradictory testimony from our hearings has been woven into a narrative that leads inescapably to clear findings. This is the strength of the independent inquiry process. This is where the painstaking, expensive, confusing, and often tedious collection of evidence pays off.

Bit by bit, by placing one piece of testimony against another, by referring to documents when verbal testimonies are in conflict, we have built up a detailed picture of the incident. Now, standing back from it, the overall design and the patterns of individual behaviour within it suddenly become clear, as if we are viewing a stained-glass window from a distance for the first time.

This chapter shows that the death of Ahmed Arush on March 4, 1993, was unnecessary – a tragedy with origins deep within the history and structure of the Airborne regiment and the military as a whole, a tragedy created by a lack of leadership in Somalia and Ottawa. It also reveals the full extent of the cover-up and damage-control operation that was mounted in Somalia and Ottawa after the incident. The conclusion that this set the stage for the even more horrific murder of Shidane Arone is inescapable.

Next week we listen for five days to final submissions from some of the parties while continuing to work on our report in the evenings. We actually are near the end. I find myself beginning to reflect on this long journey and what it has meant to everyone who has been involved.

Thursday, April 10, 1997
Ottawa

The legal rituals in our hearing room are slowly drawing to a close. We'll hear the last of the final submissions tomorrow morning. When they address us, each lawyer pays formal tribute to our integrity and diligence. We, in turn, thank them for assisting the inquiry. Then they open their notes and proceed to lambaste us, always "with respect," for running an unfair process that is little better than a kangaroo court, for victimizing their military clients, and for various other sins that, in their view, should make us thoroughly ashamed of ourselves. Then they gather their notes at the end and thank us once again for the great service that we are providing to the country.

No matter how bitter the questions that divide various parties and how high their feelings might run, the formulas of courtroom procedure enforce a certain level of decorum. Hypocritical it might seem, but I suppose it's better than hurling rocks at one another.

I came across a reference today to a report on Canadian peacekeeping in Central America by retired general Ian Douglas, a former member of the Airborne. This was in the early 1990s. Douglas wrote that, in that instance, Canadian peacekeepers were inferior to those supplied by Spain and Venezuela. That gave me a bit of a jolt. I thought peacekeeping was our national specialty.

Saturday, April 12, 1997
En route Ottawa–London

We "de-commissioned" our ninth-floor hearing room yesterday, shortly after the final lawyer presented the last oral submission on behalf of one of the generals. Then we had a sandwich lunch for the simultaneous translators, stenographers, ushers, computer technicians, and television cameramen from CPAC, who have lived with us in this room since August 1995.

CPAC had logged 181 days of coverage, but the network only started to televise our hearings in the fall of 1995. If you add our initial policy hearings in the summer to that total, the total of hearing days must approach 200. It felt quite strange this morning to gather in the adjacent conference room, line up in our usual order – Judge Rutherford first, then the chair, and then me – and follow the usher into the hearing room for the last time. Even stranger when we rose shortly before noon, bowed to the court, and filed out. My last appearance as a quasi-judge.

After lunch, we continued with lawyers and consultants to work our way through more of the 2,000-plus pages of our final report. We finished after 6 P.M., when I tucked another sheaf of papers into my briefcase and left the building.

In recent weeks I've taken to stopping at a coffee bar on Elgin Street for a decaf latté or cappuccino at the end of the day. I know I'm putting off the return to the hotel.

No one pays attention to the greying man in the tan raincoat at the back of the coffee shop, his fountain pen poised over a thick pile of papers. Yesterday I read about the Rules of Engagement governing the use of deadly force by our soldiers in Somalia. And, behind the hissing of the espresso machines, I seemed to hear the crack of rifle fire in the darkness of a Somali night and the screams of the wounded Somali as he stumbles in the sand, tries to rise, and is cut down again by the bullets from the Canadian C-7s. My pen descends, alters a few words in the text, adds a stronger adjective, and sharpens a judgement that may affect someone for the rest of his life.

A middle-aged woman at the table next to me is marking exam papers.

We started at 9 A.M. to review the chapter on Rules of Engagement, moving on later to the first part of the huge narrative section that chronicles the whole Somalia affair from beginning to end. The pressure of deadline is almost palpable. At one point, wrestling with a particularly stubborn bit of text, one of the two judges swears softly under his breath, "That bastard!" I'm puzzled and ask him who. "The minister," he growls.

At the mid-morning break, I run across the street to get a coffee to take out. Another customer, a man in his forties dressed casually for a Saturday, starts to talk to me. He wants to congratulate us for trying to do a good job. Then he identifies himself as a veteran of twelve years' service in the military. He starts to talk to me about a friend of his, in the reserve, who was involved in the gathering of documents for our inquiry. He tells me that his friend asked to be relieved of his task because he was concerned about the destruction of documents that should have been handed over to the inquiry.

"All kinds of stuff," he tells me, "including photographs. He thought it was terrible, what they were doing. It really upset him."

I ask whether he knows how I could get in touch with this man. He says that he has lost contact with him, but that he is still in the reserve and would lose his job there if he went public with this story. I suggest that he might change his mind, one of these days.

"The story is going to come out, sooner or later," I tell him. "That's the worst part of it, for the military. It won't just go away."

"I hope so," he said. "I'm completely fed up with the system. But they'll never learn, those guys at the top."

Thursday, April 17, 1997
Ottawa

The farce is over. The last act has been played out.

Peter Geigen-Miller, a reporter with the *London Free Press*, has reached me at the hotel to give me the news. The Senate committee has just disintegrated. The Tory senators have walked out. So much for the government's plan to have the Senate take over our interrupted inquiry.

The idea was the Liberals' final, cynical postscript to their decision to close us down. According to the script, the Liberal-dominated Senate would hold a quick series of hearings next week before an election call disbanded the committee. This would give the committee little more than a week to hear from such witnesses as former deputy minister Robert Fowler, former chief of the defence staff John de Chastelain, and others from National Defence Headquarters – just enough time to place their denials that there had been a cover-up on the record. Then the government could claim that the case was closed as it moved into its spring election campaign.

The Tories were almost sucked into this manoeuvre. Because former defence minister and prime minister Kim Campbell had been demanding an opportunity to clear herself of cover-up charges, the Tory senators initially must have thought that this would present a chance to embarrass the government and they naïvely went along with the idea. But as the opening date approached, it became clear that the Liberals were simply organizing another whitewash. Even if Campbell and her aides were given a chance to testify, they would be overwhelmed and discredited by the massed phalanx of government witnesses.

Having belatedly seen the trap, the Tories stormed out of an organizational meeting tonight at which the committee was to agree on procedures for the hearings next week.

I couldn't say what I thought of this to Peter Geigen-Miller. I and the other two commissioners have agreed not to comment on the Senate committee while we complete our own report. So I write it down here out of sheer frustration. I can't wait for the end of June and a chance to speak out.

Friday, April 18, 1997
En route Ottawa–London

Sitting in the in-transit lounge at Pearson airport, at the end of another week of reading, editing, and discussing the final report. Most evenings and mornings are spent reading and marking text. In the afternoon the three of us get together with researchers, editors, and writers to review and correct the text, page by page. It will take between 4,000 and 6,000 manuscript pages to fill the final report and, in most cases, we are reading various sections at least three times. That makes . . . I don't want to think about it. The other morning, when I got up and looked in the mirror, I could see the red marks from my glasses still on the bridge of my nose from the night before.

It's bearable only because there's an end in sight. The horizon keeps on receding slowly – at one time we were told that we should finish this week – but we're gaining on it slightly, day by day. By the end of the month, that should be it.

EPILOGUE
———•———

July 1997
London

On the evening of Canada Day 1997, I sat on the curb of a bridge over the Thames River near my home in London with my two grandchildren from Ottawa, fifteen-year-old Cymbria and ten-year-old Arthur, our upturned faces illuminated by the traditional fireworks display. We were surrounded by thousands of spectators, all of us conscious to some degree of our good luck in living in one of the wealthiest, healthiest, safest, and freest countries in the world. But on this Canada Day, my thoughts were already turning toward the next morning and the story that we would tell Canadians, a story that would run counter to everyone's ideas of what this country represents.

On my sixty-fourth birthday, July 2, I got out of bed before dawn to catch the first flight to Ottawa. The press conference scheduled for 11 A.M. was to be preceded by a meeting of the commissioners and staff. Normally, to be on the safe side, I would have flown to Ottawa the night before an important morning appointment. On this occasion, the Canada Day festivities and my grandchildren had taken precedence. But my heart sank when I arrived at the airport and learned that flights had been delayed because of morning fog at Toronto Island Airport, our scheduled touchdown on the way to Ottawa.

At a quarter-past seven, already a half-hour late, I was still in London, about ninety minutes flying time but seven hours' drive from Ottawa, and starting to panic. When Air Ontario began shifting Toronto-bound passengers to another airline, I almost ran to the counter, expecting to hear that my flight had been cancelled.

"Not at all," the attendant assured me. "Your plane is just going to skip Toronto and fly straight to Ottawa. You'll be almost on time."

Near-panic had become a way of life for all of us on the inquiry since the end of March. We had done the impossible in the past three months by agreeing on 160 recommendations, discussing, writing, editing, and proofreading our 1,600-page report, translating it into French, and printing its five volumes in sufficient number for an initial distribution on the day of its promised release at the end of June. Never had a royal commission of this scope been forced to complete these final processes at such breakneck speed.

By the morning of the press conference, we were exhausted, but the five volumes of the report were on the table before us, their dark-blue covers showing a soldier of the disbanded Airborne regiment with bowed head, behind him in ghostly outline his comrades on parade in front of the barracks at Petawawa, and in the sky above the faint silhouette of a helicopter. Superimposed in white was the title that was to draw immediate fire from the government, "Dishonoured Legacy – The Lessons of the Somalia Affair."

On this July 2 morning, the final day of our collective existence, Judge Gilles Létourneau was still worrying over some flaws in the French translation that he had spotted in the first copies of the report to leave the press. Later that day, after some of these copies had been released to the media, we discovered that a discussion paper in one of the English volumes had somehow been omitted. As soon as this was detected, printing was stopped until revisions had been made. The subsequent delays in delivery of the report to the many people who had requested copies sparked rumours that it was being suppressed by the government. In view of the initial reaction, this wasn't surprising.

But our job was over. On the previous Saturday night, we had gathered in the backyard of the Ottawa home of our secretary, Stanley Cohen, for a barbecue and an informal backward look at more than two years of life aboard the Somalia inquiry. Despite the political pressures that we had endured, perhaps because of them, it had been a memorable and rewarding personal experience.

On that evening, I expressed surprise that not a single word of the report had leaked to the media. This was unusual in Ottawa. The day before, a desperate journalist had begged me to give him just the title, or even the number of words in it.

"Is it something like, 'The Shame of the Past'?" he had asked.

Dozens of people – lawyers, writers, translators, designers, and production staff – had had access to portions of the final report. That none of them had leaked a word to the media vividly illustrated the group's *esprit de corps*.

At the backyard barbecue we also discussed the government's final manoeuvre to sabotage the report. Up to the end of the previous week, we had been given to understand that the official release would be a few days after we had submitted our report on Monday, June 30, probably on the Wednesday or Thursday after the Canada Day holiday. Earlier on Saturday, we had suddenly been told that the report would be released on Monday as soon as we turned it over to the government. This would allow us no time to organize the usual media lock-up before the press conference to give journalists an opportunity to study the report. Since many journalists already had left Ottawa for the long weekend, few would be on hand for a Monday release, and many newspapers were not publishing on Canada Day. If you were a government wishing to bury a report, this would be the best day of the year, next to Christmas Day, to rush it out to oblivion. In the end, only a threat to hand over the report at 11:59 P.M. on Monday produced an agreement with the government for a Wednesday release. As it was, the report wasn't transmitted officially until the end of the afternoon on Monday, as a precaution against early release. This unseemly and embarrassing harassment right up to the last minute provided a fitting conclusion to the government's treatment of the inquiry in the final part of our mandate. We discovered that even at that point, when we thought we were beyond surprise, the government still had the ability to make us shake our heads in disbelief.

Shortly before 11 A.M. on Wednesday, we walked three blocks north from our offices to the National Press Building facing Parliament Hill. The television cameras picked us up as we approached on Wellington Street and followed us into the building and the press conference theatre where I had spent so many years on the other side of the lights and cameras. The last act was beginning.

For almost two hours before we arrived, the journalists had been locked up with copies of the report. Their initial reaction, our advisers had been told, was surprise at its scope and uncompromising tone. For months they had been reporting the story of the inquiry that had been crippled and aborted by the government. They had forgotten that in fact we had completed most of our mandate – 85 to 90 per cent was my estimate, although the missing 10 per cent or so was obviously vital. If they had expected us to be intimidated, the report showed how mistaken they were.

The opening words of our executive summary set the tone: "From its earliest moments the operation went awry. The soldiers, with some notable exceptions, did their best. But ill-prepared and rudderless, they fell inevitably into the mire that became the Somalia debacle. As a result, a proud legacy was dishonoured."

The summary concluded: "We can only hope that Somalia represents the nadir of the fortunes of the Canadian Forces. There seems to be little room to slide lower. One thing is certain, however: left uncorrected, the problems that surfaced in the desert in Somalia and in the boardrooms at National Defence Headquarters will continue to spawn military ignominy. The victim will be Canada and its international reputation."

Unlike the Krever inquiry into the national blood supply, which had started before us and was still bogged down in legal wrangling, we had ended our work with most of our Section 13 notices intact. Accordingly, we described the failures of senior officers in detail. Right up to the previous week, lawyers for these officers had argued in court that the cutting short of the inquiry had made it impossible for their clients to get a fair hearing. They wanted the Section 13s withdrawn so that we couldn't lay blame on individuals. Apart from a few paragraphs in the notices sent to two senior officers, the courts upheld our procedures. This meant that we could release the 104 pages of the fourth volume of our report detailing the failure on the part of eleven senior leaders, starting with two former chiefs of the defence staff, John de Chastelain and Jean Boyle, and including almost every member of the high command in Somalia and Canada who had been involved with the mission. In six of these cases, we concluded our list of failures by making the most serious charge that we could bring against an officer: "Failure in his duty as a Commander as defined by analogy to Queen's Regulations and Orders article 4.20 and in military custom."

On the March 4 shooting in Somalia, the only one of the fatal incidents that we were permitted to investigate, we provided a clear accounting of cover-up, placing the responsibility on the chain of command in Somalia and Ottawa and describing actions that were "weak, untimely, inadequate, self-serving, unjustifiable, and unbecoming the military leadership that our soldiers deserve and the Canadian public expects." We also stated our belief that the failure to deal promptly and decisively with the March 4 incident had probably contributed to conditions that caused the torture and death of Shidane Arone on March 16.

If the media were surprised by the tone of the report, the government was outraged. Within a few hours of our press conference, Art Eggleton, the defence minister appointed only three weeks earlier, essentially rejected the report. His criticism concerned two minor points. He took issue with the "Dishonoured

Legacy" title, which he characterized as a general slur on the military, and our statement that some soldiers and senior military officers had lied during our public hearings. Eggleton insisted that we should have named the liars. He ignored the specific failures that we had attributed to senior officers and simply denied that there had been a cover-up of incidents in Somalia. Two days later, Prime Minister Jean Chrétien repeated that "there is no cover-up" in the Somalia affair. When reporters asked him about specific findings of cover-up in the report, he replied, "I don't know what you are talking about."

The initial battle for public opinion lasted for the next twenty-four hours. Hurrying between radio and television studios in Ottawa, I did about twenty interviews between the end of our press conference at noon and 9:30 P.M. The other two commissioners were equally active. At 6:30 A.M. the next day, I was back in the CBC studios of the National Press Building for the first of eleven more interviews, including an hour-long session for the public affairs channel, CPAC, and two radio interviews for the BBC. From the lounge at the airport in Ottawa, I took part in a Halifax phone-in show; the last two interviews of the day were done from a pay phone at the airport in London before I took a taxi home to face an answering machine filled with requests for more interviews in subsequent days.

It was easy to answer Eggleton's charges. Most Canadians, I said, would agree that Canada's proud tradition of peacekeeping had been dishonoured by the Somalia affair. In fact, we had paid tribute in our report to the outstanding work of most of our soldiers in Somalia and had endorsed the government's decision to award a Somalia campaign medal. It was primarily officers rather than soldiers whom we had criticized. I also explained that thousands of Canadians had seen soldiers and officers under oath give conflicting versions of events in Somalia and at National Defence Headquarters during our televised hearings. That some of them were lying was no news to these Canadians, or to the journalists who had covered the hearings. In any case, I pointed out, the government had asked us to investigate problems related to Somalia and that's what we had done.

I tried to focus attention on some of our 160 recommendations, particularly those dealing with the need for renewed leadership, clear lines of authority and accountability at all levels, and reforms of the military policing and justice system.

Unfortunately, this book became an issue when Eggleton attacked me in the course of his initial press conference. He said that I was hardly in a position to lecture the military on ethics when I was intending to profit from my experiences as a commissioner, claiming that the book would be "based on information [I had] received, information at public expense, and as part of the performance of a public duty." According to Eggleton, this was "strange behaviour" on my part. When a journalist immediately cited the precedent of Prime Minister Chrétien's highly successful book of political memoirs, Eggleton had no response.

I had already said publicly that the book would contain no confidential or privileged information, that it was simply a personal journal reflecting my own impressions of events during the inquiry and my own conclusions about the process. In interviews where the book was mentioned, I tried to dampen expectations created by Eggleton that it would be some sort of *Somalia Confidential*. I explained that I had kept a journal during our hearings to chronicle the phases of my growing disillusionment with the government and the military, and my gradual realization that we live in a less democratic country than I, an experienced and at times sceptical observer of the political process, had believed when I became a commissioner.

I was puzzled by the minister's tactics. While I understood that he probably couldn't have simply endorsed our report, because that would have raised immediate questions about the government's decision to cut us off, I couldn't understand why he hadn't given a more neutral response. After all, it was clear that he was going to have to make real changes in the military to prevent another Somalia from occurring. The recommendations in our report will be useful in this process. Surely it would have made more sense for him to keep some of his powder dry, to maintain some leverage with the high command, rather than immediately adopting the military's defensive posture.

By the end of that week, it was clear that we had won the initial battle. Not a single caller on any of the open-line talk shows that I took part in had anything favourable to say about Eggleton or the government. Letters to the editor over the following week were almost as uniform in their condemnation. In response to my comments at the press conference that I was still puzzled by Canadians' lack of outrage over the unprecedented closing of our inquiry, many people wrote to newspapers to say that this did not apply to them and to reassure me that they were in fact furious.

It was impossible to tell what serving soldiers as well as junior- and middle-level officers thought of the report because Vice-Admiral Larry Murray, the acting chief of the defence staff, forbade any of them from giving unsupervised comment. This followed an earlier general directive from Vice-Admiral Murray, issued the previous December and clarified in June, that his approval had to be obtained before anyone in the military at any level committed to "a press conference or to a media interview or prior to issuing a press release." Another indication of what Murray had called "an open and active communications program" was the unprecedented secrecy, only a short time before the release of our report, surrounding the court martial and conviction of a Canadian officer charged with offences while serving in Haiti. Courts martial are public proceedings, and news media are routinely notified about them in advance, but not in this case. The media only learned about and reported the secret June 25 trial in Valcartier after it occurred.

Murray's directives seemed to confirm that the military was drawing all the wrong lessons from its recent experiences.

If serving officers and soldiers were gagged, their comrades who had retired from the Forces were under no such restraint. One of the few heroes of the whole Somalia affair, Dr. Barry Armstrong, spoke out in the days following the release of our report. In an interview with Allan Thompson of the *Toronto Star*, he had "withering comment to make about his former bosses, whom he accused of cover-up and conspiracy."

The *Star* reported that "his harshest criticism was reserved for the man who currently heads Canada's Armed Forces as acting chief of the defence staff, Vice-Adm. Larry Murray, who was deputy chief of defence responsible for overseas operations in 1993." Under Murray, as the *Star* explained, five weeks elapsed between the March 4 shootings and the ordering of a military police investigation.

"It's atrocious that they're keeping that man on in charge of the Forces, a person that has such a questionable role . . . he has had no sense of the public good whatsoever," Dr. Armstrong was quoted as saying.

Everything that I heard and saw in the weeks following the release of the report told me that military veterans agreed with us. If we had slandered the Armed Forces, as Art Eggleton claimed, and if we had misjudged their senior leaders, presumably the first to contradict us would have been their old comrades, but I was aware of none who sprang to their defence. On the contrary, they spoke up clearly in support of our findings.

The previous minister of defence, Doug Young – in the news the week our report was released for establishing himself in Ottawa as a lobbyist looking for clients who would pay for his familiarity with government processes and personalities – had been aware of this at the end of 1996 when he commented on the number of retired officers who were taking shots at the current leadership. His remarks moved a recently retired lieutenant-colonel to respond in a letter sent to Young last January. A week after the release of our report, Greg Taylor of Pickering, Ontario, mailed a copy of the letter to me along with congratulations on our work. It was typical of others that I had received during the course of the inquiry.

Taylor's 2,400-word letter to the minister provided his analysis of a failure of leadership at the top of the system that was close to what the commission had concluded, but was written from inside the system.

"Unfortunately the army, like the other services, has consciously cultivated a general officer corps that is supposed to be politically astute," Taylor wrote. "The irony of course is that this is the group that has stumbled so badly of late.

"In my experience, at least at NDHQ, searching for the 'correct' political decision goes hand-in-hand with assuming that general's rank automatically bestows omniscience. . . .

"Omniscient generals searching for the 'correct' decision of course produces yes men and not nay-sayers. No one wants to be the subordinate who says no, or, further up the chain, the CDS who says no to the government."

Letters such as this, phone calls, and personal contacts over the course of the inquiry had confirmed that our conclusions were accurate and that, as Colonel Taylor said in his letter to me, "You have got it right." But this was small comfort in the face of the government's apparent hostility and many indications of public boredom and indifference. When the closing down of our inquiry had caused not a ripple of uncertainty in Canadians' support of the government last spring, and played virtually no role in the subsequent election campaign, it sent a clear message to government and military leaders. They took this to mean that if it was subsequently shown that there had been a cover-up of events in Somalia, they could simply deny that they knew anything about it. If the inquiry blamed the military's most senior leaders, they could simply ignore it. So that's what they did when our report came out and, despite the initial media and public reaction, experience would seem to indicate that in the long run their cynical self-assurance would be justified.

Back in London, when the phone stopped ringing, I was left with a deep sense of futility and a long list of unanswered questions. At the top of the list, still, were questions about the shutting down of the inquiry. I knew that if I could understand that, the rest of the picture would become clear.

Of course I had some partial answers. Former defence minister Young had admitted that the government didn't want our hearings to continue during the election campaign. Senior military leaders clearly were unhappy with the inquiry. The public was growing tired of all the bad news about Somalia. But none of these reasons seemed strong enough to justify the government's action. I kept thinking that I was missing something obvious.

Something like, for instance, a bombshell hidden in the evidence that we had gathered on the March 16, 1993, murder of Shidane Arone. If the military and the government knew that hearings would reveal explosive and politically embarrassing material, that would explain everything. But as far as I was aware, there was no such bombshell. And no one else among the lawyers and journalists reading these documents had spotted anything like that.

This material did contain indications of cover-up of the March 16 murder. In fact, these had started to emerge in 1994 when the magazine *Esprit de Corps* claimed that former prime minister Kim Campbell, then defence minister, had been informed soon after the event of suspicious circumstances surrounding Arone's death. This had drawn an immediate correction from John Dixon, a Vancouver academic who was one of Campbell's senior policy advisers at the time and who claimed that he and other members of Campbell's staff were not given meaningful information about Arone's death until March 31, 1993, more than two weeks later. This was subsequently contradicted in a memorandum written in November 1994 by Capt. Fred Blair of the Judge Advocate General's Office at National Defence Headquarters and later released by our inquiry. Captain Blair claimed that he had briefed Dixon and another Campbell aide, Marianne Campbell, on March 26 – which was still ten days after the event – and that this briefing had included reports of the possible torture of Arone before his death.

Other documents made public by our inquiry showed that military authorities in Somalia, within two days of the event, were concerned that "excessive force" had been used against Arone. In fact, the first Significant Incident Report on Arone's death, sent from the Canadian camp at Belet Huen to Canadian Joint Force Headquarters in Mogadishu early the following morning, March 17, stated that "body marks include contusion on lips and bruises to right of lower rib cage" but that "cause of death believed to be the result of internal head injuries." The report also noted that when Arone had been caught by Airborne soldiers the night before, a "scuffle occurred resulting in what was originally believed to be quote minor unquote injuries to local Somali." For reasons still unknown, this initial report of head injuries causing death was omitted from subsequent communications from Joint Force Headquarters in Somalia to National Defence Headquarters in Ottawa so that later that day, in a memo sent to Prime Minister Brian Mulroney by Clerk of the Privy Council Glen Shortcliffe, the only injuries to Arone mentioned were "one bruise in the area of his mouth and another on the right side of his chest." As a result of these early, incomplete reports, information was slow to reach Ottawa, at least through formal channels, but, by March 24, National Defence Headquarters knew that this was probably a case of homicide. In his November 1994 memorandum, Captain Blair indicated that he knew on March 26 that Arone had been "visited" by soldiers of Two Commando on the night of March 16 and that, in Blair's words, this " 'visit' had possibly included torture, and certainly had led to the unconsciousness, transfer to a medical facility, and death of Arone." Despite this, Kim Campbell and her staff maintained that the minister had not been informed of any suspicious circumstances surrounding Arone's death until five days later, on March 31.

Amid these conflicting and confusing claims, one fact emerged clearly: there was a major problem between the defence minister and her own department immediately following these events. The department accused its own minister of interference. In response, Campbell took the unusual step of going outside her own department for legal advice.

Blair's memorandum stated that "the Minister and her staff [in particular, Campbell minor and Dixon himself] only accepted the necessity to keep their hands off the process grudgingly, slowly, and with extremely bad grace."

On April 4, 1993, Captain Blair had sent a memo to John Dixon, with copies to the chief of the defence staff and the deputy minister, to explain why "the Minister must remain apart from the investigative/judicial processes now under way after the death of a Somali national in the custody of the Canadian forces at Belet Uen." Because the minister's responsibilities include decisions affecting military justice, Blair explained, "the application, direct or indirect, of ministerial influence on the process of making these decisions would be improper. . . ."

"Moreover," he added, "one may imagine the effect on the minister's present situation should it be revealed that she had interfered, or attempted to do so, with the course of military justice in this highly sensitive case."

At that time, Kim Campbell had just started along the path that was to take her briefly to the leadership of her party and the nation.

Later in his letter, Blair referred to a phone call by Campbell to the chief of the defence staff, Admiral John Anderson, the previous week. "It is well that she did no more than express her urgent interest in the serious case at hand."

In his application last January to appear before our inquiry, Dixon stated that this note "was understandably construed by Minister Campbell as an attempt to intimidate her from exercising her proper authority."

After hearing of Captain Blair's memo, Campbell wrote to her deputy minister, Robert Fowler, on April 22, 1993, "about a possible conflict between my responsibilities for the governance of the Canadian Forces, and my limited official role with the system of military justice." She expressed dissatisfaction with advice that she was receiving from lawyers at National Defence and informed Fowler that she had decided to consult the deputy attorney general.

"When she did that," John Dixon told me during a telephone conversation, "she was in effect firing her own lawyers at National Defence Headquarters and going outside for advice. It was a very serious thing for her to do."

I had reached John Dixon on his cell phone at an isolated cottage at Refuge Cove, B.C., about an hour's flying time from Vancouver. At home in London, a private citizen once again, I was still mulling over some of the documents that we had made public in the dying days of the inquiry, still trying to understand why we had been shut down. It was clear that the Arone incident had created serious tensions at National Defence Headquarters and that these would have been a primary focus of our hearings if we had been allowed to continue.

Dixon, who has returned to teaching at a college in Vancouver and is also head of the B.C. Civil Liberties Association, was spending the summer writing a book on freedom of expression. Our telephone conversation itself might have provided an illustrative chapter. He started by telling me that our conversation was certainly being recorded somewhere in Ottawa, and that I should be aware that all my phone calls had been monitored since my appointment to the commission.

Usually I ascribe this kind of remark to paranoia, but when it comes from someone who enjoyed the highest security clearance when he was an aide to the defence minister, it makes you think. He then said that he had read press reports about my book and wanted to warn me about the possibility of frivolous but expensive libel suits intended to hamper the book's publication. This didn't surprise me, as I had already learned that the government was unhappy about the book; this had been stated in no uncertain terms by officials in the Privy Council Office to some of my colleagues, almost a week before Art Eggleton had seen fit to attack my book in public.

Dixon said he had little to add to the material that he had already provided to the inquiry and which we had made public, except to say that it was clear from this material that information about Arone's death had taken a long time to reach Kim Campbell, that he is convinced that a cover-up had occurred, and that I should ask myself why there had been a cover-up and who would have benefited from it.

Another of Kim Campbell's aides, lawyer Marianne Campbell, supported Dixon's version of events following March 16 in an affidavit tabled by the commission and in a phone conversation. I reached her in Ottawa a couple of weeks after the release of our report. She still sounded shaken by the events in the Defence Department three years earlier. She described that period as unlike anything she had experienced since she had gone to work in Ottawa in 1990. By the end of March 1993, she was experiencing symptoms of stress.

"I was physically scared," she said. "No one actually threatened me, but that's how I felt. I had never dealt with anything like this before in my life."

In her previous positions with ministers of science and industry and with the Department of Justice, she had been accustomed to formal procedures for decision-making – the production of position papers, oral and written debate on proposals – a relatively open, above-board, and civilized process.

"But in the rigid and hierarchical culture at Defence, you have to face down these giant men to get anything done," she recalled. "And they don't like to write anything down. They're insulted if you ask them to write it down."

She remembered an episode when she was trying to reconcile the contents of her file on the Arone murder with the file held by Col. Ulrich Neugebauer, the executive assistant to the chief of the defence staff. When this phone consultation revealed that Colonel Neugebauer's file contained an important message about March 16 that she had somehow not received, she asked for a copy of it immediately.

"I said, 'You give that to me right now.' He froze. 'I'm not sure if I can,' he said. 'Then I'll come right down and get it,' I told him. So I went to the executive suite, and I sat on a couch in the waiting room for forty-five minutes while the chief of the defence staff [Admiral John Anderson] and the deputy minister [Robert Fowler] tried to decide what to do. Finally they turned the piece of paper over to me."

Even such a powerful and well-connected cabinet minister as Barbara McDougall, minister of foreign affairs during this time, found it difficult to extract information from Fowler.

"I had a lot to do with him and I was not a fan of his," she told me over the phone from her office in Toronto. "He always tried to filter everything, and I liked to be well-briefed. I didn't like my information filtered."

If any politician were likely to find this secretive and male-dominated world inimical it was former prime minister Kim Campbell. When I phoned her at the Canadian consulate in Los Angeles, she answered her direct line herself and seemed quite ready to talk. This surprised me because *Maclean's* had just reported that she had refused to talk to its reporters "further fuelling speculation that the government had told her to keep quiet." In fact, she had been publicly taciturn since January, after making it clear that she was furious that the inquiry had been cut short. But she explained that her subsequent silence was the result of realizing that "I could not as a senior public servant come out and criticize the government."

"But it was a huge frustration for me not to be able to testify," Campbell said. "For two years I had been muzzled because of my commitment to provide evidence only to the inquiry. If the inquiry had continued, you would have had all the papers and memoranda and you would have seen what questions to ask. You would have seen who knew what, and what never got answered."

Resigning from her position as consul general in Los Angeles, after the inquiry was interrupted, would not have answered the question: "How do I get my story out?" Events since then, particularly the release by the inquiry of the Dixon–Blair exchange of letters and memos, had helped to explain her position.

"During the 1993 election campaign, they said I covered up in Somalia. It really bothered me. I wanted to make it clear that we were pro-active. I wanted to respond. Canadians should know that an elected minister behaved properly, but the press was not interested in listening to me.

"I was so mad when I got the Blair memo [of April 4, cited above]. I switched lawyers. Yes, I went to the Justice Department. Justice lawyers know that I do what's right. The Justice Department had a lot of integrity when I headed it."

During our hour-long phone conversation, she looked back on her brief period as minister of defence as one of unusual difficulty and tension.

"At Justice, I had had superb relations with the deputy minister. There was a lot of respect between me and the bureaucracy. Even at Indian Affairs, the deputy minister, Harry Swain, was a typically complex career bureaucrat, but I learned a great deal from him. When I went to Defence, I assumed I would get on with the deputy minister, Robert Fowler.

"But Defence is a *ménage à trois* – the military headed by the chief of the defence staff, the department headed by the deputy minister, and the minister as the hypotenuse of the triangle. I never had a falling out with Fowler, but I still don't know what he knew.

"Clearly," Campbell added, "some person or persons in the department knew that I wasn't being given the whole truth. I really don't have the answer, but a terrible injustice was done to me."

Campbell told me that she had her suspicions about what had happened after March 16, but nothing that she was willing to say publicly.

"The real issue was their careers," she explained, referring generically to senior people at National Defence Headquarters. "If you want answers, look at the people whose careers were on the line.

"If the inquiry had continued, at least the loop would have been completed," Campbell concluded, remarking that the attempt to blame her for the cover-up helps to explain why "Canadians are so cynical about their politicians."

Kim Campbell wasn't the only protagonist in the March 16 affair and its aftermath to be concerned about the closing down of our inquiry. Her former deputy minister, Robert Fowler, Canada's ambassador to the United Nations, went public last April with complaints that the inquiry was lending credibility to "spurious speculation and allegations" by referring in public to possible cover-ups of events in Somalia.

Speaking through his lawyer, Fowler blamed us at the inquiry for not giving him a chance to appear again at our hearings – he had given evidence during the pre-deployment phase – and said that the commission "must refrain, in its report and in its public statements, from making any comment adverse to Mr. Fowler."

The warning was unnecessary because the hearings on the murder of Shidane Arone never happened. Our report barely mentioned the man who had been the top civil servant at National Defence Headquarters during the whole Somalia episode. Many of the news stories referred to "Teflon Bob" but always as an enigma. The *Maclean's* account of our report gave his picture equal prominence with the minister and the acting chief of the defence staff but had almost nothing to say about him in the text of the story. After three decades in the public service, the fifty-two-year-old ambassador had demonstrated a talent for survival equalled by few others in Ottawa. A personal friend of both Pierre Trudeau and Jean Chrétien, he had thrived during the two terms of Prime Minister Brian Mulroney, staying on in 1984 as a foreign and defence adviser at the Privy Council Office until he moved to Defence in 1986. As deputy minister there, he survived six ministers before receiving his ambassadorial appointment from the Liberals in late 1994.

When the first Somalia campaign medals were awarded to Airborne veterans last June, they were pinned to the chests of the soldiers by Fowler's brother-in-law, Governor General Roméo LeBlanc.

And now Robert Fowler has become the only top-echelon figure to serve at National Defence Headquarters during the Somalia affair to emerge unscathed. If he was unhappy about the unanswered questions about his role during those difficult months, so was I.

He had never given an interview about these events. According to *Maclean's*, he didn't respond to requests for an interview after our report was issued. I made a similar request in a fax to his office in New York on Friday, July 11. He phoned the following Monday morning to express his unhappiness with "innuendos" about him contained in the "unanswered questions" section of our report and to say that he would talk with me in his New York office that Friday.

I could still sense the anger beneath his cool bureaucratic manner when we sat down in his office. Outside, it was a steamy 35°C, and inside, despite the air-conditioning, the atmosphere was almost as torrid as I explained how the government's decision to abort our inquiry had made it impossible to hear him. He didn't accept that.

"You might have picked up the phone and said, 'Hey, Fowler, did you cover this up?' "

I suggested that lawyers for other parties might have objected to this special treatment.

"I don't care how you did it," he replied. "Before you lambaste somebody with such innuendo, wouldn't it be reasonable to ask me? You might have taken the pains somehow, through a lawyerly letter or somehow, to say: We can't complete our investigation; it looks like you guys might have covered up something; did you? I guess what I'm saying is nobody approached me."

Fowler then told me he would welcome the opportunity to clear the air. "I hope you do appreciate that for four and a half years, I have sat on this damn thing."

First there were the courts martial after Somalia, Fowler explained, then the Defence Department's internal board of inquiry, then our inquiry, followed by the possibility of a Senate inquiry. All these conspired to make him wait for his day in court.

"But at least at the moment there is no Senate inquiry, so I'm not going to wait for it. I'm going to tell you because you've asked me, and I've been waiting to be asked these questions a hell of a long time."

Later in the interview, when he realized that the publication date of this book was four months away, he indicated that he would probably make the information public in some fashion before this book appeared.

The two-hour taped interview – the ambassador's press secretary, Ralph Jensen, monitored and also taped our conversation – began with a preliminary discussion of the role of deputy minister of defence. Near the end, Fowler commented angrily on press reports that had linked him to the closure of the inquiry and labelled him "Teflon Bob" because of his survival skills in Ottawa and his reputation for being politically well-connected.

"I have no politics of any kind and no, I have never golfed with Prime Minister Chrétien," he said, referring to a frequently repeated story. "I have never golfed at all, in fact.

And yes, my sister married the guy who became the governor general after I was posted down here, and I'm afraid she didn't consult me on who she should marry."

But the central part of our conversation focused on the March 16 murder of Shidane Arone and subsequent events. I wanted to know what Fowler had known about the incident, when he learned the details and whom he had informed. The key conversation, it soon became evident, had occurred on the Friday after the murder, March 19. It involved Fowler, Vice Admiral Larry Murray, and Richard Clair, Defence Minister Kim Campbell's acting chief of staff.

"My first engagement with the death of Shidane Arone was on Friday the 19th," he said, explaining that he had been skiing at Quebec's Mont Tremblant with his daughter Justine from the morning of Wednesday, March 17, until he returned to Ottawa late in the afternoon of the following day, Thursday, going directly to a meeting of senior officials on personnel issues.

"So I came into the office for the first time since Tuesday on Friday morning," he said, "and I don't recall exactly what was said at the daily executive meeting that morning – certainly the death of Arone was an issue much alive in the hallways of DND that morning – but I had been away for two days and I was catching up on other things. I recall that late in the afternoon, four-thirtyish on Friday the 19th, Admiral Murray came in to see me and said, 'Have you heard the latest?' I said no, and he said, 'Well, Matchee tried to commit suicide.' Matchee, who had been arrested the day before, had been ... I didn't know who Matchee was, so he told me.

"At this point I said to him, 'Stop,' and got my staff to call in Miss Campbell's acting chief of staff, Richard Clair, to come and join Murray and me. We sat down, and Murray began again and told Clair what Murray had just told me."

The gist of this critical conversation, as related by Fowler, was "that Arone had died in Canadian custody, that he had died as a result of foul play at the hands of Canadians, and that Matchee was somehow involved in all of that."

Richard Clair denies that there was any mention of "foul play" during that conversation.

When I talked with him, Kim Campbell's former acting chief of staff was the only one of her former triumvirate at National Defence Headquarters – John Dixon and Marianne Campbell were the other two – who was still a public servant. He was corporate secretary, executive services, at Correctional Services in Ottawa. Unlike Dixon and Campbell, he had not become publicly involved in disputes about the flow of information at NDHQ after Arone was murdered on March 16. When I tried to contact him after my conversation with Fowler, he was on vacation with friends and family in Toronto and Montreal. Through his lawyer I sent word that I wished to talk with him. He called me on July 30.

"I don't remember that phrase being used at all," Clair said, when I related Fowler's "foul play" version of the March 19 conversation, "because I had specifically asked how he [Arone] had died, because he had two small wounds . . . there was no mortal wound on his person. So it was still mysterious at the time."

"On March 19, I was called by Mr. Fowler to this meeting," he confirmed. "They [Fowler and Murray] started talking about the situation in Somalia, and I had my pen and a piece of paper, and I put it down and I said, 'Okay, I want it in writing exactly what the situation is so I can properly brief the minister.

I don't want to miss any of the nuances.' And that's why the memo of the 19th was prepared."

Clair was referring to a memorandum signed by Murray on March 19 and tabled during the final weeks of the inquiry. Marked "Secret," and distributed immediately to the minister's staff, the deputy minister, the chief of the defence staff and his vice-chief, and two assistant deputy ministers, the memo reports the death of a Somali civilian "while in the custody of the CF," the imminent departure of military investigators and a lawyer for Somalia, and the detention and attempted suicide of an unidentified master corporal at the Canadian camp in Belet Huen. Murray's memo contains no mention of "foul play" in connection with the Somali's death.

"So I specifically asked for that piece of paper, because the death of Mr. Arone at that time was a mystery," Clair told me. "The memo was written that evening so that I could bring it home and contact the minister, who was in a plane between Toronto and Winnipeg at that time. So that's what I did. I didn't leave the office until I had the memo in hand, and she got that on Saturday morning when I talked with her."

At some point in April, Clair became aware that the "foul play" version of the March 19 conversation was circulating, and he and Dixon contacted Fowler. In his interview with me, Fowler referred to this.

"In fact, I remember we had a subsequent discussion, Richard Clair and I, about what the message we had transmitted was," Fowler said. "And he said, 'Well, you've clearly suggested foul play,' and I said, 'Well, it's not a term I often use, but that, sure, that sums it up.' I wouldn't have said murder. Murray wouldn't have said murder, because we didn't know that, and we didn't know what Matchee's role exactly was. It wasn't clear that Matchee was the perpetrator. But it was clear, late in the evening of Friday the 19th, that Arone had died in Canadian custody, that he had died as a result of foul play at the hands of Canadians, and that Matchee was somehow involved in all that. Fairly serious stuff."

I did have a conversation with Mr. Fowler afterward," confirmed Clair. "There were a couple of conversations that I remember, but definitely there's one in April, when Admiral Murray and Fowler are saying, 'We told Mr. Clair that there was foul play,' and I said, 'Excuse me?' John Dixon and I actually phoned Fowler at home, and there is a memo that we wrote to file about exactly what we had discussed – he backed away from that – that he told me there was foul play and all that . . . "

Clair insisted, as did Dixon and Marianne Campbell, that he first learned of torture, murder, and Matchee's involvement on March 31, twelve days after the March 19 conversation with Murray and Fowler.

The disputed conversation is critical because it relates closely to concerns about cover-up, about the state of Kim Campbell's knowledge of the March 16 event at the time, the obligation of various officials to keep her informed of all important matters, and, ultimately, the principle of civilian direction of the military that is central to democratic government.

I asked Fowler if he had ever thought of picking up the phone to brief Kim Campbell personally about an event that even then promised to have horrendous consequences for the military.

"Well, of course, I could have," Fowler said. "I'd called her before on other issues, but I'd called her on issues where I required an answer from her on something. I'd passed information through these guys before to her. The system worked. I don't know if what was happening in her life was relevant to all this or not. I mean, yes, I suppose you're right, I could have . . .

"But to suggest that there is some type of cover-up there, I find simply appalling."

If Defence Minister Campbell, who opened her leadership campaign on March 25, 1993, didn't become aware of these crucial aspects of the Arone murder until the end of the month, as she has claimed, the origins of the cover-up of this information from the minister and, through her, from the Canadian people lie somewhere in the conflicting versions of the March 19 conversation. Everything else flows from that, including the disagreements over whether the Campbell staff were informed much more fully on March 26, as Captain Blair claims. Perhaps not surprisingly, Fowler said he believes the Blair version.

All this made the cutting short of our inquiry even more frustrating. Now I understood more clearly what we would have encountered if we had been allowed to investigate the Arone murder. I felt even more confident that we would have uncovered and explained exactly what had happened, as we had for the March 4 killing. But I was really no further ahead in understanding why the inquiry had been shut down, although it was even clearer to me that if I or someone else should ever penetrate that mystery, most of the other questions would be answered.

In the end, no one seems very happy about the inconclusive conclusion of our inquiry and the Somalia story except, perhaps, the re-elected members of the Chrétien government, the surviving members of the high command at National Defence Headquarters, and the journalists who are continuing to poke and prod at the story, and who, I'm sure, will eventually find answers to most of their questions. I will be surprised if some of them haven't been published or broadcast before this book appears.

With my background, I was particularly conscious of the role that journalists played in bringing events in Somalia to light. With all its flaws, our news media are still the one part of the "system" that leaders of our society do not totally control and that they fear. I'm confident about leaving the rest of the Somalia story to my colleagues in the Fourth Estate. The truth will eventually emerge. It almost always does.

ACKNOWLEDGEMENTS

—————•—————

I think that my fellow commissioners, Judge Gilles Létourneau and Judge Robert Rutherford, were intrigued when I told them that I was keeping a personal journal of the inquiry – an activity favoured more by writers than judges. I think that they liked the idea of having this informal record of our work, and they trusted my discretion. I have respected their privacy and the confidentiality of our work. If there are any errors in my account, they are my responsibility.

Although this journal was entirely my own project, done on my own time and using my own computer, I benefited as a commissioner from the work of many of our staff. In particular, I would like to thank the secretary, Stanley Cohen; the director of research, David Pomerant; Linda Cameron, our library technician; and Kim LaViolette, who was my own secretary.

At the University of Western Ontario, Dr. Greg Moran, then dean of graduate studies and currently provost and vice-president (academic), encouraged me in this public service, even when it became more prolonged and time-consuming than either of us had expected. My thanks also to Dr. David Spencer, who succeeded me at the helm of the Graduate School of Journalism during the course of the inquiry.

My biggest debt of gratitude is to my wife, Hazel. Neither of us had expected such a drastic and prolonged interruption of our life together at this stage of our careers. I depended constantly on her support, as I have for the past twenty years.

The many months in Ottawa were made a little more bearable by my children who live there: my daughter Michelle, her husband, Dave, and children, Cymbria and Arthur, my son Nicholas, and my daughter Jane.

CHRONOLOGY

1968

– Creation of Canadian Airborne Regiment.

Oct. 1970

– French-speaking 1er Commando of the Airborne serves in Montreal during the October Crisis.

1974

– Canadian Airborne Regiment goes to Cyprus for UN duty, remains there for three tours.

1985

– Canadian Airborne Regiment moves from Edmonton, Alberta, to Petawawa, Ontario. The "Hewson Report" outlines disciplinary problems in the regiment.

July 1992

– After downsizing, the Airborne consists of a headquarters commando (124 soldiers), three company-sized commandos (119 soldiers each), and a service commando (120 soldiers).

Aug. 1992

– 1er Commando conducts extreme hazing as part of initiation ceremony at Petawawa. Videos of this hazing are broadcast on national television in January 1995.

Oct. 2-3, 1992

– Car-burning and other illegal activity by Airborne soldiers at Petawawa.

Oct. 21, 1992

– Lt.-Col. Paul Morneault is relieved of his command of the Airborne; Lt.-Col. Carol Mathieu replaces him.

Dec. 2, 1992

– President George Bush phones Prime Minister Brian Mulroney in Ottawa to invite Canada to participate in a U.S.-led mission to Somalia.

Dec. 3, 1992

– UN Security Council authorizes the first peace-enforcement mission since the end of the Cold War to invade Somalia in response to mass starvation as a result of civil war.

Dec. 5, 1992

– Canada promises 900-person contingent for Somalia mission. The Canadian Airborne Regiment receives a warning order for Operation Deliverance in Somalia.

– Col. Serge Labbé is appointed commander of the Canadian Joint Force Somalia.

Dec. 15, 1992

– Advance party of Canadian Airborne Regiment Battle Group arrives in Somalia. Temporarily stationed at Baledogle.

Dec. 28, 1992

– First Canadian soldiers arrive at Belet Huen, Somalia, to occupy airfield and establish permanent camps for Canadian Airborne Regiment Battle Group.

Jan. 10, 1993

– Canadian Joint Force headquarters established in the devastated capital city of Mogadishu, 350 kilometres from Belet Huen.

Jan. 28, 1993
– Lt.-Col. Carol Mathieu, commander in Belet Huen, issues verbal orders permitting soldiers guarding the Canadian camp to shoot at thieves under certain conditions.

Feb. 10, 1993
– Soldiers of Two Commando fire warning shots to disperse crowd at Red Cross distribution centre in Belet Huen.

Feb. 17, 1993
– Airborne soldiers fire at Somali demonstration in Belet Huen. One Somali is killed and two wounded. The incident is not investigated by military police until May.

March 3, 1993
– U.S. soldier based at Belet Huen is killed when his vehicle explodes an anti-tank mine near Balem Balle to the north. First fatality of soldier known personally to some Canadian soldiers.

March 4, 1993
– Soldiers of the Airborne's reconnaissance platoon, led by Capt. Michel Rainville, kill one Somali thief and wound a second during stake-out of the engineers' compound at Belet Huen.

March 5-6, 1993
– Maj. Barry Armstrong, a doctor stationed at Belet Huen, makes allegations of murder in relation to the March 4 incident to Canadian headquarters in Mogadishu and to his commander in Belet Huen, Lt.-Col. Carol Mathieu.

March 8-9, 1993
– Chief of the Defence Staff Adm. John Anderson and official party from Ottawa visit Belet Huen during tour of Somalia. Anderson visits Canadian military hospital and sees Somali wounded on March 4.

March 16, 1993
– Shidane Arone, a sixteen-year-old Somali, is beaten to death after being captured by soldiers of Two Commando in the camp at Belet Huen.

March 18, 1993

– Canadian Joint Force headquarters in Mogadishu issues a short press release stating that a Somalia man has died while in Canadian custody.

March 19, 1993

– Master Cpl. Clayton Matchee of Two Commando attempts suicide while being held in connection with Arone's death.

March 19, 1993

– Ottawa orders a military police investigation into the death of Shidane Arone.

March 25, 1993

– Defence Minister Kim Campbell announces that she will run for the Conservative leadership.

March 31, 1993

– Canadian Press carries a report on the death of Arone and the attempted suicide of Corporal Matchee.

April 2, 1993

– Colonel Labbé arrives in Ottawa with his report on the March 4 incident.

April 13, 1993

– On leave in a hotel in Nairobi, Kenya, Major Armstrong slips a note under the door of a military police officer alleging murder in the March 4 incident.

– Ottawa decides to launch a military police investigation into the March 4 incident.

April 18, 1993

– Opening of the school rebuilt by Canadians at Belet Huen, the showpiece of the Airborne's "hearts and minds" humanitarian campaign.

April 20, 1993

– The CBC reports the first allegations of cover-up of the death of Arone. Defence Minister Kim Campbell offers explanation of delay in making information public.

April 28, 1993

– Chief of the Defence Staff Admiral Anderson convenes an internal board of inquiry (the de Faye inquiry) to investigate "leadership, discipline, actions and procedures of the Canadian Airborne Regiment Battle Group."

May 3, 1993

– Canadian soldier of Three Commando dies from accidental discharge, the only Canadian soldier to die in Somalia.

June 2, 1993

– Canadian Airborne Regiment Battle Group leaves Belet Huen. Canadian withdrawal from Somalia underway.

June 1993

– Kim Campbell wins Conservative leadership and becomes prime minister.

July 19, 1993

– The de Faye inquiry report is released. Chief of the Defence Staff Adm. John Anderson is "disturbed" by its findings.

Aug. 24, 1993

– Military police report on the March 4 incident is completed indicating that police investigation of the incident had been "inexplicably delayed" and had commenced only five weeks after the incident.

Sept. 1993

– The Somalia Working Group is created at National Defence Headquarters under Maj.-Gen. Jean Boyle to co-ordinate the response to continuing Somalia-related developments.

– CBC Radio reporter Michael McAuliffe makes a verbal request for Somalia-related documents (Responses to Queries) and these are supplied to him informally after the documents have been altered to remove sensitive material. McAuliffe is not told of the alteration.

Oct. 1993

– Court martial proceedings begin against soldiers and officers involved in the March 16 incident. One private is convicted; another is acquitted. One sergeant is acquitted; another pleads guilty. One major is convicted; a captain is acquitted. Later, in connection with the March 4 incident, a major is convicted and a captain acquitted.

Oct. 25, 1993

– Liberal leader Jean Chrétien defeats Prime Minister Kim Campbell.

Nov. 4, 1993

– David Collenette appointed minister of national defence.

Jan. 20, 1994

– Michael McAuliffe submits an Access to Information request to the Department of National Defence for the same Somalia-related documents that he had received informally in 1993.

April 25, 1994

– Corporal Matchee is found unfit to stand trial at his court martial in Petawawa. He suffers from severe brain damage as a result of his attempted suicide.

May 16, 1994

– Michael McAuliffe receives the Somalia-related documents requested under Access to Information. They have been illegally altered to conform to the documents provided to him informally the previous year.

June 1994

– McAuliffe makes a second Access to Information request for more Somalia-related documents (Responses to Queries) and is told that these are no longer produced by the Department of National Defence. This is erroneous.

Jan. 1995

– CBC-TV broadcasts a videotape showing hazing activities at an Airborne initiation ceremony in Petawawa.

Jan. 24, 1995

– Defence Minister David Collenette announces the disbandment of the Canadian Airborne Regiment.

March 5, 1995

– The Canadian Airborne Regiment is disbanded at Petawawa.

March 20, 1995

– Defence Minister Collenette establishes the three-person Commission of Inquiry into the Deployment of Canadian Forces to Somalia.

April 21, 1995
– The inquiry issues an order to the minister of national defence for the production of all Somalia-related documents.

April 1995
– The Department of National Defence creates the Somalia Inquiry Liaison Team (SILT) to assist the inquiry, reporting to Maj.-Gen. Jean Boyle.

May 24, 1995
– The inquiry holds its first public hearing.

Sept. 5, 1995
– A clerk at National Defence Headquarters is discovered placing Somalia-related documents in a "burn bag" for destruction.

Nov. 1995
– Michael McAuliffe broadcasts reports on alteration and destruction of documents at National Defence Headquarters.

Jan. 1, 1996
– General Boyle is appointed chief of the defence staff.

April 9, 1996
– General Boyle orders all military units to stop ordinary duties for one day to search for Somalia-related documents.

Oct. 4, 1996
– David Collenette resigns as minister of national defence. Doug Young replaces him.

Oct. 8, 1996
– General Boyle resigns as chief of the defence staff.

Jan. 10, 1997
– Defence Minister Young orders the inquiry to complete its hearings by the end of March 1997 and submit its report three months later.

Jan. 13, 1997
– Inquiry commissioners hold press conference to announce acceptance of deadline under protest.

June 30, 1997
– Inquiry submits its final report.